Marketing
Success
Stories

FIFTH EDITION

Marketing Success Stories

FIFTH EDITION

edited by

MICHAEL CANT
Sub Department Head: Marketing and Retail Management,
University of South Africa
Holder of the Massmart Chair in Retail Management

RICARDO MACHADO
Senior Lecturer, University of South Africa

authors

Annekie Brink
Michael Cant
Michael du Toit
Cindy Erdis
Charlene Gerber-Nel
Ricardo Machado
Johan Strydom

OXFORD
UNIVERSITY PRESS

OXFORD
UNIVERSITY PRESS

Great Clarendon Street, Oxford OX2 6DP

Oxford University Press is a department of the University of Oxford.
It furthers the University's objective of excellence in research, scholarship,
and education by publishing worldwide in

Oxford New York

Auckland   Cape Town   Dar es Salaam   Hong Kong   Karachi
Kuala Lumpur   Madrid   Melbourne   Mexico City   Nairobi
New Delhi   Shanghai   Taipei   Toronto

with offices in

Argentina   Austria   Brazil   Chile   Czech Republic   France   Greece
Guatemala   Hungary   Italy   Japan   Poland   Portugal   Singapore
South Korea   Switzerland   Thailand   Turkey   Ukraine   Vietnam

Oxford is a registered trade mark of Oxford University Press
in the UK and in certain other countries

Published in South Africa
by Oxford University Press Southern Africa, Cape Town

Marketing Success Stories
Fifth Edition
ISBN 0 19 578520 7 (10-digit, current)
ISBN 978 0 19 578520 3 (13-digit, from 2007)

Previously published by Southern Book Publishers (Pty) Ltd and by International Thomson Publishing Southern
Africa (Pty) Ltd. Third edition published by Oxford University Press Southern Africa 1998. Fourth edition
published 2002.

Fifth edition published 2005
Second impression 2006

Publishing manager: Marian Griffin
Editor: Marisa Montemarano
Designer: Ian Norris
Cover design: Kerry Buchan/ Sharna Sammy
Published by Oxford University Press Southern Africa
PO Box 12119, N1 City, 7463, Cape Town, South Africa

Set in 9.5 pt on 13 pt Stone Serif by Global Graphics
Cover photo: Snapstock
Reproduction by Castle Graphics
Cover reproduction by The Image Bureau
Printed and bound by ABC Press, Cape Town

Contents

Topic Index

Preface

Marketing Success Stories was one of the first books in South Africa to provide students and teachers of marketing with real-life stories of South African businesses to help them increase their understanding of marketing.

Lecturers at universities, universities of technology, and colleges still find that students have difficulty in relating marketing theory to practical situations. The aim of these cases is to assist students to understand the real world of retailing better and to show how theory can be applied within a wide range of situations to achieve success in marketing.

The format used in previous editions was intended to help students analyse and recognise what has actually been done in real life, rather than concentrating on finding solutions to abstract or theoretical problems. The fifth edition also follows this approach.

The new edition of *Marketing Success Stories* builds on the success of the previous editions, while specific areas of interest that have been pointed out to us through research and feedback have been added. We have carefully selected new contributions that help to illustrate the major and more complex aspects of marketing and we have retained a number of cases from the previous editions. This was due to the encouraging support from the contributors, the positive feedback received from the readers, and because all these cases are based in a South Africa marketing context. We have also sourced new stories in specific areas of interest. These areas include competition and intellectual property. Other topics cover some of the new buzz-words emerging from marketing theory such as relationship marketing, integrated marketing communication, and loyalty programmes. The book has therefore been improved in the sense that it now covers the whole scope of marketing from consumer to industrial, and from large to small marketers.

The key difference of this edition from the previous ones is that the case studies have been divided into four parts: Socio-economic parameters in South African retailing, Classic cases, Contemporary cases, and Overcoming marketing obstacles. The aim of this approach is to make it easier for the reader to refer to areas of interest and study, as cases studies similar in nature are grouped together, thereby refining the focus of each case.

The cases included in this edition, in our opinion, offer insight into marketing theory and practice. They link together to form a cohesive whole that affords those teaching marketing the opportunity to vary the complexity of the use of the cases, from simple recognition to evaluation and comparison. The readings are therefore often interconnected, and reinforce or complement each other in a number of cases.

However, we were still limited by the fact that we could obviously only include those stories that company executives were willing to share, as revealing sensitive information may affect the competitive edge that companies have in the market.

We would like to thank those executives who willingly offered information, time, co-operation, and encouragement. We encourage those who are reading this book to be more amenable to case study research collection in the future in order to enlarge the case study base in South Africa.

A Topic Index has been compiled to assist the readers in cross-referencing the topics covered in each case study. A list of marketing features has also been added in the beginning of each chapter to help readers determine which specific marketing concepts will be addressed in each case. We would still encourage students to use a sound textbook to gain the theoretical background necessary to understanding the marketing actions described in the cases.

THE EDITORS

PART ONE

SOCIO-ECONOMIC PARAMETERS IN SOUTH AFRICAN RETAILING

Introduction

Unlike any of the previous editions of *Marketing Success Stories*, the fifth edition has divided the 32 case studies into four parts, grouping together case studies which are similar in their nature or in their objectives, thereby refining the focus of each case. The aim of this approach is to make it easier for scholars, students and casual readers to refer to areas of interest and study.

Part 1: Socio-economic parameters in South African retailing does not contain case studies of *companies*, but rather comprises a selection of commentaries on different aspects of retailing within South African society. The idea is that this overview creates a context within which the case studies of companies can be placed and analysed. It is necessary to have a good grasp of the macro-environment in which they function in order to understand the problems these companies have faced, the particular opportunities they have had, and the changes they have been through.

Chapter 1, for instance, deals with the structural changes in the South African consumer market, examines the attitudes and preferences of consumers and predicts how they may react to new and different forms of retailing, services or products. It outlines a general profile of South African consumers, which forms a prototype for the profiles built up in other case studies.

The chapter on retailing moves from a theoretical and historical perspective on retailing in South Africa to a description of recent developments and the effects of local and global change on the industry.

The chapter on Generation Y considers using age-based segmentation as a means of dividing and categorising the South African market and its needs and wants. It concludes that age-based segmentation may be viable, at least, in terms of identifying a Generation Y target market.

Although global trends and general marketing theory support these chapters, the focus remains on South Africa since the bulk of the case studies in this book concerns South African companies and the South African context in which they achieved their success.

Structural changes in the consumption patterns of South African consumers

Introduction

Retailers in South Africa have adapted through the years of sanctions and are now flourishing in a democratic South Africa. The economy is currently in a phase of steady, if unspectacular, growth with the increase in the GDP ambling along between two and three per cent per year. Retailers, however, recognise that structural changes are taking place in the economy and that 'traditional' retailers are competing in a dynamic environment. Factors leading to this increased competition include changed buying habits: customers are spending more money on cell phones and gambling and less on 'traditional' products and services such as clothing and shoes. Another reason lies in the new forms of competition in retailing, such as e-retailing (also called e-tailing). Let's then take a brief look at how these products and services have influenced the spending patterns of South Africans.

Cellular phones

Mobile cellular services in South Africa started in 1994 with Vodacom launching its cellular service. It is estimated that the market size by March 2004 was 16,4 million cell phone users, with 80% being classified as active users. The potential number of South African subscribers in 2006 is predicted to be more than 19 million,[1] dispelling previous predictions that the South African cellular market has reached maturity. The rapid growth of cell phone subscribers is an extraordinary feat with more cell phones in operation in South Africa than all the fixed-lines provided by Telkom – an indication of the success story of cellular phones in South Africa and the previously untapped demand for affordable telecommunication services in South Africa.

Some of the reasons for the success of cellular phones can be ascribed to the long period that fixed-line subscribers had to wait for the instalment of a telephone service, the high incidence of crime necessitating immediate communication, the general lack of security in South Africa and the introduction of prepaid packages by the cellular providers which made it easier for potential subscribers to acquire cellular services. It was especially the introduction of prepaid packages in November 1996 that boosted sales of cellular phones in South Africa. During the first few years there was slow growth in subscription rates, as the service providers demanded that customers sign a two-year contract agreement. There were also credit checks on potential subscribers, limiting the market for cellular phones. All this changed with the introduction of the first prepaid packages – suddenly customers that were previously disqualified due to a poor credit rating could also afford a cellular phone. All that was needed was an amount of cash that could buy airtime minutes and the initial outlay to acquire a handset. By the middle of 2004 more than 90% of new subscriptions were by prepaid customers.[2]

The cellular role players

The cell phone industry is a major industry in South Africa. Cellular expenditure was R15 billion in the 2001 financial year, up R3 billion from the 2000 financial year. The South African market was estimated to be worth R45 billion in 2004.[3] Currently there are three service providers in South Africa providing services to 18,2 million subscribers. In classic economic terms the competitive situation in South Africa can be described as an oligopoly. An oligopoly is described as a competitive situation where there are few suppliers of the service. These suppliers formulate their strategies with an eye to the effect on their competitors.[4] Vodacom obtained a first-mover advantage and commenced with cellular services on 1 June 1994, followed a few months later by MTN, and Cell C entering the market as a laggard some seven years later in November 2001. Let us take a closer look at the competition between these three players.

Vodacom

Vodacom is currently the largest of the three competitors – largely attributed to the first-mover advantage that it had when cellular services were launched in South Africa. The shareholders in Vodacom are Telkom SA (50% – majority shareholding), Vodaphone AirTouch Plc (an international service provider operating in 23 countries which provides technological support and operates in countries such as the UK and in Australia – 31,5%), Hosken Consolidated Investments (5% market share, controlled by the labour unions, Sacwu and NUM) and Rembrandt (famous, inter alia, for its involvement in the South African tobacco industry – 13,5%). Vodacom is also pursuing growth in southern Africa and has subsidiaries in the DRC, Lesotho and Tanzania. The success of Vodacom can further be ascribed to the introduction of prepaid packages (marketed under the Vodago brand name) with more than two thirds of its customers using the prepaid cellular option. In the year to March 2004 Vodacom's total subscribers grew 29,7% to 11,2 million subscribers. Vodacom's revenue was up 18,7% to R23,5 billion in March 2004.[5] At the beginning of 2004, 94% of Vodacom's turnover was generated in South Africa.[6] Contract churn (defections) was down to 10% and prepaid churn was 41%, although prepaid churn is a low cost expense, because of the interconnect charges that recover most of the cost of defecting customers. The average revenue per user (Arpu) of Vodacom is R177,00 per month.[7] Vodacom suffered a setback early 2004 when it exited out of the lucrative Nigerian market. This was due to some pressure from its shareholders, namely SBC Communications of the USA and Telkom Malaysia, which holds 30% market share in Telkom, which in turn holds the majority share in Vodacom. The hasty exit from Nigeria was ascribed to 'corporate governance problems'.[8]

It would seem that Vodacom has redirected its strategy by pursuing technology advances in its quest to maintain the growth rates of the past. In its quest to obtain this they are working closely with Telkom in the areas of Wi-Fi (wireless Internet) and high-speed high margin data services. This is in reaction to the speed in which information technologies converge. Vodacom is also testing the next generation cellular technology in South Africa, called 3G in close collaboration with Vodaphone, which is supplying state-of-the-art technology.

MTN

MTN's holding company on the JSE is M-Cell. M-Cell in turn is owned by Johnnic (majority shareholder) and Transnet (the public transport utility). MTN commenced its services a few months after Vodacom and initially followed a classic follower strategy. Today it is following a different growth strategy, which could be classified as an international growth strategy. MTN is more active in growing the market into Africa. It has subsidiaries in Swaziland, Uganda and Rwanda as well as in Cameroon and Nigeria. By March 2004 MTN had 9,5 million subscribers. At the same time MTN's turnover increased by 23% to R23,9 billion. In this process MTN has overtaken Vodacom in the turnover stakes, because of significant growth in Nigeria, indicating that the growth strategy followed by MTN is succeeding. There is obviously a higher operating margin outside South Africa that discounts the risk taken in these countries. Nigeria currently contributes 36% of revenue and 46% of headline earnings of MTN.[9]

Cell C

The third cellular service provider was introduced on November 2001, operating on both the traditional GSM 900 as well as the 1800 Mhz frequency. The ownership of Cell C consists of the Saudi Arabian group Oger (majority shareholder) and Cellsaf (a domestic grouping of 33 empowerment groups). By March 2004 they had 3 million subscribers of which 1,9 million were active users. Some 84% of their subscribers are prepaid users. Average revenue per user (Arpu) was R62,00 for prepaid and R409 for contract users with a blended (average) Arpu of R110 per month.[10]

The success of Cell C in the South African cell phone market is hard to believe since it was the late entrant with its two competitors having a seven-year advantage. The sustainable competitive advantage of Cell C is believed to be in its approach to the domestic market. It targets two segments in the market, namely the middle to higher segment in the prepaid market and the middle to lower segment in the contract market. It is focusing specifically on the younger, lower income segment of the market with an innovative pricing structure and a hip branding strategy. Cell C introduced greater flexibility to contract options, per second billing and one-rate plan fees to waive the connection fee. In its quest to be perceived as being different from its two competitors, Cell C has been very successful, with 65% of its customer base wooed away from Vodacom and MTN.[11] Another reason for the success of Cell C is the strategic alliances that it formed in the development of its distribution channels. It has agreements with the leading retailing groups in South Africa, which contribute an important share in the sales of Cell C packages. Other channels of distribution include selling directly to corporate customers, telesales, a franchise operation and sales through a wholesaler and dealer network.

With respect to branding, Cell C followed a dynamic approach to obtain brand consciousness. It commenced with an advertising campaign on 21 June 2001 to announce the launch of Cell C. This was also the date of the sun-eclipse and Cell C used this C-shaped eclipse to great effect in its advertisements using the tag line 'We'd like to thank Mother Nature for announcing our imminent arrival'.[12]

The customers

As part of the census of October 2001 by Stats SA, South African households were asked about their possession of certain household goods. One of the items asked about was cell phones, which are perceived to be a status product in South African society. In this census it was ascertained that 32,3% of all South African households had a cell phone in the household. This figure is impressive when compared to the number of households with a fixed-line telephone from Telkom. Fixed-line penetration has fallen from 13% of the population in 2000 to 10% in 2004. Fixed-line connections have been in a steady decline from 2001 onwards. In the 2003–2004 financial year the total number of fixed lines was 4,8 million, which includes pay phones and ISDN data lines. By contrast, mobile penetration (Vodacom, Cell C and MTN) increased from 12% in 2000 to 39% of the population in 2004.[13]

Overall, mobile telephones have proven a far more efficient technology in providing telecommunication access, especially for the lower income population of South Africa. As part of a mandatory obligation by Telkom, with the renewal of their license, they had to install 2,7 million land-lines especially in rural underserviced areas. For the following five years from 1997 Telkom installed 2,8 million new land-lines in the designated areas but disconnected more than 75%, due to consumers moving to cell phones or not being able to pay their monthly bills.[14]

The changes in the South African consumption patterns

Changes in the South African retailing environment over the past few years can be summarised as follows:
- A large amount of the disposable income of consumers is spent on cell phones, the lottery (Lotto) and gambling.
- The income of the debtors book of retailers has reduced due to the dramatic decline of the usury rate (i.e. the maximum rate of interest that retailers can charge on outstanding amounts).
- Increasing cell phone bills, higher medical and education costs, spending on gambling and higher fuel prices have reduced the disposable income of the average customer in South Africa.
- The influence of emigration and AIDS deaths are eroding the customer base of retailers.
- Growth in South Africa was characterised by a decrease in employment (jobless growth).

Let us now take a look at the role of gambling and its influence on changing South African consumer expenditure patterns.

The role of gambling in the changing of consumer expenditure patterns

Gambling was previously limited to places such as Sun City and the Wild Coast Sun, which were relatively far away from the major cities of South Africa. Some of the more recent casinos were built within easy reach of poor neighbourhoods in the major cities, giving rise to concerns about the impact of gambling on these disadvantaged communities. Gambling has, however, become a major moneyspinner for the national economy. In Gauteng alone gambling generated R3,2 billion in the 2003 financial year, contributing almost 1,5% to the province's GDP.[15] Since 1996 the South African casino industry has been responsible for R12 billion in new investments and has created 30 000 direct and 64 500 indirect jobs in South Africa. It also pays annually more than R1,7 billion to government in taxes.[16]

There is, however, still concern in South Africa that gambling leads to social problems. One of the major problems is that compulsive gambling is leading to financial, social and health problems for a growing part of the South African population. What is also of concern is that these problem gamblers are mostly in the lower income groups – the part of the population that can ill afford to squander money on games of chance. In a study done in 2003 it was determined that 72,3% of South Africans played the lottery regularly (i.e. once a week). Participation in playing scratch cards also increased to 15% of the population. Participation in other forms of gambling was slightly down, including slot machines at 14,1%, horseracing at 5,7% and table games at casinos at 1,4%.[17]

There is, however, a positive side to gambling also – Uthingo, the company that operates the lottery has paid more than R7 million to 8 000 small retailers in South Africa, which are used as distribution outlets for the sales of lottery tickets. The R7 million was earned from the 6% commission that these retailers obtain by selling Lotto tickets for Uthingo.[18] Overall, it can be said that expenditure on gambling has stabilised in South Africa.

E-retailing in South Africa

In 2001 South African customers spent R162 million online, which made up less than 0,1% of South Africa's total retail sales of R188 billion.[19]

By May 2002 Webchek[20] reported that 26% of South Africans that have access to the Internet have shopped online. Approximately 338 000 South Africans have purchased products on the Internet. The range of products sold on the Internet ranged from books, software, CDs, gifts, flowers and groceries. The most popular product bought online was books.

Towards the end of 2003 the situation regarding sales and products on the Internet had improved with turnover up to R341 million. There were 700 South African websites involved in e-tailing up 500 from 2001. Online grocery shopping was the top-seller. The dominant online retailers are Pick 'n Pay Shopping, Kalahari.net, Woolworths In-the-bag, Netflorist, Cybercellar and Streetcar.com. The most popular online shopping malls were MWeb Shop Zone and the Digital Mall.[21]

South African retailers are, however, concerned about the relatively slow growth of e-tailing in this country. There are a few reasons for the slow growth, namely:

- **The limited access of customers to the Internet.** In research done by the Bureau of Market Research in South Africa it was found that of 500 households listed in the telephone directory, 53% had access to a computer, while only 34% had access to the Internet (mostly at work) and about 15% made use of online shopping facilities.[22]
- **The telecommunication restrictions.** South Africa's monopoly by Telkom is inhibiting the growth of the Internet. This is due to the limited and expensive bandwidth available, which is detrimental to ordinary South Africans using the Internet.

It would seem that e-tailing has a place in South African retailing but that external factors are inhibiting the growth of this distribution channel. Most online retail sales are an extension of an existing physical retail operation such as In-the-bag of Woolworths.

Conclusion

The discussion centred on the changing consumption pattern of South African consumers and how this influences South African retailers. The examples indicated that there are changes in the way that customers in South Africa are spending their disposable income. A few years ago cell phones were unknown – today they are a must-have accessory for everyone, from scholars to workers, managers to housewives.

What we are seeing is a permanent change in the way people are spending their money. South African retailers have to recognise the fact that these structural changes are here to stay and they have to adapt accordingly. Retailers who provide the products their customers want, even those products such as cell phones which may not be not part of their traditional product range, will reap the benefits of adapting to change, especially if customers can buy on credit.

The same trend apples to gaming. More and more retailers are getting involved in selling gambling tickets such as Lotto. There are more than 7 000 retailing outlets selling Lotto tickets currently and a few thousand gambling machines (aptly called 'one-armed bandits') will be placed at various retailers in the near future.

E-tailing is slowing down at present due to problems out of the control of online retailers. This situation will only change if the cost related to online purchasing declines. Nevertheless, e-tailing has the potential to become a powerful instrument for South African retailers in the future. Successful retailing now and in the future remains a matter of adaptation by South African retailers and the old marketing tenet of supplying the needs of your customers.

References

1   This case study was written by Johan Strydom.
    Internet: Statistics of Cellular in South Africa.
    Http://www.cellular.co.za/stats/statistics_South_Africa. Date accessed: 30 April 2004.
2   Internet: Statistics of Cellular in South Africa.
    Http://www.cellular.co.za/stats/statistics_South_Africa.htm. Date accessed: 30 April 2004.
3   Op. cit.
4   Mansfield, E. & Yohe, G. 2000. *Micro Economics: Theory/Applications* (10th ed.). New York: Norton, p 383.
5   *Sunday Times*, Business Times. 13 June 2004.
6   *Financial Mail*. 11 June 2004. p 24.
7   *Financial Mail*. 11 June 2004. p 23.
8   Op. cit., pp 22-23.
9   *Sunday Times*, Business Times. 13 June 2004.
10   Op. cit.

11 Htttp://www.bday.co.za/bday/content/direct/1,3523,1224469-6078. Date accessed: 5 March 2004.

12 Http://www.brandchannel.com/print_page.asp?ar_id=78&section=profil.
Date accessed: 6 July 2004.

13 Bidoli, M. 11 June 2004. *Financial Mail.*
http://free.financialmail.co.za/04/0611/cover/coverstoryc.htm. Date accessed: 8 July 2004.

14 Op cit.

15 Http://www/sabcnews.com/Article/PrintwholeStory/0,2160,73480,00.html. Date accessed: 4 April 2004.

16 Casinos create 64 500 jobs. iafrica.com.10 November 2003.

17 Http:www.sabcnews.com/Article/Printwholestory/0,2160,66100,00html. Date accessed: 30 April 2004.

18 Http:www.sabcnews.com/Article/Printwholestory/0,2160,75577,00html. Date accessed: 30 April 2004.

19 http://www.theworx.biz/retail02.htm Date accessed: 14 July 2004.

20 http://www.nua.ie/surveys/index.cgi?f=VS&art._id=9053579548rel=trie

21 SABC News file://A:\0,2160,82720,00.htm. Date accessed: 30 June 2004.

22 Behavioural aspects of users of e-commerce in South Africa. Bureau of Market Research. 2003. *Research Report* no 320. Pretoria: UNISA, p 1.

2

Retailing

A future perspective[1]

Retailing in South Africa is in an exciting period of dynamic growth and expansion, supported by an economy strengthened by lower inflation and interest rates relative to recent years. According to a recent report, retailing is being shaped by 'vocal consumerism, saturating markets and globalisation'.[2] Not only is the South African retailing industry regarded as the leading retailing body on the African continent, the same report states that 'the retail market in South Africa faired far better than its global counterparts, aided by favourable economic factors, buoyant consumer confidence, and the benefits of a competitive currency'.[3] The following quick facts reflect this positive situation:

- South African retail sales in 2003 totalled R234,3 billion,[4] an increase of 10,7% on 2002.
- The retail trade contributes 12,5% to GDP, the third biggest sector behind Manufacturing (18,1%) and Finance (19%).
- The retail sector employs 2,46 million people, of which 65% are employed in the formal sector, with the balance in informal employment.

The core challenge for the South African retail sector is to grow profitably in an increasingly competitive market. This drive is fuelling the dynamic changes we are seeing in this sector.

Retailing defined

The retailer is the last link in the distribution chain, bridging the gap between the manufacturer and the final consumer. It is, in fact, the most important link in the distribution chain, since almost all of our gross national product (GNP) reaches us through some form of retailing.

Retailing is omnipresent (everywhere all the time), dynamic, and challenging. It is found in small towns and big cities, at local and regional levels, as well as at national and international levels. Whether an enterprise sells to the consumer in a store, through the mail, over the telephone, via a television shopping network, from door to door, or through a vending machine, it is a form of retail. In fact, retailing occurs every time a consumer spends money.

A number of definitions of retailing can be found in the literature. The definitions of Lusch, Dunne, and Gebhardt (1993:4); Mason, Mayer, and Ezel (1994:6); Ghosh (1994:4); and Lewison (1994:5) all have a common thread, namely that retailing helps to make products and services available to the final consumer. For the purpose of this discussion, retailing is defined as the set of business activities that adds value to the products and services sold to consumers for their personal or family use. Most people think of retailing as the sale of products in stores only. However, it also involves the sale of services: for example, overnight lodging in a hotel, a visit to a doctor, a haircut, a videotape rental or a home-delivered pizza. Not all retailing therefore occurs in stores. Examples of non-store retailing are the direct sales of cosmetics by Avroy Shlain, catalogue sales by Music Direct, and TV shopping by Verimark.

Let's now consider the classification of retailers.

Classification of retailers

Kotler and Armstrong[5] distinguish between two basic types of retailers, namely store retailers and non-store retailers, a viewpoint that also applies to the South African retailing scene.

Store retailing

Retail stores come in all sizes, from very small to very large. A store retailer could be classified in terms of one or more of several characteristics.

Extent of service

Self-service was introduced in South Africa by the Checkers group of supermarkets in the early fifties. Full service obviously results in higher operating costs and therefore must have an impact on the price structure of the retailer. Full service in

South Africa is found in exclusive retailing outlets such as upper-class fashion boutiques where high-value durable products are sold.

Product assortment

Retailers can also be classified according to the width and depth of their product assortment (product line sold).

- Specialty stores such as bookshops and toyshops carry a very narrow product line with a deep assortment.
- A department store carries a wide variety of product lines and each line operates as a separate department in the overall shop, for example the Edgars and Stuttafords department stores, and large hardware stores such as PG Timber.
- Supermarkets are large, low-cost, low-margin and high-volume stores that provide a wide variety of food, clothing, and household goods. In South Africa the best examples of supermarkets are the Pick 'n Pay, Spar, and Shoprite/Checkers groups of supermarkets.
- Convenience stores are small stores carrying a limited line of convenience products such as milk, bread, and cigarettes. They are located in or near residential areas and are open for long hours each day, seven days a week. The best examples are the greengrocer and the café on the corner, 7-11 retail outlets as well as petrol forecourt retailers.
- The hypermarket and superstore are both larger than the supermarket, with the hypermarket being the largest. Both carry food as well as non-food products and render basic services to the consumer.

Pricing structures

Classifying retailers according to the pricing structure is another way of distinguishing between the different retailers. Discount stores have been in operation in South Africa since the early sixties, with Massmart's Game and Dion brands being the most visible example. The products sold are national brand names, while lower prices are universally applied to the product range.

Store clusters

Another way of categorising retailing is according to the type of store cluster. Most retailers these days form clusters to attract customers, offering a wide variety of products and services. In the past, most of the retailers were located in the Central Business District (CBD). However, owing to socio-economic changes, retailers began moving to regional shopping centres (such as Eastgate in Gauteng and Canal Walk in Cape Town) and to the suburbs.

Non-store retailing

According to Kotler and Armstrong,[6] three types of non-store retailing can be identified, namely direct marketing, direct selling, and automatic vending.

Direct marketing

Direct marketing uses the advertising media to call upon the consumer to respond to the advertisement and includes catalogue marketing, direct marketing, and electronic shopping.

- Catalogue marketing involves selling by mailing catalogues to selected customers.
- In the case of telemarketing, the telephone is used to sell direct to the customer.
- Electronic shopping is still in its infancy in South Africa. The telephone, personal computer, and Beltel are used to contact the retailer to place an order. The order is processed and the goods required are then delivered to the customer.

Direct selling

Another form of non-store retailing is direct selling, also called door-to-door selling. Examples in South Africa include the selling of vacuum cleaners and encyclopaedias, as well as Tupperware parties held at the home of an agent.

Direct vending

The last form of non-store retailing is automatic vending, a 24-hour method of selling convenience products such as cigarettes, cold drinks, and snacks. Vending machines are found in easily accessible places and help to distribute convenience products at a premium to the consumer.

Any discussion on the future of retailing is, however, incomplete unless the evolution of retailing is included.

The evolution of retailing

The earliest form of retailing in southern Africa is the bartering that took place between local tribes. After the European settlers had landed at the Cape, sole traders of fresh fruit, meat, and vegetables began selling these products to the local population. After colonisation of the hinterland, a new retailer, the pedlar, was born. The pedlar took basic necessities such as sugar, tea, coffee, and cooking utensils around the country areas on his wagon. Following the first pioneers, he travelled through the country taking products and services to the interior.

When the first diamonds – and later gold – were discovered in the interior, the first retailers such as general dealers, hotels, and brothels, were opened. At this time certain needs were perceived, for example for capital equipment, especially mining equipment, and for more formalised distribution channels. This resulted in the establishment of wholesalers in the former provinces of Transvaal, Natal, and the Northern Cape. Importers situated at the coastal harbours were at this stage still dominant in the distribution system, owning some of the wholesalers and retailers in the interior. With the development of an infrastructure in the Johannesburg area, the importers were obliged to locate in this area since this was the growth point in southern Africa and also the key to the rest of South Africa.

General dealers, who were the major store retailers at the turn of the twentieth century, began to expand, opening branches in different locations. This resulted in the chain-store groups as they are known today.

The next development was the introduction of department stores such as Greatermans and Ackermans. During the late forties and at the beginning of the fifties, discount stores and the first supermarkets were introduced. At this stage there was a growing trend toward urbanisation and the development of suburbs further away from the CBD. This led to the development of suburban shopping centres.

At present, South Africa has a sophisticated retail infrastructure in the urban areas which compares very favourably with American retailing. As stated previously, the rural areas are not fully developed, since a great deal of reliance is still placed on the older forms of retailing such as the general dealer, while in the rural areas, even the pedlar still supplies the retailer and also sells direct to the public. However, this is changing as large retail groups have begun acquiring rural chains and actively targeting these markets. Mainstream retailers realise the potential these areas hold as well as the need to expand in markets outside of an increasingly saturated urban sector.

Against this background it is important to look at the factors that inhibited the development of black retailing in South Africa. This will be done by looking firstly at the development of black retailing in three phases (from before 1976 until 1994), and secondly at the present situation of black business in South Africa.[7]

The period up to 1976

Most authors (Louw 1979; Van den Berg 1984; Rammala 1989) agree that politics tended to dominate the lives of black people and cloud business issues to such an extent that the normal functions of black retailing became impaired. According to Rammala,[8] the development of black communities who settled around the country's major white cities was discouraged and even ignored. He referred to the first investigation by the Stallard Commission in 1921 into the desirability of the presence of black people in the urban areas and the doctrine which was subsequently laid down that black people in the urban areas existed solely for the purpose of providing labour for their white counterparts. The result was that black townships around white cities and towns remained undeveloped, and that black retailing suffered and was discouraged.

In 1948, when the National Party came into power, apartheid became official government policy. Mazwai[9] wrote that since 1948 'black business has been hammered into penury by various enactments'. After 1948 the introduction of severe restrictions hampered the entry of black retailers into the formal business sector in the white cities. Even in the townships the freedom of entrepreneurs to establish and expand their business undertakings was seriously curtailed.

Many additional restrictive measures on black business since 1959 retarded the growth of black retailers and discouraged black people from entering business.

Some of the most significant measures were as follows:[10]
- The nature of business that black people could conduct was limited because they were not allowed to run more than one business, even in a different residential area.
- Black businesses were confined to meeting the daily essential needs of local communities.
- The establishment of black companies and partnerships was prohibited.
- All buildings necessary for business activities were to be erected by local authorities and not by black businessmen themselves.

The effect of these restrictive measures in the political and constitutional fields excluded black people from participation at all levels of government. The official view that black towns were transient dormitory locations which would one day disappear, had a great influence on the planning and provision of essential infrastructure and militated against the development of black retailers in these areas. Backlogs in education, for example, were created since the policies produced wide disparities between the black and white population groups both in the context of educational programmes and in the provision of educational facilities, resulting in a poorly educated section of the population unable to understand and appreciate the elements of business.

Prior to 1976, according to Negota,[11] there was a lack of awareness by black consumers that black business needed their concerted support to make it viable in the face of current political and economic conditions. Black business also suffered because consumers believed that it was more expensive to buy in the townships than in the towns and cities, and that most black businessmen were predominantly food retailers. Black business was reduced to the level of convenience stores where only small amounts were spent, with the bulk of the money being spent in towns and cities. The many and various types of businesses found in white areas to cater to the needs of the communities, simply did not exist in the black business context.

The period 1976 to 1985

In the years following the Soweto riots, various restrictions affecting black business were lifted. The government felt a need to hold discussions with black leaders and acknowledged the importance of black business leaders for the first time.[12] As a result of this feeling, initiatives were taken, including a sharp focus on the need for expanding the scope of black business. In 1976 the range of business permitted in urban black townships was increased to 26 from the original seven. Another important change was that partnerships in which black people held at least 51% of the shares, were permitted from then on.

During 1984 the country experienced the most widespread black civil unrest since the Soweto riots in 1976. The underlying causes of the violence were continuing dissatisfaction with black education, anger at the exclusion of the black population group from political power, and the persistence of high inflation and deepening unemployment. The violence escalated over the years to a point where the black retailer's turnover was savaged and the rate of entry of new black retailers was in a steep. One of the reasons why black businesses were often destroyed, according to Motsuenyane,[13] was the lack of appreciation of the importance of black business or the suspicion that business contributed nothing towards the realisation of black political aspirations. Those running businesses in the townships were often looked upon as an extension of an exploitative, unjust and corrupt system.

According to Gama,[14] black retailers had attempted to gain the black consumers' buying power by launching 'Buy-at-home' or 'Buy Black' campaigns for many years before 1984, but these campaigns had proved unsuccessful. However, the boycotts of white-owned businesses during the early eighties proved to be a non-violent but effective tactic in encouraging black consumers to buy from black retailers.

The period 1986 to April 1994

The desegregation of trading areas took a step forward when the central business districts in Johannesburg and Durban were opened to trading by all races in 1986. This meant that members of all population groups could now freely obtain occupation and ownership rights of premises in the proclaimed area. By the end of 1986 a total of 29 central business districts had been opened to retailers of all races.

The repeal of major apartheid laws in 1991 helped pave the way for multiracial constitutional negotiations which began in December 1991. These developments ultimately impacted on black business.[15] The Group Areas Act and other major statutory pillars of apartheid and discrimination were repealed, paving the way for black business to operate freely for the first time.

Although the remaining legislative barriers had now been removed, the Race Relations Survey said black business continued to have to deal with the legacy of apartheid and with the volatile political situation which had undermined economic growth and stability. The boycotts had affected township business because wholesalers had been unable to obtain access to many townships, and prices had escalated to offset the risks of entering townships on account of the violence. Other problems experienced by black retailers during this period included the establishment in 1991 of large supermarkets on the peripheries of townships and the emergence of the informal sector which competed with these businesses, as well as the reluctance of major institutions to grant loans to black businesspeople because they were considered a high risk. Businesses destroyed during the violence had usually not been insured, resulting in heavy losses.

The period April 1994 to date

South Africa's first multiracial election took place in April 1994. The African National Congress (ANC) won the election with the support of 62,6% of the electorate.

With political change came social change, and the new government spearheaded a number of initiatives aimed at normalising South African society and its economy. These included broad policy frameworks, such as the Reconstruction and Development Programme (RDP), and Black Economic Empowerment (BEE) aimed at increasing the participation of Historically Disadvantaged South Africans (HDSA) in the economy.

BEE received a large amount of criticism during its early stage of implementation. For while BEE promoted empowerment through a redistribution of ownership, a lack of capital amongst HDSAs resulted in the empowerment of a few while most continued to be excluded from the economy. This has slowly been addressed with the introduction of the new Broad-based Black Economic Empowerment policy which advocates a shift away from an emphasis on the redistribution of ownership, towards the redistribution of economic opportunities.

Broad-based Empowerment measures the development of HDSAs across the areas of ownership, control, skills development, employment, and preferential procurement. With this new focus we are beginning to see real change (although not as fast as some would like), which is having an impact at community level. The new BEE policy promotes the adoption of Empowerment Charters which enable sectors to set their own targets and ensure that as an industry group, they promote the participation of HDSAs in their industry.

BEE and retail

At the time of writing, charters were active in over five sectors, and under construction in many others. The retail sector is not one of these.

The government has carefully and successfully encouraged the creation of Industry Empowerment Charters through a combination of its roles as customer, regulator, and licensor. By doing so it has been able to avoid the use of legal means. However, government has limited influence over the retail sector through the above roles, and many claim that for this reason the sector has been slow to transform. While it is true that the sector is presently not involved in a charter process, many retailers have active BEE programmes within their organizations, and have done so for many years. However, research[16] has shown that the main factors hindering this process include: the sheer size of the industry, the heightened level of competition between retailers, the shortage of necessary skills, the difficulties in verifying BEE credentials and the power of brands in the South African market.

The retailing environment

Adapting to change

Change constantly presents an organization with opportunities and threats; it is how one responds to these opportunities and threats which determines success in the retail market. An analysis of the marketing environment is essential if organizations are to take advantage of the opportunities, and circumvent the dangers. The essence of retailing is the management of change.

Retailing deals with many societal changes. If a popular singer adopts a unique clothing or hairstyle, this influence will almost immediately be seen in the fashion-forward sections of South African stores. With the advent of globalisation, the rate of change is accelerating in our society, profoundly affecting the way we live, dress, socialise, communicate and even think about ourselves. Political trends have worldwide influence, and competition from foreign markets challenges the retailer's ability to stay on the cutting edge of these changes. Retailers face the inevitable fact that quick and appropriate response is the only way to stay current, to differentiate oneself from the competition, and to avoid becoming a 'me-too' retailer.

Retailing is one of the most sophisticated businesses in our country – featuring state-of-the-art computerised merchandise control and distribution systems, magical merchandise presentation, in-depth consumer and market research, and representation of merchandise from worldwide markets. The ever-present constant in this equation is change. Growth, on the other hand, is optional. Retailing cannot grow and expand as a profession unless South Africa commits itself to trend (change) management. Retailers continually strive to understand their customers – to renew their marketing strategies or replace them when they no longer serve their customers. Too many retailers exercise their egos by telling customers what is good for them. Marketers ask customers what they want and give it to them. Therein lies the major difference!

In the end, like any other successful element in our workplace, the strength of retailing comes from achieving an appropriate balance between continuity and change, between consistency and innovation, and between traditional and breakthrough ideas. In the world of retailing, consumers buy satisfaction and at the same time generate profit for the sellers. Because retailing institutions must be as dynamic as the environment in which they exist, retail strategies are subject to constant change.

Two components of the market environment which are of cardinal importance to retailers and which change constantly are consumers and intermediaries.

Consumers

A market has two sides: a supply side and a demand side. On the demand side are all the possible consumers of the products or services the retailer offers, and on the supply side are all the retailers (competitors) offering more or less similar products on the market. Competing retailers thus vie with one another in the market to satisfy consumer demand.

Consumers are probably the most uncontrollable of all the variables with which retailers have to contend. Retailers serve consumers from varied walks of life who display different patterns of behaviour, and these are manifested in their purchasing behaviour. Since the success of retailing lies in customer contact, understanding customers' motivations, buying habits and lifestyles is a prerequisite for successful retailing. Retailers' marketing planning should therefore be driven by their perception of how and why customers behave as they do, and how they are likely to respond to the various elements of the marketing mix. Knowledge of their customers' behaviour patterns would enable them to make need-satisfying products available in suitable packaging, at prices which they are willing to pay, and in places which they prefer to patronise.

There have been some changes in consumer purchasing behaviour. We have seen a rise in the number of convenience shops as consumers have decreased their reliance on monthly shopping trips and are prepared to pay a premium for convenience. The surge in choice and competition has afforded customers to be less loyal and hunt for bargains when they are to be had. There has also been a national drive to promote local products, specifically through the Proudly South African campaign. While patriotism in South Africa is definitely on the rise, the truth is that for many South Africans, price and branding remain the major consideration in their purchasing decisions.

Intermediaries are also important to retailers because they form an essential link between manufacturers and consumers.

Intermediaries

Intermediaries are found in the demand side of the market and include wholesalers and retailers, commercial agents and brokers and, in the Third World, also spaza shops.[17]

It was estimated that there were in excess of 200 000 licensed hawkers trading in the metropolitan areas in South Africa – 8 000 of them in Johannesburg – while spaza shops were said to number more than 100 000 in the country as a whole employing almost 300 000 people with a further 1 000 000 dependents.[18] About R32 billion of retail trade's annual turnover is attributed to hawkers and spaza shops. Sustainability remains a challenge in this sector. In a five-year period, 36% of spaza shops and 20% of hawkers remain in business.[19] On average hawkers show a monthly surplus of R600 per month on R2 400 worth of sales, while spazas retain R1 300 on goods worth R7 700.[20]

The penetration of national retailing chains into black residential areas remains negligible. While there exists an opportunity for these retailers to develop these areas, lack of access and infrastructure, uncertainty and aggression are significant barriers to their involvement. In addition any development would need to be done in conjunction with the community and its leaders, the demands of whom include sourcing labour from the community as well as ensuring any development does not harm spazas and hawkers in the surrounding region. To date successful development has been limited to the establishment of cash-and-carry outlets close to black townships and to supplying the small black traders in these areas. Coca-Cola has also been successful in establishing a supply chain into the townships through its driver network.

Holt and Horne[21] maintain that the person wanting to open a retail outlet in the townships faces huge disadvantages, such as lack of education, low standards, poor credit track records, and unsuitable premises. However, there are advantages. Markets are concentrated, they are convenient for shoppers, and they have better credibility than potential opponents in white areas.

The variables in the macro-environment exert a strong influence on retailing and should thus be monitored regularly. Some of the more important variables are discussed next.

The macro-environment

The forces in the macro-environment represent the uncontrollable factors with which marketers do not deal directly but which directly or indirectly influence both their organization and market environment. These factors include the social, economic, political, technological, and international variables which impact on retailing in various ways.

Social environment

While South Africa is a culturally diverse society with divisions along language, race, culture and religion, there is a drive to build a sense of nationalism of different people in one country. This is the social mix in which retailers currently operate and they need to be sympathetic to cultural and regional differences.

South Africa has urbanised at a rate faster than most countries and well ahead of the global average; however, this growth is beginning to slow. Figures on this subject do differ due to differences in the definition. However, using the 2001 Census, the UN estimates current urban levels to be around 57% (growing at 1,4% per annum). The UN also predicts that South Africa's urban population will top 70% in 2030. Over this period the growth will continue to slow, with rural growth figures in the negative.

Education category	Asian/Indian		Black/African		Coloured		White		Average	
Tertiary	14,9	(10)	5,2	(3)	4,9	(4,3)	29,8	(24,1)	8,4	(6,2)
Grade 12	34,9	(30,4)	16,8	(12,1)	18,5	(12,3)	40,9	(40,7)	20,4	(16,4)
Some secondary	33,0	(40)	30,4	(32,8)	40,1	(42,5)	25,9	(32,8)	30,8	(33,9)
Complete/some primary	11,9	(13,1)	25,4	(27,8)	28,2	(30,7)	2	(1,2)	22,4	(24,2)
None	5,3	(6,5)	22,3	(24,3)	8,3	(10,2)	1,4	(1,2)	17,9	(19,3)

Sources: StatsSA, 1998; 2000; 2003

Table 2.1: Percentage of adult South Africans (20 and older) in each education category by population group, 2001 census with 1996 census figures in brackets

South Africa is in an unenviable position of having both high unemployment, and severe skills shortages. Education levels differ vastly between communities as a consequence of years of exclusion. This is changing as the government strives to make education both accessible and affordable to all. Refer to Table 2.1 for statistics on the education levels among different race groups in South Africa.

Unemployment remains one of the biggest black marks on an otherwise outstanding social scorecard. While the total number of people employed has increased 25% over the past 10 years, almost half of that growth has been in the informal sector, while unemployment has grown 106% in the same time (from 20,3% to 28,2% according to the strict definition). It should be stressed, however, that unemployment levels have dropped during the past few years as South Africa has enjoyed significant growth in the construction, trade, and financial services industries.[22]

HIV/AIDS remains the other concern affecting social development in South Africa. Many businesses remained unconvinced as to the impact HIV/AIDS will have on their businesses. The effect in the mining industry is well documented, and these operators have already begun to make significant changes to address the challenge, but by and large stakeholders remain critical of current progress by government and the public sector at large in this regard.

The social variables referred to above (population, urbanisation, education, and employment) jointly and separately affect trends in income and expenditure patterns, which are crucial issues impinging on retail decision-making.

Economic environment

The South African economy went through a torrid time in 1998/9 with the Far East crisis and its impact on developing markets around the world. The crisis triggered a number of years of high interest rates and spiralling rand. However, South Africa weathered this storm and is now reaping the benefits of some tight fiscal management and investment.

The expansion of the tax base has widened the tax burden while at the same time allowing an increase in social grants and service delivery. Due to a stronger rand (helped by a weakened US dollar), inflationary pressures have come down and, with them, interest rates. On the back of these factors, consumer and business confidence has steadily risen, resulting in both an ability and propensity for people to spend. Extraordinary factors (such as the successful 2010 Soccer World Cup bid) continue to underpin this rise.

However, there remain some voices, if soft, of concern. The stronger rand has had a negative influence on a range of sectors (most noticeably tourism and manufacturing), as well as widening the balance of payments deficit. South Africa benefited this last year from an influx of foreign investment, but a high proportion of this investment was once off and therefore not sustainable. Finally much of the spending power is being supported by easily accessible credit. While rising incomes and higher net worth (through higher property prices) is supporting this growth, it needs to settle at a sustainable level. South African savings as a per-centage of GDP also remains dismal by global comparison.

Political environment

While there remain some concerns around the lack of a significant opposition party to the ANC, the successful transition from an exclusive government to open democracy cannot be questioned.

South Africa is a major player in African politics and is doing much to improve the perception of Africa in the rest of the world. It is understood that if Africa wants to develop, it needs the rest of the world, if not to provide aid, then to provide the social and economic environments that are conducive to such development.

In doing so, the government is building a continent with growing opportunities for South African businesses. Already mining and telecom companies have expanded speedily into new markets in Africa. Shoprite has grown into the largest retailer in Africa, now looking to new opportunities in the sub-continent.

Political intervention in the retail sector is at a minimum; however, there have been a number of key incidents over the past two years. In the first instance, there was the move to charge for plastic bags at the paypoint counters of supermarkets in an effort to reduce the negative impact that freely available carrier bags were having on the environment. The second incident was the opening of the pharmaceuticals sector to non-pharmacist owned businesses, as well as new pricing regulations. At present this issue remains unresolved in the South Africa courts, but it has provided retailers with a new avenue for growth (although rather less profitable).

Technological environment

The technological environment is responsible for the rate of innovation and change. The retailer's technological environment incorporates improvements in processes which increase the productivity and efficiency of existing systems while reducing the demand on manual labour.

New technologies being developed with regard to retailing include: electronic shelf-edge labels that can be updated automatically from a central computer net-work; wireless communications that will enable retailers to be more flexible in the layout of their stores; and RFID (Radio Frequency Identification), an alternative to bar-coding which allows tags to be read by scanners without line of sight. This sys-tem is particularly topical after the adoption by Wal-Mart and its top 100 suppli-ers in the US, and the cascading effect this will have on manufacturers and sup-pliers around the world.

Such technology promises major advantages for retailers: it drastically reduces shrinkage which has been attributed mainly to employees and customers; it pro-vides invaluable marketing information on customers, which enables retailers to respond quickly and effectively to changes in consumer buying patterns; it can readily link information from regional branches and distribution centres to head office; it leads to better stock control and the ability to cut stock-holding, since stock levels can be related to the correct anticipation of changing purchasing patterns; and it improves customer service, notably the speed of service, which is becoming increasingly important in an era when the prices of products in the major supermarket chains differ very little.

International environment

Technological innovation in the fields of transport and communication has brought the nations of the world closer together in terms of distance and time. Organizations that operate internationally find themselves in a far more complex business environment because every country has its own unique environmental factors, with its own technology, culture, laws, politics, markets and competitiveness, which are different to those of other countries. Nations are also more dependent than ever on each other's technologies, economies, politics, and raw materials, so that the developments in these fields inevitably influence the decisions of management. In the light of the above discussions, some future perspectives of trends in retailing in South Africa are now presented.

Global trends

The lure of globalisation

Global retailers hit by sagging growth prospects in their home markets or lack of suitable acquisition targets due to competition constraints have looked for opportunities abroad. American retailers have been particularly active in the European markets as well as in the Far East (along with other European retailers).

Global retailers are particularly interested in developing markets, which are highly fragmented, with a large consumer base and with large opportunities for the use of supply chain efficiencies to compete. There is particular interest in Asian and Eastern European markets.

Africa remains largely untouched by these retailers; however, South African retailers are taking their advantage of vicinity to these markets, and similar markets to set up retail chains in a highly fragmented market, the best example of this trend being Shoprite. South African retailers have historically also had an interest in the Australian market with its similarities to the South African retail environment. Players in that regard include Pick 'n Pay and Metro Cash & Carry.

Favourable trade agreements such as Nafta (North American Free Trade Agreement) and Gatt (General Agreement on Tariffs and Trade), as well as political developments in the rest of the world, support this global trend.

Private sector adopting non-core functions from the public sector

With a change from exclusive to open democracy, we have seen the focus of government change, specifically from maintaining an elite minority while suppressing a majority, to an emphasis on social development, service delivery and upliftment for all. However in doing so, there have had to be some concessions made.

In many instances the private sector is having to adopt new non-core functions as part of day-to-day business in South Africa. Public safety is one area where retailers are employing security personnel, or outsourcing these services to security companies, to improve the level of safety for customers and reduce the risk of crime in their stores.

Education and skills is another area in which retailers are taking an active step to improve the development of their staff. Management courses have always been a part of this process; however, retailers are now designing courses in conjunction with universities which are accredited by these institutions in areas of financial management, store management, and computer literacy courses to name but a few. By doing so employees are developing the very skills that their employers require, making the process far more efficient and beneficial for both parties.

Savings and financial assets rise

Despite historically high valuations, financial markets should do well over the next few years. Baby boomers will increase their level of savings as they reach their peak earning years and focus more on saving for retirement. This increase in savings will provide a foundation for financial markets, putting downward pressure on interest rates. At the same time, higher savings will be a drag on retail spending.

Deflating the domestic economy

After many years of higher inflation, retailers have to get used to operating in a lower inflationary environment. Certain sectors have been experiencing deflationary pricing over the past three years, notably the apparel sector (due to poor merchandising and the need to push volumes) and electronics (due to the stronger rand and lower import prices). The food sector is also under threat as retailers fight for volume share. Retailing in a lower inflationary environment does require a shift in focus to an emphasis on increasing volume sales.

Deflation poses a significant risk to the health of the economy. Deflation favours creditors over debtors, not a positive development in a heavily indebted economy such as South Africa.

Digital economy

The development of the digital economy is having a profound impact on the traditional 'physical' or 'atom-based' economy. The digital economy is far more flexible and responsive to changes in the business world, thus making this sub-economy less vulnerable to recessions (without taking into account the type of goods retailed). For instance, retailers in the digital economy are not hit by a sudden overcapacity when a recession hits; instead, through selling and moving goods through virtual channels, and often outsourcing their supply chain, they are able to adapt to the business cycles. Also there are few physical limits to growth in the digital economy, where the marginal cost of producing an additional unit of output approaches zero.

The digital economy in South Africa is small and will remain small for many years to come. While a number of clicks-and-bricks companies have moved into this sector, their motivation has been mainly to prevent part of their market share (the techno-savvy level) from jumping ship to a retailer which that market segment may consider to be more in tune with its needs. However, there will be an additional benefit for these companies: the digital economy does provide new and innovative ways of both retailing and connecting with the market. Success will come to those retailers that use this medium to challenge the traditional ways of doing business and combine the best high volume businesses with the level of information and intimacy available in the digital space.

Technology and the importance of place

For the growing number of knowledgeable workers who can operate in a virtual world, technology will greatly expand the choice of where to live. Telecommuting will liberate workers from the confines of a specific location. It will allow workers to define their own work-spaces, working conditions, and even hours of work.

The shift to virtual work space will reduce the importance of location for conducting business. It will redefine the concept of a good location. Quality of life will take on greater importance in deciding where to locate. As a result, population growth will shift. Growth will occur in the cities, where access to the arts, amenities, and community will attract people.

Falling real estate prices

Over the past 15 years, retail space has grown faster than both population and consumer demand. Retailers continued to chase this new space; however, that is changing and recently, for the first time, a new shopping centre failed to secure more than one major anchor tenant (others did subsequently move in). The net result is that landlords are having to provide very attractive agreements to entice major anchors. To subsidise these agreements, smaller and independent traders have been hit by rising rentals resulting in many having to close or move to less expensive (and less profitable) locations.

The result is a homogenised mix of stores across regional malls. To differentiate themselves malls will look to include entertainment as part of their package; this includes central stages, big screens, entertainment courts and even mini fun parks.

Regional shopping malls

Regional shopping malls are receiving some investment as a result of the current upsurge in consumer spending. However, this is due to the buoyant economy, and in the longer term we can expect malls to lose market share to smaller neighbourhood shopping centres. This is partly due to consolidation in the retail sector, which is resulting in regional malls taking on a very similar store profile to each other.

In order to sustain their market share and continue to draw consumers, new mall developments are incorporating an element of entertainment and adventure to provide customers with a more fun, complete, and emotive shopping experience. Gateway Mall in Durban has a wave pool and a climbing wall, while Canal Walk shopping centre at Century City includes Renaissance-inspired frescoes decorating the domed ceiling, as well as a skating and water park. Century City itself is rapidly being populated with residential apartments and marketed as a lifestyle village with adjacent shopping facilities.

Urban retail renaissance

City planners are encouraging companies and people back into the city centres. For many years now we have seen the migration of people and businesses into the suburbs, creating mini CBDs in suburban districts. The result is an under-use of inner-city property. Many of these buildings are being converted into loft apartments, attracting younger professionals, and with them attracting late night shopping, restaurants and nightlife back into the CBD.

Rise of the blade-runner society

South African society will continue to splinter into increasingly smaller groups that are more diverse in their education, wealth and income, ethnicity, characteristics, tastes and shopping behaviours. The traditional middle-class family will decline in number and importance.

The fastest-growing division in society will be along the lines of educated versus not-educated. The educated will live and work in a controlled-climate, controlled-access world dominated by information and knowledge. They will be engaged in the manipulation of images. Theirs will be a world of bit-based digital reality. The uneducated will live in a world dominated by physical labour and the physical reality of the atom-based world. Neither access to nor the environment of their world will be controlled.

The wealthy, the educated, those who live in the digital world, will increasingly remove themselves from the physical world. They will control public access to where they live, where they work, where they shop, and where they play. They will shop more by catalogue and other electronic means.

The rise of the single-person household

Staying single for longer, rising rates of divorce, living longer and increased work demands (particularly on women) are all changing the traditional shape of the South African household. Smaller and single-person households have very different life styles, needs and wants. Retailers have identified this and are adjusting their merchandise and marketing approach to target a growing sector with money to spend.

Youth: Financially independent market

In line with global trends, retailers are targeting the youth market, which is becoming increasingly financially independent. They have very different purchasing criteria from their parents, and retailers focusing on this market have adjusted their approach accordingly. This includes a more fashion-conscious approach and aligning sponsorships with teen celebrities.

The middle-aged: Changing needs

The number of middle-aged South Africans will also increase over the next few years. The chief barrier to greater consumer spending by this group is not so much income as energy. While at the peak of their earnings, this group is more income-constrained than they appear. Facing the high cost of education for their children and the need to increase savings for their own retirement, spending at retail will be a declining priority. This group will be a source of many new business startups.

An increase in the number of middle-aged South Africans also means an expanding waistline in a large segment of the population. Thin may be in, but for the growing number of middle-aged South Africans, fat is where it's at. The changes this group will create in consumer spending include:
- more high-end thrill-seeking
- redefinition of large-size apparel
- casualisation of society
- rising prices of financial assets
- rising savings rate
- redefinition of careers
- more time-for-money trade-offs.

The young elderly, aged from 55 to 64, are the most overlooked group of consumers relative to their spending potential.

The changes this group will create include:
- redefinition of old
- beauty at any age
- rise in value of vacation homes
- boom in travel
- extended work life
- boom in health care.

Changing retail format

In the grocery retail sector there has been an explosion in the convenience-retailing format. With the buoyancy in the economy, people are beginning to pay a premium for convenience retailing. The larger retail supermarkets are also expanding into this section, bringing prices down in this format. The rollout of new stores is also a case of retailers moving the store to the customer to win the battle for premium retail space.

Addition to retail market

Retailers are expanding into new product areas using their expertise in certain facets of their existing businesses and leveraging off large customer databases and information. The changes are blurring the lines of what is traditionally considered a retailer into the financial and business support services sectors.

Expansion into lower market

As the market saturates around more traditional market segments, retailers are seeing the opportunities that lie in targeting the lower-middle and lower income markets and attracting these people as customers earlier in their development. This has been done through acquiring chains that are aimed at this market in both urban and rural markets, and expanding these networks with more easily accessible funds.

References

1   This case study was updated by Mark Wilson, industry analyst, Ernst & Young. Case study procured by Michael Cant.
2   http://www.ey.com/global/download.nsf/South_Africa/Jun03_SA_Retail_Industry/$file/S.A.%20 Retail%20Industry.%20June%202003.pdf.
3   Ibid.
4   The retail market, as defined in this chapter, is given as all instances in which a transaction takes place (e.g. not only foods and goods, but services as well). However, the figure provided for the size of the retail market (R234bn) relates only to the sale of retail goods and not wholesale or services. Figures taken from StatsSA.
5   Kotler, P. & Armstrong, G. 1991. *Principles of marketing*. Englewood Cliffs: Prentice-Hall.
6   Ibid.
     Lewison, D. M. 1994. *Retailing*. New York: Macmillan.
7   Brink, A. 1997. The marketing perception of grocery store retailers belonging to black business associations in Gauteng. Unpublished thesis for the D.Com degree. Unisa.
8   Rammala, S. T. 1989. The development of black communities and the role to be played by small business entrepreneurs. *Juta's South African Journal of Property*, 5(1):4-9.
9   Mazwai, T. 1991. Township tragedy. *Finance Week*, 49(10):24-26.
10 Van den Berg, G. J. 1984. Beperkinge van kleinsake-ondernemings met spesifieke verwysing na die swart entrepreneur. Unpublished dissertation for the BML degree. Unisa.
11 Negota, G. 1988. Is business really black? *African Business*, 15(1):5-6.
12 Butler, C. 1989. *The extent and nature of black business development*. Sandton: LS Associates.
13 Motsuenyane, S. 1990. *Portfolio of black business in southern Africa*. Johannesburg: Portfolio Business Publications.
14 Gama, P. 1986. The role of the black businessman. *African Business*, 13(8)31.
     Ghosh, A. 1994. *Retail Management*. Fort Worth: Dryden.
15 Race Relations Survey. 1991/92. Johannesburg: South African Institute of Race Relations.
16 Ernst & Young survey on the attitudes and perceptions of retailers towards BEE, June 2004.
17 Van der Walt, A; Strydom, J. W.; Marx, S.; & Jooste, D. J. 1996. *Marketing management*. Kenwyn: Juta.
18 BMR press release, 5 November 2002.
19 BMR Study, *ThisDay*, 11 February 2004.
20 *Financial Mail*, 27 February 2004.
21 Holt, H. & Horne, K. 1995. Multi-cultural marketing. *Marketplace*, 17(2):8-9.
22 StatsSA Labour Force Survey, September 2003.

Buy-aid societies: An unknown factor in the South African consumer society?

Background

Contemporary buy-aid societies have their roots in the commercial cooperatives which developed out of the poor economic circumstances of the 1920s. The commercial cooperatives were born out of the needs of poor communities and had the aim of obtaining cheaper prices for their members by inter alia using collective bargaining actions and the economies of scale principles. The direct advantage to a member was the purchasing discount obtained from suppliers such as retailers and other institutions. Today's buy-aid societies function in a similar way. The monetary advantage is passed on to members after operational costs by the buy-aid society are deducted and a small percentage kept in reserve. This advantage occurs in the form of a bonus payment to members once a year. However, buy-aid societies currently face challenges linked to changed demographics and a changed market-place, the implications of which are discussed later on.

The basic activities performed by the buy-aid society include:

- Being the intermediary between the member and a retailer such as a large grocery retailer (e.g. Checkers). What the buy-aid society does is to obtain a discount on the amount owing by its members from the particular merchant. The society gathers the outstanding money in full from its members and pays the difference over to the chain after a period of time. The society benefits in two ways, namely retaining the discount and receiving cash from its members which is kept on interest in a bank for a short period before being paid over to the retailer.

- Another business activity performed by the society is to be a broker between an insurance company and the members of the buy-aid society. Again the society places the business with the insurer and collects the money from the member.
- One of the most profitable business activities performed by the society is to let its members borrow money from it over a short period of time. The member borrows the money at a competitive rate and pays it back within a certain time frame. The society benefits because the interest earned is higher than the amount that it could earn in the form of a deposit at a commercial bank. Hire purchasing agreements with its members are one of the most profitable trans-actions for the buy-aid societies.

The history of buy-aid societies is in certain instances intertwined with the civil service and shows an exponential growth in the period from when they started. Pretorium Trust, a case in point, started in 1938 as the Civil Servants Mutual Aid. In the late forties it was registered as a Trade Cooperative and the membership was open to any private sector person. Today Pretorium Trust has over 27 000 house-holds using its benefits and has paid cash bonuses in excess of 5% to its members for more than 50 years.[1] However, today there are only a few of these institutions left in South Africa, with some of the most visible being Koopkrag[2] and Pretorium Trust in Pretoria and Cape Consumers in Cape Town.

In addition, the cooperative principles, originally introduced by the first co-operatives or buy-aid societies, have been taken over by other players in society. The South African government and especially the non-governmental organiza-tions (NGOs) are supporting the use of the cooperative principles in starting small businesses – especially in the disadvantaged communities of South Africa. The cooperative society in agriculture has also run its course and more and more agri-cultural cooperatives in South Africa have converted to private/public companies with major shareholding outside the farming community. Stokvels, popular and widespread throughout South Africa, follow the basics of the cooperative society principles, as do the many burial societies. The members of stokvels, burial soci-eties and other small businesses work together as a community to further the ideals of the community, doing so in a cost-effective way. In this way they are fill-ing a gap missed by the original buy-aid societies. Furthermore, all the major retailers have moved into the buy-aid area of expertise with incentives such as Loyalty Cards. All of these factors have limited the potential market for buy-aid societies. The failure of buy-aid societies to adapt to changing circumstances is a case-in-point for the consequences of inadequate environmental scanning and doing SWOT analysis. The analysis on the next page examines the changing market for buy-aid societies and further explores the reasons for the limited market share which buy-aid societies currently hold.

Benefits of membership to Cape Consumers

The following benefits of membership to Cape Consumers in Cape Town are mentioned in their website (http://www.buyaid.co.za):

- Annual bonus (the bonus consists of discounts negotiated with contracted merchants and the accrued interest on the investment thereof – a bonus of about 5% of a member's annual purchases is the norm)
- Wide variety of suppliers (more than 1 700 merchants)
- Interest-free credit (at least 30 days interest-free credit)
- Convenient and safe shopping (no cash needed to buy)
- Guaranteed transaction (payment is guaranteed by Cape Consumers)
- Exclusive insurance packages (various group scheme packages at competitive prices from Santam, Metropolitan Life and Rentmeester – the monthly insurance payments contribute to the annual bonus)
- Car hire purchases (two options available, one that helps to generate a bonus for the member)
- Travel benefits (local and international travel through contracted travel agencies contributes to bonus plus free international travel insurance)
- Personal loans
- Budget facility (paying for more expensive products over a period of up to 24 months)

The fee structure of Cape Consumers[3]

Cape Consumers levies the following monthly fees on its members:

- Annual service fee – R35 per card is levied annually
- Transaction cost – 35c per transaction
- Petrol purchases – petrol cannot be supplied on credit or at a discount and Cape Consumers must pay the petrol stations up front. Therefore a surcharge of 2,5% is levied on all petrol purchases and no bonus is earned on buying of petrol.
- Card insurance – an agreement with Santam covers members against abuse of their cards if stolen or lost. Card insurance is compulsory and costs R5,70 per annum.
- Purchases from supermarkets. As a result of low margins of these suppliers lower discounts are determined. To augment these discounts a surcharge of 2% is levied on all purchases at Shoprite, Checkers, Woolworths and selected Spar stores.

Bonus payments at Cape Consumers[4]

In the 2003 financial year it was reported that Cape Consumers had a turnover of nearly R647 million with contracted suppliers and that an amount of nearly R28 million was appropriated for the payment of bonuses to members. This bonus payment was spread over 25 500 principal account holders.

The members of the buy-aid societies

Some of the characteristics of the current members of these societies are as follows:

Elderly members
A growing number of the members are older than 60 – implying that these people are on pension with the implications of a fixed income and usually a declining income. The age grouping between 20 and 30 is, in most instances, the least representative of the membership basis.

Declining income
In direct correlation with the growing number of elderly members is a growing number of members with a very small monthly income, which means a decline in turnover from them, which affects the bonuses of the buy-aid societies.

In general the buy-aid societies are influenced by the amount of disposable income in the hands of the customers. There is, in most cases, a link between the use of any form of credit and the amount of disposable income in the hands of the customer. Over the past forty years the average disposable income per decade was 5% in the sixties, 4% in the seventies and between 1980 and 2000 the average declined to only 1,7% per year. The expectation is that the average increase in disposable income between 2000 and 2005 will be below 2% per annum.[5] Average South African customers are renowned for their quest to improve their living standards, with a notable percentage living way above their means.

The widespread use of credit and debit cards by South African consumers is another trend that is hurting the buy-aid societies as this way of doing business competes directly with their activities.

The suppliers

Not all the chain store retailers are contracted to the buy-aid societies. Significantly, the Pick 'n Pay group of stores is not contracted to the buy-aid societies. This results in a number of potential members not able or not keen to become members of a buy-aid society. The list of suppliers to the buy-aid societies is nevertheless impressive with Shoprite, Spar, Game/Dion and Woolworths being the most important chain stores forming part of supplier base. It is especially the Shoprite group that is seen as the major customer of the buy-aid organizations. In the period June 2001 to June 2002 the market share of the four major retailers was as follows. See Graph 3.1 below:

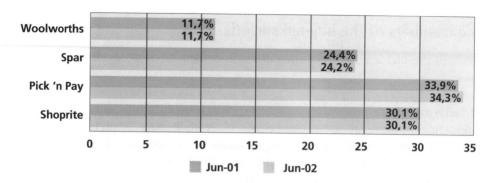

Graph 3.1: Market share of the four largest South African retailers (period June 2001 to June 2002)

As can be seen from Figure 3.1 Pick 'n Pay has the largest share of the market (33,9%) followed by the Shoprite group with a market share of 30,1% and then Spar with 24,4% and Woolworths with 11,7%.[6] The buy-aid organizations are doing business with three of the four largest retailers but the exclusion of Pick 'n Pay is obviously detrimental to the marketing efforts of the buy-aid societies.

The question why Pick 'n Pay is not interested in the affiliation with the buy-aid societies can be found in the way it operates. In the past there were a few times where Pick 'n Pay was accused of being more of a bank than a food retailer. Stock turnover figures of between 12 and 14 times a year were attained whilst creditors were paid between 45 and 60 days.[7] Obviously there were a few weeks that the money of the creditors was earning interest in the bank accounts of Pick 'n Pay. Raymond Ackerman was quite clear on this issue when he said: 'Managing cash and interest has always been our business'.[8]

To this end Pick 'n Pay diversified in the late nineties to deliver a financial service together with Boland PKS bank. One of the activities was to be the deposit taking arm where customers of Pick 'n Pay could invest money in the bank. At the end of the association with Boland Bank there were at least 100 000 customers that had deposited R150 million through the Pick 'n Pay branch network. Thereafter, Pick 'n Pay started a partnership with Nedbank, called 'Go Banking'. This was done in order to attract further deposits as well as to entice customers to do online buying at www.picknpay.co.za. Nedbank also scored with partnership because they suddenly had a drastic increase in 'branches' with more than 400 super- and hypermarkets fronting as representatives of the bank. The bottom line why Pick 'n Pay is not interested in an association with the buy-aid societies is because of the long lead time in getting its money back from the customer through the buy-aid societies. This lead-time is rather used by Pick 'n Pay to gather interest for its own account.

Reasons why members are resigning from buy-aid organizations and why new members are loath to join

Any rational person would think that an organization that provides you with an interest-free loan to buy from a retailer, which you only need to pay back within a period of between 30 and 45 days, and on top of which you can earn a once-off bonus at the end of the year, should have a flood of potential members applying every day. This is, however, not the case. Some of the reasons why potential customers are not applying or why existing customers are resigning are as follows:

- **Financial problems:** A number of existing members resign because they do not have the financial discipline to be able to manage the account on a monthly basis. It is especially new members that don't have the financial discipline to manage the buy-now-and-pay-later principle. This problem was also encountered particularly by clothing retailers when they went on a drive to open new clothing accounts a few years ago.
- **Geographic location:** One of the major problems of the buy-aid societies is that their customer base is centred in the major urban areas with limited membership outside of these areas. One of the complaints of rural members is that there are not enough suppliers/retailers available in the rural towns such as Lichtenburg, Nelspruit and Beaufort West to make it viable for members to enrol and to reap the benefits of the buy-aid organizations.
- **Paying in cash:** Another reason why the membership of buy-aid societies is declining is that for various reasons customers often prefer to pay in cash. For some customers cash is the only way they want to do business, despite the great risk incurred by carrying large amounts of cash on your person.
- **Convenience and preference:** Customers may want to buy from a Pick 'n Pay store, either due to preference or because it may be the nearest store to where they live (a matter of geography).
- **Loyalty card:** An additional reason given by some ex-members is that a large number of retailers – such as Edgars – have their own store loyalty card which provides a payback incentive to customers who use the Edgars cash card. Every few months the cash card customers get a free voucher for R50 (or multiples of R50) in the post, which ties in with a new sales promotion effort of Edgars. The sales promotion has the objective of encouraging the customer to visit his/her nearest Edgars store – hopefully to spend more than the amount given as a free voucher. There are a growing number of retailers that are using the store loyalty card concept to attract and maintain customers.
- **Emigration and old age:** These factors also lead to members resigning.

Summary

The buy-aid society was born during a time when the South African consumer was struggling to make ends meet. By pooling their resources (buying power) buy-aid societies leveraged discounts from participating merchants and eventually received a cash back bonus, which helped them to survive during difficult economic periods. What is interesting is that the same economic situation occurs today and yet the buy-aid industry is not benefiting from this. This is partly due to investment by government and by other small business societies taking over some of the gaps in the market left by buy-aid societies. In addition, the dynamic competitive environment of credit-supply now provides a variety of financial options for the consumer, whose needs are not all served by the buy-aid society. These factors have changed the demographics of buy-aid society members, the majority of whom are now lower-to-middle income pensioners. As a result of their failure to adapt to the changing socio-economic circumstances, buy-aid societies are limited to a particular market segment and are no longer the driving force of consumer life in South Africa.

References

1   This case study was written by Johan Strydom.
     Pretorium Trust. http://wwwprettrst.co.za. Date accessed: 19 June 2004.
2   Koopkrag. http://www.wierda.co.za. Date accessed: 19 June 2004.
3   Cape Consumers. http://www.buyaid.co.za. Date accessed: 19 June 2004.
4   Cape Consumers. http://www.buyaid.co.za. Date accessed: 19 June 2004.
5   Bureau of Market Research. 2002. National personal income of South Africa by income and population group, 1960–2005. Report 299. Pretoria: Unisa.
6   Shoprite Holdings, Financial results, June 2002.
7   Strydom, JW. 1991. Innovasie in die Suid-Afrikaanse groot voedelkleinhandel. Unpublished DCom dissertation, Pretoria: Unisa
8   Shoprite Holdings, Financial results, June 2002.
9   Keenan, T. & Harris, S. 17–23 April 1997. *Finance Week*, p 33.

MARKETING FEATURES:

ADVERTISING

LEGISLATION

PRODUCT STRATEGY

PROMOTION

SOCIAL MARKETING

SPONSORSHIPS

4

Smoke gets in your eye – Marketing a pariah product

Introduction

Smoking is one of those habits everyone has a definite opinion about. On the one side there are those who say that smoking is a bane and the ultimate vice of humankind. These are the people that will tell a smoker: 'If you want to smoke in my home, don't exhale!' Case studies have proved that smoking is bad for your health, is addictive and will shorten your life span. Given all this information we may well ask: 'Why are people still smoking?' This brings us to the five million or more smokers in South Africa who are being hounded by the press, their family and friends, their bosses, as well as the government, to stop smoking. So, why do these people smoke? Various theories have been put forward as to why people smoke – from an Oedipus complex, peer pressure or individualism, to a badge of honour. Most of the smokers agree that they would love to stop smoking – and eventually many of them will, but only a lucky few have enough willpower to do so immediately. Some smokers say smoking is so addictive – and the withdrawal symptoms so bad that they cannot stop smoking. Let us then take a look at the marketing of a reviled product and the influence of legislation (a macro-environmental variable) on this product.

The marketing of tobacco products until 2000

The Tobacco Control Act of 1993 was the first real step in the war against smoking. This Act banned the sale of tobacco to any person under the age of 16. It furthermore outlawed smoking in various public places, curbed the free advertisement of cigarettes and introduced the use of health warnings on tobacco packaging and in advertisements for tobacco products.[1] This act influenced the large tobacco organizations in South Africa. Rembrandt and British American Tobacco inter alia was forced to demarket their products through informative advertising about the negative effects of smoking. For the period between 1993 and 2001 the tobacco companies were allowed to operate only within these restrictions. There was a lot of publicity on dire warnings about the link between smoking and cancer and other negative statements on cigarette packaging.

The South African reaction was a direct result of the growing clamour in America that culminated in the Tobacco Settlement reached in June 1997. In this settlement the tobacco companies Philip Morris, RJR Nabisco, BAT, Brown and Williamson and Loews reached a resolution with the attorneys general of nearly forty states in America in which the industry had to pay $US368,5 billion over the next two decades in compensation, changing their marketing programmes and submitting to the regulations of the American Food and Drug Administration (FDA).[2] This was a public admission that tobacco is a deleterious product and that everyone including tobacco companies must help prevent people from smoking. This famous court case was followed up with another verdict in July 2000 against the cigarette companies in the USA. This class action was heard in Florida and the jury awarded $150 billion in punitive action against the tobacco companies. The tobacco companies were found guilty of knowingly selling products that cause illnesses to 700 000 residents of the state of Florida. Although the tobacco companies instituted a youth smoking prevention campaign in 1998 after the initial Tobacco settlement between the 40 states of America and the tobacco companies, they continued a massive advertising campaign. One of the lawyers for the plaintiffs illustrated the point by mentioning that Philip Morris spent $100 million on the youth prevention campaign whilst proceeding with a R6 billion investment on advertising tobacco products.[3]

Very limited promotion was possible for tobacco companies in the USA and the icons of some of the most well-known cigarette brand names such as the Malboro Man and Joe Camel were put out to pasture, because of reforms to human and cartoon forms in advertising negotiated under this settlement.[4] To illustrate the effect of the reforms in January 2000 a Boston judge upheld state regulations that prohibit tobacco companies from placing outdoor billboards advertising cigarettes, smokeless tobacco and cigars within 300 metres of schools and playgrounds in the state of Massachusetts.[5]

Older South Africans were well accustomed to cigarette marketing messages originating in America. In cinemas, where a major part of the South African cigarette advertising budget was spent, the focus was on using international advertisements. Products such as Peter Stuyvesant and Chesterfield were advertised using international models and exclusive vacation spots of the glitterati of the world. The message was similar to the American range of cigarette advertisements discussed above – showing healthy, beautiful people, enjoyment and action and concluding with the message that smoking is an inherent part of the basic enjoyment of life.

Smoking legislation in South Africa

On 1 June 1995 the South African legislation in terms of the Tobacco Products Control Act of 1993 was introduced stating that the following regulations regarding the advertising must be adhered to:

* Tobacco companies are to display one of eight health warnings on packs of cigarettes.
* Health warning signs on billboards are to cover 10% of the surface area.
* An additional 2% of the billboard is to be covered by the tar and nicotine content notice.
* The script of the health warning must cover between 60 and 70% of the surface area set aside for the warning as a whole.[6]

This resulted in a decline of advertising, initially with billboard advertising being hit most severely. That form of advertising declined by approximately 70%, leaving empty billboards right across South Africa.[7] The explanation for this was the huge costs involved in changing the advertising material. There were eight different health warnings and existing material had to be changed to accommodate these warnings – add-ons were not allowed. The same applied to the printed media (newspapers, etc.). A loophole in this legislation used by tobacco companies was radio advertising. There was a moratorium on the original government regulation enforcing a warning message to be flighted after the commercial message, using the same presenter and the same tone of voice. This regulation was, however, never put to practice and was substituted with a ruling whereby cigarette advertising on radio could be flighted without the prescribed warning. The provision was that a similar amount of free airtime (advertisements) should be granted to anti-smoking lobbyists.[8]

Examples of South African health warnings on cigarette boxes
* Tobacco is addictive
* Pregnant? Breastfeeding? Your smoking can harm your baby
* Danger: smoking can kill you
* Warning: don't smoke near children
* Danger: smoking causes cancer
* Your smoke can harm those around you

One of the advertisements by anti-smoking lobbyists used these health warnings to great effect in a radio spot. The customer (a male) is asking for a package of cigarettes from the counter assistant. The assistant then starts reciting the above-mentioned warnings such as 'Danger: smoking causes cancer'. The customer hesitates after each quote, saying that it sounds bad. Finally the customer decides to buy a packet of cigarettes with the warning 'Pregnant? Breastfeeding? Your smoking can harm your baby' saying that this sounds the most harmless of the lot!

Stricter government legislation in 1999

During the nineties the size of the South African cigarette market was about 30 million cigarettes per year with 75% of adults not smoking. At this stage Steven Jurgens, managing director of British American Tobacco in South Africa said that the South African market was a medium-size market with a low volume but with a high value potential. According to Jurgens the industry was at this stage highly regulated and severely penalised. Excise duties increased 52% in 1997,[9] way up from the 18% increase in excise in 1996.[10] In 1996 the excise duty contributed R220 million to state finance. At that stage, tax rates on tobacco products were still of the lowest in the world. South Africa's total tax on cigarettes in 1996 was 42% of the retail price, against Japan (60%), 74% in Brazil and 76% in the United Kingdom.[11] In 2001 the government collected more than R2,5 billion in taxes on tobacco products.[12] In 2004 the excise duty rate stood at 52% with the price of a pack of 20 cigarettes costing around R12,50.[13]

After the hefty increase in excise duty over the past few years, the question arises how the double-barrelled attack of government (excise duties and legislation) affected the tobacco industry in South Africa. At the end of 1996, Rembrandt Group chairman Johann Rupert openly attacked the anti-smoking campaign of the government and private lobbyists. This attack came after the Minister for Health said in parliament that the Rembrandt Group, United Tobacco (now BAT), RJ Reynolds and Imperial Tobacco were 'evading regulations'. These evasions were 'importing cigarettes that do not have the prescribed warnings', 'posting bill-boards with warnings that are not visible at night or do not show the nicotine and tar content as per the regulations' and 'advertising in newspapers and magazines with adverts that do not have the tar and nicotine content'. The Minister threatened to 'ban tobacco advertising if the tobacco industry continues to violate regulations'.[14] This threat at that time could have lead to a loss of R150 million in promotions spent by the tobacco industry in South Africa.

The crux of Rupert's attack centred on the fact that while tobacco companies were not importing cigarettes without the necessary health warnings, smugglers were making a fortune bringing in illegal cigarettes, particularly through Swaziland, facilitated by poor border controls and the high price of domestic cigarettes. Cigarettes smuggled into South Africa were available at 99c per packet of 20 in 1996, less than 25% of the official price of cigarettes at that time. He further said that 'a criminal can earn over R4 000 from one carload, and nearly R1 million from a container of smuggled cigarettes'.[15] At that stage each smuggled pack represented a loss of R1,60 in excise revenue.[16] Jurgens, MD of BAT in South Africa concurred with this, adding: 'Prices have been going up way above what is reasonable, driven largely by a political agenda'. He further said that this had backfired, 'because of the large price differential between South Africa and its neighbours'. 'There is a large influx of smuggled cigarettes into the local market. Marlboro, for example, is not legally imported, but has a 1,5% market share. While there has been no significant change in consumption habits, manufacturing has declined by 6% to 8% and the difference is taken up by contraband.'[17]

The above allegations are hotly debated in 2005, with a yawning gap between the price of local manufactured cigarettes and illegally imported cigarettes.

In 2004 it was reported that cigarette consumption dropped on average by 5,7% per annum during the period 1991 to 2001, which was the latest available statistic. For the same period it was reported that the number of smokers declined by nearly a third and that total cigarette consumption declined from a record of 2 billion packs in 1991 to 1,3 billion in 2001.[18] According to the tobacco industry the decline can be ascribed to the increase in cigarette smuggling, which is not reflected in the official sales figures of the country.

New legislation in January 2001

By January 2001 legislation that prohibits all advertising, sponsorship and promotion of tobacco products was in place. Added to this legislation was the introduction of designated and limited smoking facilities in public places. According to this law, any indoor or enclosed public space is allowed to designate a maximum of 25% of the establishment's floor area for smoking. Smoking areas must have a solid partition and entrance door between smoking and non-smoking rooms and forced ventilation to the outside. This legislation caused problems for owners of bars, restaurants, coffee shops, hotels, shopping malls, trains and workplaces in general. These establishments received a six-month deferment in order to adhere to all the prescriptions of the legislation. The initial fine for individuals contravening this law was R200 but was increased to R500 in 2004 for a first offence and up to R1 000 for a second offence. Fines for contravening the laws by the owner of an establishment (public space) increased from R10 000 to R20 000 whilst the fine for advertising and promoting tobacco products increased from R200 000 to R500 000 for a first offence and up to R900 000 for subsequent offences.[19]

Legislation planned for 2004

A second Tobacco Products Amendment Bill was planned for the end of 2004. This bill proposed:[20]
• To impose a R50 000 fine for selling tobacco products to anyone under the age of 18 years of age.

- To ban children under 18 from entering designated smoking areas.
- To extend the smoking ban in public places to include the area within 5 metres of building entrances.
- To empower the Minister of Health to ban or restrict smoking at specified outdoor venues where crowds may gather.
- To force shops selling tobacco products to keep it out of direct sight of customers.
- To forbid tobacco companies to fund events, buildings, programmes or scholarships.
- To forbid the display of any 'brand element' that might suggest a product or logo.
- To forbid the use of terms such as 'light', 'low-tar' or mild on tobacco products.

Results of the legislation

The results of the smoking legislation are still under investigation but there are already indications of what is happening on the ground level:

Loss of employment

Some of the unintended consequences of the banning of the Tobacco Control Act are to be found in the impact on agriculture and rural employment. One of the regulations of this legislation instructed the tobacco industry to lower the tar and nicotine content of cigarettes in South Africa to respectively 12 mg and 1,2 mg per cigarette by 2006. Tobacco grown in the warmer climate countries, such as South Africa tends to have higher nicotine and tar content. Obviously it will not be possible to lower the tar content within such a short space of time because 99% of cigarettes smoked in South Africa is manufactured locally and 60% of the tobacco used is grown locally. It will take on average five to ten years for farmers to produce new tobacco cultivars with a lower nicotine and tar content. To adhere to the time frame of the legislation will mean that lower tar and nicotine tobacco will have to be imported. The Tobacco Institute of South Africa (TISA) claimed that tobacco was the fifth largest cash crop in 2000 in South Africa and employed 48 710 workers who had 150 000 dependants. Tobacco production is also labour intensive; on average two workers per hectare are employed, while maize farming requires one worker for every 100 hectare.[21] The concern was that the legislation would cause thousands of job losses. The threat of job losses was not limited to South Africa alone. Countries in southern Africa, such as Malawi, Mozambique and Zambia, also raised concerns about job losses.[22]

Reaction by the tobacco companies

Philip Morris, major manufacturer of tobacco products in the world diversified into unrelated products and services. There are concerns that the negative publicity and advertising bans are decaying the brand equity of some of the most famous brand names such as Malboro. In 2003 Malboro was ranked 9th most valuable brand in the world (estimated brand value in 2003 was $22,18 billion, down from $26,38 billion in 2002).[23] The Marlboro diversification will take place outside the USA, because the tobacco companies agreed not to put their brand names on clothing and other products in the local market. They are however free to leverage the brand name in other countries. Phillip Morris has already followed the diversification tract – they own Kraft foods (the manufacturer of Kraft margarine in South Africa), Miller Brewing (brewers of Millers light and other beers in the USA which was subsequently sold to SA Breweries), and Jacobs Suchard, the Swiss coffee and chocolate manufacturer.[24] Rembrandt of South Africa is also diversifying out of tobacco-related products towards more upmarket luxury goods such as jewellery and watches.

Tobacco companies stand accused by the World Health Organisation (WHO) of targeting the developing world countries in a drive to grow the sales of tobacco products.[25] In 2004 the WHO estimated that there were 1,25 billion smokers worldwide which constituted one third of the world's population, and of which the majority lived in developing countries.[26]

Another accusation against the manufacturers of tobacco products is that they concentrate on guerrilla marketing which can be described as more inventive, unconventional but still legal ways to market their products. Some of these 'guerrilla' activities of South African tobacco companies include:[27]
- Sponsoring an online lifestyle magazine in South Africa.
- Bringing out foreign music bands to South Africa.
- Using arts and clubbing venues to promote cigarettes.
- Using the Benson & Hedges ampersand '&' – on its own in a campaign to promote the brand of cigarettes.
- Targeting the wealthy part of the population by giving cigarettes away on university campuses and at major sports events.[28]

Effect on the South African hospitality industry

The hospitality industry in South Africa has its own particular problems with the implementation of the new smoking laws. Some non-smoking restaurant owners are complaining about declining sales. Restaurants with smoking sections (a maximum of 25% of restaurant space is allowed for smokers) are complaining that the smoking space is too small and that they are facing abuse from angry customers. What is especially frustrating for these restaurants is that smokers tend to spend on average 20% to 30% more than non-smokers per sitting – resulting in some restaurants losing revenue due to the legislation. The bottom line is that some of the restaurant owners are publicly ignoring the new laws.[29] Restaurants with outdoor areas have an advantage because smoking outdoors is permitted – and their revenue is not influenced at all.

At casinos the feeling is similar to that of restaurants. The problem is also the 25% allocation of space to smokers in casinos. According to one of the casinos, more than 50% of the patrons in gaming environments smoke – this creates a problem by effectively limiting the potential income of these gaming institutions. Hotels who for some time have rented out smoking and non-smoking rooms are more sanguine about the new smoking laws.[30]

The influence on sponsorships

Tobacco companies have been major sponsors of a whole series of sporting events, ranging from surfing to horse racing. The introduction of the new legislation has resulted in BAT being forced to severe its sponsorships of the following events:

- Soccer's Rothmans Cup.
- The Dunhill Symphony of Fire (a pyrotechnics display).
- The Gunston 500 surfing contest. [Mr Price, the clothing store, has taken over the sponsorship of this event.]
- The Peter Stuyvesant Music Spectacular, which brought many musical mega-stars to South Africa.
- The Rothmans Durban July, the South African premier horseracing event.[31] [Vodacom, the cell phone company, has taken over the sponsorship of this event].

Decrease in cigarette consumption by South Africans

In particular, poor customers in South Africa are kicking the habit; this indicates that the steep increase in the price of tobacco is having the desired effect. The drop in consumption by population group is reflected in Table 4.1 below:

Population group	Consumption in 1993	Consumption in 2000
Blacks	28,1%	22,7%
Coloureds	49,3%	48,7%
Indian	32,3%	28,2%
Whites	35,6%	36,6%

Table 4.1: Smoking habits of the four major population groups (1993–2000)[32]

All the population groups have a decline in consumption patterns except the white population. Speculation has it that this anomaly is due to the success of the marketing efforts by the tobacco companies to the wealthy segment of the population, which is still mostly white.

The next target: Alcohol products?

As a social marketing issue, the misuse of alcohol-related products has been intensely debated by civil society in South Africa. Over a period various suggestions were raised on how to encourage responsible consumption of alcohol. Suggestions ranged from banning the promotion of alcohol products in total to placing certain restrictions on the advertising of alcohol products. One of the major manufacturers of alcohol-related products in South Africa is SABMiller, which has currently about a 98% share of the South African beer market. They have already anticipated the groundswell and have instituted an advertising campaign to combat alcohol misuse. The liquor industry maintains that the restriction on advertising will reduce customer choice and entrench existing brand names' dominance in the marketplace whilst having no effect on alcohol misuse. It is further maintained that advertising restrictions may create insurmountable barriers of entry to new entrants entrenching the current quasi-monopolist competition in South Africa. Research in France has shown that advertising restrictions have little effect on the misuse of alcohol in that country.[33]

Conclusion

Tobacco marketing in South Africa has changed dramatically in the last decade since the introduction of the new legislation. This legislation has resulted in a drastic drop in the advertising revenue of, among others, newspapers and journals. On the other hand there are claims that 89 000 South Africans died in 2001 due to smoke-related deaths.[34] By law, the government must fulfil its responsibility to look after the interests of its citizens. Government sees its role as extending further than controlling smoking and is taking a careful look at related industries such as the liquor industry and associated problems such as alcoholism in this industry. The effects of possible government intervention on marketing within the liquor industry are yet to be seen.

References

1   This case study was written by Johan Strydom.
    Sunday Times. 6 June 2004, p 6.
2   *Time*, 30 June 1997, p 21.
3   Internet: US smokers seek $154bn.
    Http://bdfm.co.za/cgi-bin20/07/12.
4   *Time*, 30 June 1997, p 21.
5   Tobacco billboards restricted.
    Http://bdfm.co.za/cgi-bin20/01/26.
6   Internet: *Independent online*. Tough-talking Zuma threatens to ban all cigarette adverts.
    Http://www2.inc.co.za/Archives/96/10/29/smoke.html.
7   *Marketplace*, 19 June 1995, p 1.
8   *Marketplace*, 17 June 1996, p 4.
9   *Business Times*, 6 July 1997, p 12.
10 Internet: Independent online. 1996 Budget – Tobacco tax lights up a fire.
    Http://wn.apc.org/wmail/issues/960315/BUS49.html.
11 Loc. cit.
12 *Sunday Times*. 6 June 2004, p 6.
13 Loc. cit.
14 Internet: *Independent online*. Tough talking Zuma threatens to ban all cigarette adverts. Op. cit.
15 Internet: Zuma, Rupert square up in smoking war. Http://www2.inc.co.za/Archives/9610/29/smoking%20war.html.

16   Internet. Rembrandt takes tough stance. Http://www.bday.co.za/961126/ special/d1.htm

17   *Business Times*, 6 July 1997. loc. cit.

18   *Sunday Times*. 6 June 2004, p 6.

19   Loc. cit.

20   Loc. cit.

21   Internet: Draft tobacco laws will affect rural employment.
Http://www.bdfm.co.za/cgi-bin/200527.

22   Internet: Tobacco revenue is expected to fall.
Http://www.bdfm.co.za/cgi-bin/200630.

23   *Business Week*. 4 August 2003. Special Report: The Best Global Brands.

24   Internet: Phillip Morris may diversify Marlboro brand.
Http://www.bdfm.co.za/cgi-bin20/03/06.

25   Internet: Tobacco industry targets youth in developing countries, says WHO.
Http://bdfm.co.za/cgi-bin01/01/29.

26   *Sunday Times*. 1 May 2004.

27   Internet: Tobacco firms light way underground.
Http://bdfm.co.za/cgi-bin00/01/03.

28   *Sunday Times*. 6 June 2004, p 6.

29   Internet: Restaurants feel bite of the law.
Http://bdfm.co.za/cgi-bin01/01/29.

30   Not time for smoke signals yet.
Http://bday.co.za/bday/content/direct/1,3523,765306-6078-0,00.html.

31   *Sunday Times,* Business Times, 25 March 2001, p 9.

32   *Sunday Times*. 6 June 2004, p 6.

33   *Financial Mail*. 25 June 2004, p 70.

34   Internet: It is not clever to cheat the law.
Http://bday.co.za/bday/content/direct/1,3523,717369-6078-0,00.html.

The importance of subcultures: Putting Generation Y into perspective

Identifying market segments

There are many different ways of identifying market segments, for example the Living Standards Measures (LSM) system, which divides consumers into ten categories based on their income and standard of living, functions on the basis that these factors are related to their buying and consumption patterns. This case study looks at how culture and subcultures can be used to identify market segments within South African society and, in particular, it focuses on the subculture of age as a useful means of identifying generational differences between market segments in South Africa.

Culture is one of the important factors that influence customer behaviour. Culture is described as a complex system of values, norms and symbols that have developed over time in a society and in which the members share. These values, norms and symbols are created and shared by people and passed on from generation to the next.[1] Culture therefore can be seen as setting loose boundaries for individual behaviour which impacts on families, societies and countries. The boundaries that culture sets on behaviour are called norms, which are seen as rules that specify or prohibit certain behaviour patterns for members of society. Cultural beliefs are those widely held beliefs that affirm what is desirable in a society.[2] South Africa is a melting pot of different cultures, within which different subcultures can be identified. There are several different ways of identifying subcultures, based on variables such as nationality, age, religion, language grouping, racial grouping and geographic regions and these subcultures relate to important market segments in South African society. For instance, using language as a variable, one could identify an Afrikaans-speaking subcultural group with preferences for 'braaivleis' (barbecue), biltong and rugby; using racial groups as a variable, one could identify 'Asians' as a subcultural group, with their unique preferences regarding strong curry dishes; similarly geographic regions could identify rural versus urban subcultures.[3] In this case study we take a closer look at the age-based subculture phenomenon and how it influences one of the identified generations, namely Generation Y. Finally we will look at the economic impact of age-based groups in South Africa.

Age-based subculture

The age-based subculture is the focus of this discussion and can be described as a generation or a group of people 'who have experienced a common social, political, historical, and economic environment.'[4] In consumer psychology reference is made to the fact that generations, described as 'groups of persons that are roughly subdivided in 20-year blocks', can help explain different consumer behaviour patterns. The Generational model postulates that every person has a value system that is moulded by the family and community in which the individual grows up.[5] What is further of interest is that significant events that occurred during this groups' life will also influence the individuals of this group. Significant events such as World War II, the Vietnam War, the Cold War and 9/11 all had an influence on the generations during which time it occurred. Five basic generations are identified, namely:[6]

Pre-Depression generation
Born before 1930, this is a generation that experienced the Great Depression as children and who were adults during World War II. Some of this generation volunteered to fight in World War II, whilst others joined the nationalist organization called the Ossewa Brandwag that was sympathetic to Nazi Germany. This generation today includes the people in old-age homes and those living as the matriarch or patriarch of the extended family. They have unique needs, related to health and trying to cope with an ever-increasing burden of medical costs and trying to make ends meet. Famous South Africans that form part of this generation include Mr Nelson Mandela and Archbishop Desmond Tutu. Ex-president Ronald Reagan of the USA was also a member of this generation.

The Depression generation
Born between 1930 and 1946, this generation grew up in the relatively affluent years in the 1950s and 1960s, experiencing Rock 'n Roll first hand as well as Elvis Presley. They are just retired or in the last stage of their career. They are the grand-

parents of the Generation Y children. This generation is called the silent generation – they believe in hard work, are conservative in nature and like order, rules
and a clearly-defined hierarchy.

The Baby Boom generation

Born between 1947 and 1964, this is one of the largest generations in South
Africa. They experienced the rise of the National Party, the Apartheid years, the
Rivonia trail, Sharpeville, racial discrimination, sexual revolution, the Flower
Power and Hippy era as represented in the Woodstock music happening, recre-
ational drugs and the effect of divorce creating single parent households, pop
groups such as the Beatles, the Rolling Stones and The Who, which took Rock 'n
Roll further than ever expected. They were also the generation that saw the effect
of Communism, the Cold War and the Vietnam War. They were adults when the
Berlin Wall fell and they saw the demise of Communism in Eastern Europe and
Russia. They have a live-for-today attitude. Well-known South African politicians
that form part of this generation include President Thabo Mbeki, Mr Tony Leon
and Ms Patricia de Lille.

Generation X

This is the generation born between 1965 and 1978. The term comes from a book
of the same name written by Douglas Coupland. In this book Coupland described
the fictional characters in the book as 'underemployed, overeducated, intensely
private and unpredictable'. The stereotype of Generation X is seen as 'cynical,
hopeless, frustrated and unmotivated slackers who wear grunge clothing, listen to
alternative music and still live at home because they cannot get real jobs.' [7] In real
life Generation X want options and flexibility and they dislike close supervision
in the workplace. They prefer an output driven system where they believe the
organization that they work for has bought their output – the mechanics on how
and when they do their work is irrelevant – they want the freedom to do the work
in their own time.[8] Famous people that form part of this generation are actors
Brooke Shields, Halle Berry, Jennifer Aniston and model Cindy Crawford, enter-
tainers such as Janet Jackson, Kurt Cobain and P Diddy, the boxer Mike Tyson and
the football stars David Beckham and Ronaldo. Their cultural legacy includes Hip
Hop and Grunge music and their contribution to the film noir is inter alia the
Lord of the Rings Trilogy (Peter Jackson).[9] This is the generation that experienced
dual income households with both parents away during working hours. They bore
the brunt of single parent households, which left emotional scars, and experienced
a deteriorating environment and the Aids pandemic. In South Africa they were
the first generation influenced by television, which was introduced in 1976. They
were young adults when South Africa became a democracy in 1994. Well-known
South Africans that form part of this generation are soccer stars Lucas Radebe and
Quentin Fortune, the Academy award winner Charlize Theron and the astronaut
Mark Shuttleworth.

Generation Y
This is the generation born between 1979 and 1994, the children of the baby boomers and which grew up as the first generation that reaped the fruit of democracy in South Africa. They grew up with computers, the Internet and saw their parents losing their jobs in an economic slowdown period. Generation Y exuberate independence and are much more optimistic, confident and social than previous generations. They are also much more street-smart and technology-minded than the previous generations. The South African Generation Y form part of the global youth culture that transcends all boundaries in the world – they are truly part of the global village in their needs, attitudes, perceptions and lifestyles. Well-known South Africans that form part of this generation are the South African cricket captain Graeme Smith and Natalie du Toit.

Let us now take a look at the customer behaviour of Generation Y.

The customer behaviour of Generation Y in South Africa

There is a belief that brand awareness of children can start as early as age three. We therefore see young children being targeted in marketing campaigns for about every imaginable product. Generation Y are seen as the ideal target market because they have a basic desire for anything new and fresh and they are increasingly able to influence their parents' spending habits.[10]

According to Stats SA, the youth market (defined as consumers under 24 years of age) of today make up more than half of the South African population and have influence over the spending of between 6 and 7 billion rand a year.[11] It is estimated that the pocket money of the youth market amounts to R5 billion per annum.[12]

Preliminary research in a town in the Western Cape province found some interesting results regarding the consumer behaviour patterns of an upmarket school where 98 13-year-old learners were interviewed as part of the Generation Y group.[13] The group was predominantly white with 26 learners in Grade 7 and 72 in Grade 8. Qualitative research was done and one-on-one interviews were performed. It must be borne in mind that the results of the study are not representative of all the population groups in South Africa and can at the most be extrapolated to the customer behaviour patterns of upmarket white Generation Y customers.

Looking more specifically at the household structure in which these Generation Y respondents live it was found that 88% lived in a traditional household structure consisting of both parents whilst 12% lived in a single parent/guardian household.

Even at this young age 73% had already thought about their future plans, with 10% indicating that they intended to take a gap year (i.e. spending a year not studying after school and in some cases going overseas) whilst 7% indicated that they intended to be involved in business.

On average 92% of the respondents received pocket money of which 10% received R400 per month, 20% received R200, and 18% received R100 per month. In total these respondents received R209 940 per year in pocket money. The major items on which the pocket money was spent included:

- Airtime for cell phones: Females spent on average R80 per month on airtime whilst males spent on average R60 per month.
- Movies: Females spent R50 while males spent on average R40 per month.
- Magazines: Females spent R30 whilst males spent on average R55 per month.
- Savings: Females saved on average R65 whilst males saved R110 per month. Nearly 81% of the respondents had a savings account.

The major reasons for receiving pocket money were for doing chores (15%), as a living allowance (30%), and for no apparent reason (43%). On the issue of the amount of influence on their parents spending, 68% responded that they had an influence on what their parents/guardians purchased. They had a larger amount of say in the food that their parents bought but they were also of the opinion that they exerted an influence regarding the purchasing of more expensive products such as clothing, cars, furniture, electronics, and upholstery.

Looking at brands, the favourite brand being mentioned by these Generation Y teenagers was Billabong, followed by Levi's, Diesel, Roxy, Quiksilver, and Adidas. Just more than 60% said they followed the fashion trends and bought accordingly. The major sources of information for this generation's decisions regarding brands and what to buy were friends, magazines, and television, in that order, indicating the importance of word-of-mouth communication. With regard to the preferred mass media types, these youngsters preferred television, followed by magazines, followed by radio, to gather information.

South African retailers are already starting to target Generation Y in their advertising campaigns and marketing strategies. An example would be the Cell C adverts, particularly the one which showcases a range of Generation Y South Africans about their business on the busy streets of a South African city centre (possibly Johannesburg). The youngsters are different in terms of home language or family background, race, religious background, and possibly geographical origin and spending capacity; however, they share similarities in their style of dress, style of music, their attitude toward life, way of moving, their way of speaking (fast-talking jargon), and of course their use of cell phones – the target of the Cell C campaign. Certainly they are all different from their parents' generation and share this commonness of generational difference. Edgars has a similar strategy, targeting their youth clothing brands (Free2BU, Roxy, Bad Boy) at South Africa's Generation Y. It would seem that targeting Generation Y is a particularly good strategy with regard to the marketing of non-essential or luxury goods and services.

The economic impact of age-based groups in South Africa

Having discussed the different age-subcultures let us now take a look at the economic impact of age groupings in South Africa. In a segmentation exercise by the
Bureau of Market Research the household expenditure of South African households was determined using life stage and life plane determinants. The life stage
determinant breaks the life of consumers up into 5 year segments, i.e. age 1 to 5,
6 to 10, etc. These life stage groupings were banded together to obtain the following five life stages as depicted in Table 5.1.

Life stage	Age group of household head
1	Less than 26 years
2	26 to 35 years
3	36 to 45 years
4	46 to 55 years
5	56 years plus

Table 5.1: Life stages of South African households[14]

The life plane determinant refers to the level of education of the consumer and is
used in segmentation because education influences attitudes and perceptions,
expectations and aspirations. There is also usually a direct correlation between
level of education and income. Six broad life plane categories were determined as
indicated in Table 5.2 below:

Life plane	Level of education of household head
A	Degree, postgraduate degree or diploma
B	Diploma, certificate with Grade 12
C	Grade 12 ('Matric')
D	Grade 10, Grade 11, National Technical Certificate
E	Grade 9, Grade 8
F	Below Grade 8

Table 5.2: Life planes of South African consumers

Combining the life stage and the life plane information gathered, the following
information was developed (see Table 5.3).

Life plane	<26 R'000	26–35 R'000	36–45 R'000	46–55 R'000	56+ R'000	Total R'000
A	3 733 787	37 823 859	48 456 646	37 829 122	26 137 391	153 980 624
B	4 785 391	27 986 735	32 606 799	17 508 578	13 565 478	96 452 984
C	10 312 978	40 355 400	40 786 731	30 390 723	20 105 509	141 951 342
D	4 646 804	26 221 910	37 658 690	25 106 230	19 923 554	113 557 190
E	2 899 843	10 978 942	19 965 399	18 917 187	18 871 810	71 633 182
F	2 699 605	15 921 870	31 887 739	32 607 365	54 669 186	137 785 767
Total	29 078 410	159 288 718	211 361 825	162 359 208	153 272 929	715 361 092

Table 5.3: Annual household expenditure by life plane and stage (2004)

From the above table the following interesting observations can be made:
- Households with a tertiary qualification have the highest household expenditure of the six groups proving the point that there is a direct correlation between the level of education and income.
- The Baby Boom generation (i.e. the age categories between 36 to 45 and 46 to 55) are the households with the highest level of expenditure.
- The Pre-Depression generation and the Depression generation's (i.e. category 56+ years) household expenditure makes up a substantial part of the total expenditure in South Africa and both these groups have unique needs.
- Generation X's (i.e. the age grouping between 26 to 35 years) household expenditure is more than that of the Pre-Depression and the Depression generation together.
- Generation Y's (i.e. the age group younger than 26 years) household expenditure is the lowest of the five life stages, which is understandable as they are still entering the job market and working their way up in the job market. It is also the segment of the market that currently has a very high unemployment rate.

Conclusion

There is a growing belief that people with a common social, political, historical and economic environment have commonalities regarding consumption patterns. This holds especially true for first-world countries such as the USA, the UK and countries in Europe. There is however doubt as to the extent to which age-based subcultures can be used in target market analysis in the South African context, especially in the older life plane categories. This is partly due to the skewness of the income distribution between the different race groups, especially in the age groups in which the Baby Boomers, the Pre-Depression and the Depression generation fall. The skewness can be calculated by looking at the Lorenz curve, which gives a measure of the amount of inequality in income distribution. This measure is called the Gini Coefficient. A Gini Coefficient of 0 indicates perfect income equality between all members of the population, whilst a Gini Coefficient of 1 points to a situation of perfect inequality in income distribution. The Gini Coefficient of South Africa increased from 0,596 in 1995 to 0,635 in 2002,[15] indicating that the divides of the past are further entrenched.

Nevertheless, the use of age-based subculture as a segmentation variable may be useful for the younger generation, especially for Generation Y that is growing up in a non-racial society in South Africa. Certainly, marketers are taking notice of Generation Y South Africans as a consumer group. They may in future be the first generation in which age-based subculture may be used to help segment a certain part of the South African population.

References

1   This case study was written by Johan Strydom.
    Strydom, JW, Jooste, CJ & Cant, MC. 2000. *Marketing Management* 4th edition. Cape Town: Juta, pp 90-91.
2   Hawkins, DI, Best, RJ & Coney, KA. 2001. *Consumer Behavior: Building Marketing Strategy.* Boston: Irwin McGraw-Hill, p 42.
3   Cant, MC, Brink, A & Brijbal, S. 2002. *Customer Behaviour: A Southern African perspective.* Cape Town: Juta, p 49.
4   Hawkins, et al. p 173.
5   Mulrooney, B. May 2001. *Marketing Mix*, p 24.
6   Adapted from Hawkins, et al, pp 172-182
7   Http://ww.jour.unr.edu/outpost/specials/genx.overvw1.html. Date accessed: 25 June 2004.
8   *Sunday Times,* Business Times, 20 June 2004, p 2.
9   Http://www.wordiq.com/definition/generation_X. Date accessed: 25 June 2004.
10 Von Bornman, T. 2004. Tweens and Teens – sacred cash cows. *Journal of Marketing,* vol 10 no. 1.
11 Stats SA. Http://www.statssa.co.za. Accessed: 20 May 2003.
12 Stats SA. 13 November 2002. Income and expenditure of Households. P0111.1.
13 Based on an unpublished field study by JL Rose-Innes. 2004. Pretoria: Unisa.
14 This section is based on Maartens, JH. 2004. Total household expenditure in South Africa by income group, life plane, life stage and product, 2004. Research report no. 326. Pretoria: Unisa, pp 13-15.
15 Http://www.wsws.org/articles/2004/may 2004/safr-m21_prn.shtml. Date accessed: 9 July 2004.

PART TWO

CLASSIC CASES

Introduction

In its definition for the word 'classic', *The Concise Oxford Dictionary* includes the following explanations: 'of acknowledged excellence', 'remarkably typical', 'in accordance with established forms', and 'not much affected by changes'. These descriptions lend themselves to the cases grouped together under **Part 2 Classic cases** because they continue to be of enduring relevance for marketing students. In other words, because the focus is on the time-tested solid principles and key strategies of marketing, the case studies are unlikely to date. These marketing success stories are not 'typical' in as far as they are common; rather they form the archtype of marketing success, which other companies can aspire to. The companies have established forms and structures which have proved foundational within their respective markets. The focus for these companies is now on maintenance and consolidation.

Turning to the fourth definition of the word 'classic', that is, 'not much affected by change', this is true of the classic companies, but only, ironically enough, because they have moved with the socio-economic and political changes which have affected the marketplace in South Africa. For example, Pick 'n Pay's family-owned structure, which has proved key to its success in establishing its brand, has evolved to include professional management as a way of meeting the challenges of the present and the future. Similarly, Game, a familiar feature on the South African retailing landcape, has consolidated its market position in South Africa and is expanding into Africa by applying and adapting its characteristic classic marketing strategies.

In all of the classic case studies, the companies involved have proved that being classic examples of success involves not only the consistent implementation of good marketing principles and strategies but also adapting to, and growing with, marketplace changes in order to ensure continued success.

6

MARKETING FEATURES:

ENTREPRENEURSHIP

INNOVATION

MARKETING CONCEPT/ PHILOSOPHY

MARKETING STRATEGY

MISSION

PERSONAL SELLING

PRICING

RETAILING

SEGMENTATION

STRATEGIC MARKETING

TECHNOLOGY

Pick 'n Pay –
An entrepreneurial legend

A legend is born[1]

Raymond Ackerman, the chief executive officer of Pick 'n Pay, became the founding father of the modern Pick 'n Pay when he bought a group of four supermarkets in Cape Town from Jack Goldin and Mark Hoffman for R620 000. By 1968 Pick 'n Pay had become a public company with 529 170 shares that were offered to the public. This issue provided much-needed additional working capital to start four new stores in 1969. By 1970 Pick 'n Pay was ready to take on the might of South African retailing in its own backyard when it opened its first supermarket in Gauteng. This opening was the start of an aggressive store-opening campaign that saw Pick 'n Pay breaking out of its regional boundaries, and paved the way for this company to challenge the established national food retailers (at that time OK Bazaars and Checkers).

Early in 1973 Pick 'n Pay realised that the supermarket, as a retail institution, was reaching maturity in South Africa and that the innovations that succeeded in Europe and the USA should also be introduced to the South African retailing scene. One such retailing vehicle that opened the road towards a growth strategy for Pick 'n Pay was the hypermarket. With this diversification Pick 'n Pay became a dominant player in the general merchandise (non-food) business.

The early Pick 'n Pay hypermarket can be described as a store (with a trading area of more than 8 500 m²) offering consumers food, clothing, housewares, audio-visual and domestic appliances, do-it-yourself items and, when possible, auto centres. The concept was based on the formula of self-service, discounting, with a combination of two-thirds food and one-third general merchandise, and with at least 200 000 people living within a radius of 20 minutes' driving time from the store.

The first hypermarket opened in Boksburg, near Johannesburg International Airport, on 19 March 1975. This hypermarket was so successful that a long-term programme of hypermarkets was initiated. The second hypermarket, at Brackenfell, was opened in October 1977, followed by three openings in Bloemfontein, Durban, and Norwood in 1978. By 1992, 14 Pick 'n Pay hypermarkets were in operation. Pick 'n Pay had, by far, the most of these behemoths in operation, with its main competitors Checkers and OK Bazaars left well behind!

In 1981 control of the company was placed in the hands of Ackerman through the establishment of Pick 'n Pay Holdings (Pikwik), the holding company of Pick 'n Pay. Through this arrangement the Ackerman family acquired a controlling interest in Pikwik, which in turn acquired a controlling interest in Pick 'n Pay, the percentages being 54% and 52% respectively.

By the financial year ending 28 February 1983, Pick 'n Pay's turnover exceeded R1 billion for the first time. At this stage Ackerman realised that hypermarket growth opportunities in South Africa were limited and that the time was right for international expansion as another route towards obtaining growth for the company. The opening of the first Pick 'n Pay hypermarket in Brisbane, Australia, heralded an important milestone in the quest for growth for this company. A second hypermarket was planned for Melbourne but strong trade union opposition and negative sentiments towards South Africa at the time saw the shelving of these plans. In the end Pick 'n Pay was compelled to sell its interest in the Australian hypermarkets to its Australian partner. This Pick 'n Pay hypermarket is today still in operation in the Callumvale suburb of Brisbane.

By 28 February 1986 Pick 'n Pay had reached the R2 billion turnover figure and during that year Pick 'n Pay continued its established growth strategy by diversifying into the wholesaling sector. In a move which can be labelled backward vertical integration, Pick 'n Pay started its own chain of cash-and-carry wholesalers called PriceClub. This chain of wholesalers served traders and was subsequently sold off.

In 1999, Raymond Ackerman made Sean Summers the CEO of Pick 'n Pay.

The shift from being a family-run business toward professional management (while ownership remains with the Ackerman family) reflects the company's awareness of the increasing emphasis on the importance of corporate governance over the past decade.

Pick 'n Pay today

Today Pick 'n Pay is the largest retail grocery chain in South Africa, owning approximately 34% of the market share of the formal sector grocery market. During the 2004 financial year, sales increased by 11,4 % to R29,3 billion. This was reached with 428 stores, which compares quite favourably with the other retailing giants (namely Shoprite/Checkers).[2] The different types of stores used by Pick 'n Pay are depicted in Table 6.1 below.

Hypermarkets	14	Score supermarkets	142
Supermarkets	121	Boxer superstores	45
Clothing stores	3	Boardmans (sold in 2004)	26
Pick 'n Pay family stores (franchise)	121	Franklins (NSW-Australia)	77
Pick 'n Pay Mini-markets (franchise)	41		

Table 6.1: Composition of Pick 'n Pay Stores (circa 2004)

In 2004 Pick 'n Pay employed 40 000 employees in South Africa and was still growing, which is evidenced by market development for the 2004 financial year. In this period eight supermarkets, two clothing stores, 15 Score supermarkets and six Boxer superstores were opened. In the franchise operations side the Pick 'n Pay family stores increased by 15 whilst the convenience-oriented Pick 'n Pay mini-markets decreased by 5 to 41.[3]

Reasons for the success of Pick 'n Pay

The main reason for the success of Pick 'n Pay is the growth strategy and especially the policy of diversification that Ackerman pursued. From the outset Pick 'n Pay was in the forefront of innovation; it was, for example, the first to introduce many retail innovations such as the hypermarket, the superstore, and the convenience store. On the technological front Pick 'n Pay also pursued technological innovation as can be seen by the introduction of scanning facilities which resulted in savings of between 0,5% and 1,0% on business expenses.[4]

Another important reason for the success of Pick 'n Pay is the high stock turnover rate (approximately 12 times per year).

A third reason for the success is Pick 'n Pay's diversified corporate portfolio. Ackerman does not believe in 'putting all your eggs in one basket'. Pick 'n Pay consists of several divisions, the major one being the retail division consisting of supermarkets, Score supermarkets, and hypermarkets. Each of these divisions has its own identity and competitive advantage. The remaining stores in the retail are the divisions of Pick 'n Pay family stores, Pick 'n Pay clothing stores and Pick 'n Pay Auto stores. There is also Home shopping. An outstanding characteristic is the backward vertical integration that is part of Pick 'n Pay's long-term strategy. An example is the Blue Ribbon meat company supplying meat to inter alia the super-markets, superstores, and hypermarkets.

The last but not the least important reason that can be given for the success of Pick 'n Pay is the personality cult that was built around Raymond Ackerman. From the outset he has been portrayed as the homemaker's friend and his motto of 'the customer is queen' is still firmly established in the mind of the average consumer. Pick 'n Pay's quick reaction to matters that affect the everyday consumer has also endeared the company to the masses. Pick 'n Pay's reaction to increases in the bread price is but one example of a consumer orientation that has positioned Pick 'n Pay as a fighter for the interests of the consumer.

Pick 'n Pay's reaction to the extortion scare (circa fine 2003)[5]

Towards the end of June, 2003, the CEO of Pick 'n Pay, Sean Summers, announced on TV that an extortionist had informed them that three types of products had been tampered with and were poisonous. The extortionist demanded money and requested Pick 'n Pay to remain silent. Pick 'n Pay in conjunction with the suppliers of these products, removed these prod-ucts from the shelves. No consumer backlash against Pick 'n Pay occurred and Pick 'n Pay was praised for the way it handled the situation.

Pick 'n Pay mission

The current mission statement was developed in 1996 with an aim to re-energise company spirit. The statement is threefold:

1. We serve.
2. With our HEARTS we create a great place to be.
3. With our MINDS we create an excellent place to shop.

Pick 'n Pay aims to make available to customers a combination of quality, price and service, through honest and efficient selling practices that will make the company the best from which to buy.

The company's aims are to sell quality goods at the lowest possible price, by fighting for efficiency in the market and attacking any form of monopoly or collusion, and to play the fullest possible role in social responsibility.

The retailing mix used by Pick 'n Pay[6]

The retailing mix used by Pick 'n Pay combines strategies of targeting customers from different customer bases, while continuing to appeal to a broad target market through inclusive product decisions, and following an aggressive pricing strategy.

Target markets

Pick 'n Pay, as a company, does not target itself at any particular segment of the market. It aims to serve the total South African consumer market. Since stores in specific regions are run mainly autonomously, target markets are determined by the actual location.

Pick 'n Pay establishes its image by store appearance, layout and decor, as well as the quality of its product range and services offered to customers. The advertising messages reflect the company image and Pick 'n Pay's approach to its target customers.

Competitors

Woolworths and Shoprite/Checkers are probably Pick 'n Pay's strongest competitors, with Shoprite/Checkers and OK Bazaars a close second.

Both Woolworths and Pick 'n Pay operate at the upper end of the market, and both compete for the same consumers. This is very evident in the Food Hall concept introduced in 1991 by Pick 'n Pay, which offers specialised food products to those consumers who seek convenience and have little time for preparing meals. Pick 'n Pay's rationale in establishing the Food Halls was that it already had those people who purchase specialised food from Woolworths in its stores. It therefore provided an additional customer service in allowing these people to purchase both basic commodities and specialised foods under one roof.

The competition between the two companies is clearly illustrated by the establishment of Pick 'n Pay's clothing outlets.

In addition to Woolworths and Checkers/Shoprite, the Spar chain has recently emerged as a competitor that may pose a significant threat to Pick 'n Pay. This is illustrated by the growth rate of food sales at Spar.

Strengths of Pick 'n Pay

The strengths of Pick 'n Pay are embodied in the five fundamental principles which have underpinned its history of achievement:
- Satisfying the needs and wants of its customers.
- Convenient store locations for customers.
- Design and layout of stores for maximum efficiency.

- Providing a wide-ranging and apt inventory of products at the best prices.
- Empowering its employees with training and skills to fulfil their maximum potential.

Product decisions

Pick 'n Pay considers its customers' well-being paramount. The company is actively involved with government on issues of genetic modification and provides information on its products in this regard.

Pick 'n Pay has three house brands, which fulfil its promise regarding quality and affordability. They are:

- **No Name products:** No frills packaging is used to reduce the price of these products without impairing the quality of the product.
- **Pick 'n Pay Choice products:** These products are selected for their outstanding quality – which is equal to the leading international brands.
- **Foodhall products:** There are a range of ready meals prepared to the highest standards.

Expansion into retail services

Pick 'n Pay's newest expansion is into retail services: Go Banking and Home Shopping. Pick 'n Pay is currently in partnership with Nedcor to provide customers with banking services. Not only can customers pay for goods bought using a debit card but they can also carry out a range of banking functions from withdrawals to deposits at Pick 'n Pay till points.

Although initially expensive to set up, Pick 'n Pay online shopping division is growing and currently occupies one third of the R220 million spend online in South Africa. In 2003 there were over 80 000 consumers registered to Home Shopping and on average they spend R900 per virtual shopping basket.

Both Home Shopping and Go Banking demonstrate Pick 'n Pay's awareness of changing market needs and their preparedness to capitalise on new opportunities.

Supply chain decisions (Distribution decisions)

While Pick 'n Pay negotiates the lowest price possible with its suppliers, the company realises that suppliers are also customers and therefore Pick 'n Pay strives to have ethical day-to-day dealings with its customers. Pick 'n Pay aligns itself with supply chain members ascribing to similar ethical and moral codes. Payment is made in terms of supplier contracts. Pick 'n Pay also supports historically disadvantaged suppliers and service providers, in addition to putting some Black Economic Empowerment (BEE) initiatives in place.

Pricing as a strategic weapon

Pick 'n Pay follows a pricing strategy of discounting (or low margins and high turnover).

Furthermore, Pick 'n Pay believes that consistent pricing across the range is essential to keep customers content. In the first six months of the 2004 financial year Pick 'n Pay grew bottom-line profits by 17% by reducing prices even further. This resulted in increased turnover and increased operational efficiencies. Deflation across the Pick 'n Pay group was 1% for this period. Turnover was up 9,3% to R15,2 billion and trading profit grew to R350,6 million.[7]

Pick 'n Pay's pricing strategy is extremely aggressive. The company is committed to fighting cartels, monopolies, and price fixings. Pick 'n Pay managed to break the resale price maintenance on cigarettes in 1968 and magazines in 1981. The company is still fighting for the removal of price fixing on petrol.

Pick 'n Pay does not sell on account nor does it allow any discount for cash or quantity purchased.

Promotion decisions

Apart from its unique retailing mix, Pick 'n Pay also uses sponsoring activities to maintain the good image of its brand name in the public view. Promotion and social responsibility are seen as two sides of the same coin at Pick 'n Pay. Above- and below-the-line promotion is used to communicate the Pick 'n Pay brand and to market the products.

Pick 'n Pay sponsors various sporting, educational and charitable events. It is very visible in athletics: supporting the Comrades Marathon as well as cycling, for example the Pick 'n Pay 94.7 Cycle Challenge and the Argus Pick 'n Pay Cycle Tour.

Conclusion

The fact that the company has managed to increase its turnover over the past three years from R18,8 billion to R29,3 billion and has succeeded in acquiring an approximately 30% market share of the formal-sector grocery market, proves that Pick 'n Pay retains a winning formula. In 37 years Pick 'n Pay has become a legend on the South African retailing scene. Under the vision and experience of the Ackerman family and the dynamism and innovativeness of professional management, Pick 'n Pay is set to apply its retailing and marketing strategies to future opportunities in order to grow further.

References

1   Case study written by Johan Strydom.
     Pick 'n Pay Group Annual Reports, 1988, pp 5-13.
2   Pick 'n Pay, Annual Report 2004, p 1.
3   Pick 'n Pay, Annual Report 2004, p 1 and Pick 'n Pay legacy and citizenship review 2004, p 1.
4   Pick 'n Pay Group Annual Reports, 1989, p. 4.
5   Pick 'n Pay Annual Report, 2004, p 14.
6   Based on information obtained from Pick 'n Pay, Annual Report, 2004 and Pick 'n Pay, Legacy and Citizenship review 2004.
7   http://www.bdfm.co.za/cgi-bin/pp-print.ph.

7

MARKETING FEATURES:
AGRICULTURAL MARKETING
DISTRIBUTION
INTERNATIONAL MARKETING
PRICING
PROMOTION
SEGMENTATION
STRATEGIC MARKETING

Rooibos tea:
The tea of Africa

If asked to name the top ten typically South African products, most South Africans would probably identify Rooibos tea on the list. Geographically unique to South Africa, this tea product has sprung from humble beginnings to success in the international tea market. This case study examines the story of Rooibos tea, its strengths and weaknesses, as well as the marketing strategy being used for this unique product.

African origins

The natural habitat of *Aspalathus linearis* (the Rooibos tea plant) is the slopes of the Cedarberg mountains and the surrounding high-lying areas north-west of Cape Town. At present this tea is not grown naturally anywhere else in the world; it is an indigenous South African product. Before it became a commercial enterprise, the development, production, and consumption of Rooibos tea was carried out by the local inhabitants of the Western Cape. They began harvesting the wild plants by cutting them during the summer months. The plants were then chopped with axes, bruised with wooden hammers, fermented in heaps and finally dried. The same basic method is still used today although it is now mechanised and refined.

In about 1904 a Mr Benjamin Ginsberg, a merchant and pioneer in the Western Cape region, began marketing Rooibos tea: buying it from the local inhabitants and selling it. By 1930 Dr P. le F. Nortier, a medical practitioner and nature-lover, became interested in the agricultural value of Rooibos tea. Together with some of his friends, he undertook intensive studies and investigations on seed collection and the cultivation of Rooibos tea in the Clanwilliam district. Because of their enthusiasm and skill, other farmers became interested and so began the official production of Rooibos tea. During these years the industry was hampered by a shortage of seed and after the Second World War the tea market collapsed with a producer price in 1947 of only 6,6 cents per kilogram. These fluctuations necessitated the establishment in 1954 of a Rooibos Tea Control Board, which is, however, no longer in existence today.

The unique properties of Rooibos tea

Rooibos tea is a popular drink owing to its health properties: it is rich in essential minerals and contains a low percentage of tannin and no caffeine. Because of these properties, the tea is sold in many countries as a health beverage. Rooibos tea is also used in South Africa as an everyday beverage: at mealtimes, for morning and afternoon tea, as a nightcap and also for a wide range of other purposes, for example:
- as an ingredient in cosmetics, to help prevent the ravages of the skin associated with age
- as an ingredient in slimming products
- for infants: the soothing properties of Rooibos tea for colicky babies are well known
- as a cure for insomnia and allergies
- as a flavouring ingredient in baking and cooking, and cocktails.

Nutrients	Function in the body	Per 200 ml	*RDA	%RDA
Iron (Fe)	Essential for transport of oxygen in the blood	0,07 mg	18,0 mg	0,003
Potassium (K)	Necessary for metabolic functions	7,12 mg	2 000,0 mg	0,004
Calcium (Ca)	Necessary for strong teeth and bones	1,09 mg	800,0 mg	0,001
Copper (Cu)	Necessary for different metabolic processes	0,07 mg	2,0 mg	0,032
Zinc (Zn)	Necessary for normal growth and development, and a healthy skin	0,04 mg	15,0 mg	0,002
Magnesium (Mg)	Necessary for healthy nervous system and for other metabolic processes	1,57 mg	400,0 mg	0,004
Fluoride	Necessary for healthy teeth and bones	0,22 mg	2,75 mg	0,08

Manganese (Mn)	Necessary for metabolic processes and for bone growth and development	0,04 mg	3,5 mg	0,011
Sodium (Na)	Necessary for fluid and acid-base balance	6,16 mg	500,0 mg	0,012

*RDA: Recommended Daily Allowance for people of 4 years and older

Source: Rooibos Tea Board. Information brochure, 1992

Table 7.1: Substances found in an ordinary cup of Rooibos tea

Production of Rooibos tea

Rooibos tea is produced in the districts of Calvinia, Ceres, Clanwilliam, Hopefield, Malmesbury, Paarl, Piketberg, Tulbagh, Van Rhynsdorp, and Wellington.

The climate of the Western Cape is well suited for the Rooibos tea plant, which requires a winter rainfall climate with showers during the late autumn and early summer. Its needlelike leaves make the plant resistant to cold winters and hot summers. The plant grows best at an altitude of 450 m and higher, with a rainfall from 250 mm to 500 mm per annum. A farmer can expect his first crop after two years. The bush will be in full production in its third year. Approximately 10 000 tea bushes can be established per hectare. The key production statistics for 1999/2000 were as follow (see Table 7.2 below):

Volume of production (average per year)	4500–6000 tons
Yield per hectare	300–500 kg
Yield over plant's lifetime	1200–1500 kg
Establishment costs	R325–355 per ha
Production costs	R2.80–R3.30 per kg

Table 7.2: Key production figures of rooibos tea

The production and sales figures for Rooibos tea grew impressively through the nineties. According to *Finance Week*,[3] total sales for 1991 were in the region of 4 000 tons, with exports making up 12% of the total. Retail and export values exceeded R10 million, with the growers receiving over R4 million for the year.

The total quantity of rooibos produced increased to 6 000 tons in 2000, of which nearly 50% was exported. At this time the rooibos tea industry employed nearly 5 000 people, with over 300 commercial producers. The earnings for 2000 were estimated at R70 million. The average price for conventional rooibos reached a high of R5.80 per kg in 2001.[4]

Roleplayers in the Rooibos tea industry

The Rooibos tea industry has five major role players (see Figure 7.1 below).

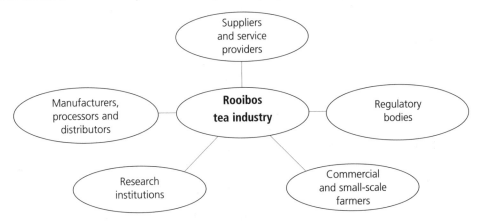

Figure 7.1: Role players in the Rooibos tea industry[5]

These role players are discussed below:

Manufacturers, processors and distributors
There are 20 small, medium and large organizations involved. The previously mentioned Rooibos Tea Control Board was transformed in 1993 into Rooibos Ltd when the industry was deregulated. Rooibos Ltd is a public company owned largely by the producers of the tea.

Suppliers and service providers
Because of specialisation there is a growing number of organizations involved in providing specialised processing machinery, packing equipment and marketing materials such as packing design and printing to the industry.

Regulatory bodies
The Perishable Export Control Board is the most important regulatory body and controls the quality and standards of Rooibos tea on behalf of the Department of Agriculture.

Research institutions
There are a number of institutions conducting research on the product. Rooibos Ltd also has an in-house research facility.

Commercial and small-scale farmers
There are over 300 commercial and less than 200 small-scale farmers involved in the production of Rooibos tea products.

Rooibos tea's position in the hot beverage market

A SWOT analysis of Rooibos tea in the beverage market produced the following strengths, weaknesses, opportunities, and threats of Rooibos tea.[6]

Strengths

- **Unique:** It is currently only grown in the Cedarberg area of the Western Cape. It is not grown naturally anywhere else in the world and is therefore indigenous to South Africa.
- **Healthy:** It contains no caffeine and very little tannin. Caffeine is a stimulant that takes between three and eight hours to be excreted from the human body, while high tannin intake results in decreased nutrient absorption, especially of protein and iron – which is particularly detrimental to the nutrient status of women who are inherently prone to anaemia. It also contains minerals, especially fluoride, and vitamin C.
- **Natural:** Rooibos tea is a natural product with a natural production process.
- **Versatile:** It can be used for various purposes (as mentioned above).
- **Economical:** Rooibos tea is the most economical hot beverage on the market with a long shelf life. It is distributed intensively through retailers and wholesalers nationwide.

Weaknesses

- **Shelf space:** The biggest weakness of Rooibos tea is the limited shelf space that the product receives. This results from intensive competition from the black and imported teas.
- **Taste:** The taste of Rooibos is not always acceptable to everybody (it is an acquired taste).
- **Low-value product:** Rooibos tea is inherently a low-value product with limited funds available for its promotion.
- **Foreign promotion:** Over 90% of exports are sold in bulk, with international buyers doing the packaging and promotion of the product overseas, selling the product at profit margins of up to 800%. South African producers generally do not invest in value-adding activities.

Threats

- **Brand vs. generic advertising:** As a result of the weakness of differentiation, the idea is to promote generic advertising. The packers with their own brand names are, however, adamant that this will inhibit brand-consciousness and result in a decline in sales of branded Rooibos tea.
- **Other hot beverages:** Competition is intense, with instant coffee and medium-grade tea being the main protagonists.

Opportunities

- **Exports:** A strategic window of opportunity at present is the export market, especially exports to Asia and more specifically Japan. European countries especially Germany and the Netherlands are the major consumers of Rooibos, followed by Japan, the UK and Malaysia. The estimate of the market potential indicates that up to 25 000 tons could successfully be exported.
- **Developing new products and new tastes:** New product development in the field of taste, e.g. honey-flavoured Rooibos tea and colourants, will help differentiate the product. The development of an instant Rooibos tea also broadens the market as well as ready-to-drink Rooibos iced tea. A new avenue for growth is the organic market for Rooibos tea.

Marketing strategy for Rooibos tea

Market trends

Rooibos tea's share of the tea market increased to 18% of the local tea market. About 85% of the tea is sold in convenient tea bag format. Flavoured Rooibos products such as lemon, honey, orange, and peach also contribute to growth.

Marketing objectives

The marketing objectives for Rooibos tea in general are:
- to create a higher awareness level for Rooibos tea
- to create an interest in and desire for Rooibos tea
- to improve the image of the product
- to promote brand awareness.

Target market

The market for Rooibos tea can be divided into primary and secondary markets. The primary target market is black consumers of all income levels in the age group 16–34 years. The secondary target market is identified as white consumers of all income levels in the age group 16–34 years. The age limit of 34 years is set because of the belief that younger consumers are more willing to change and to accept new tastes, habits, and products.

Young adults have a long tea-drinking life ahead of them and can educate their children to become the Rooibos tea-drinkers of the future.

Product decisions

Three grades of Rooibos tea are available, namely super, choice, and standard. Rooibos tea is sold to different packers who are responsible for branding the product and the actual distribution.

Price decisions

The price of Rooibos tea is determined by the comparative prices of instant coffee and medium-grade black tea. There is tacit agreement to offer the cheapest hot beverage on the market.

Distribution/ Supply chain decisions

The export market is growing, and new markets are rapidly opening up. Exporting direct to Japan and cutting out the intermediaries develops new distribution channels.

Promotion decisions

Promotion is directed at the target market, with the generic advertising of Rooibos tea to the black market being the most important facet of promotion. Above-the-line promotion consisted of advertisements on television and double-page magazine advertisements in magazines such as *Huisgenoot, You* and *Femina*. These media vehicles were used for the generic promotion of Rooibos tea.

Below-the-line promotion consisted of promotions and demonstrations by qualified food nutritionists at schools, hospitals, crèches, clinics, and women's clubs.

The future

It would seem that Rooibos tea is breaking into the world market with a unique product which could contribute handsomely towards enhancing South Africa's foreign exchange position. There is also a new local market that must be developed, namely the 200 000 traditional healers serving 70% of the South African population. This market is worth R500 million per year. Rooibos tea must therefore be positioned to unlock this market by targeting the traditional healers and convincing them of the medicinal characteristics of Rooibos tea.

References

1   Case study written by Johan Strydom.
     Rooibos Tea Board. *Annual Report*, 1986, p 3.
2   Wesgro. 2000. The Rooibos Industry in the Western Cape.
     http://www.wesgro.co.za/uploads/ssnatural_products_0800.pdf
3   Tea from the Cape. *Finance Week*. 27 February-4 March 1992, p. 28.
4   Arends, A. 2001. Rooibos Tea Trade & Small Scale Production. *Environmental Monitoring Group*, p 2.
5   Op. cit., pp 2-3.
6   Presentation by Mr A. Redelinghuys, 1991, pp. 5-6.

MARKETING FEATURES:
ADVERTISING
CONSUMER BEHAVIOUR
MARKETING CONCEPT/ PHILOSOPHY
POSITIONING
RESEARCH
SEGMENTATION
SERVICES MARKETING

8

Toyota's 'Book of Life' after-sales campaign

Background to campaign

The environment faced by motor manufacturers is very volatile. Across the world, there is a trend whereby the profits made on new vehicle sales are diminishing at a fast rate. This is caused by the introduction of new vehicles which have been very competitively priced, especially by Korean, Taiwanese, and even Romanian manufacturers. This is especially true in South Africa, with the fairly recent launch of manufacturers such as Hyundai, Daewoo, Daihatsu, and the like.[1]

Because of this trend, the 'traditional' manufacturers are finding their vehicle sales volumes decreasing and are having problems in keeping their dealer networks profitable. As a result, motor manufacturers are trying to assist their dealer networks to concentrate on different profit-generating aspects of their businesses which have traditionally had a lower priority than the vehicle-selling function. Two areas in particular are receiving attention:

- Maximising market share in the parts and accessories market.
- Maximising customer retention through the automobile-servicing area (building a long-term relationship with the customer).

Motor manufacturers have run programmes over the past few years to emphasise the importance of genuine parts. In spite of their efforts, there has been a decreasing trend in the genuine parts market share, mainly because of very aggressive marketing and pricing strategies by the non-genuine parts suppliers such as Midas.

Toyota took cognisance of the decreasing sales of genuine parts, and in order to reverse this trend, it identified the dealer service area as the one that could have the greatest impact in doing so. Improving its performance in the automobile servicing area would also assist in its objective of improving customer retention in the long term.

Promoting the automobile service aspect is not a very common practice among either motor manufacturers or franchised dealers. Toyota SA was a pioneer in this field by launching the Welcome to our World (WTOW) after-sales service programme in 1991. WTOW was an attempt by Toyota SA to improve its dealer service culture by developing a more caring attitude toward the customer, and to communicate this to the customer. The cornerstone of the WTOW campaign was the internal Toyota Touch programme, which was implemented from 1986, aimed at generating a culture of customer care and a total business philosophy based on customer satisfaction.

The WTOW campaign expanded on the success of the Toyota Touch programme by trying to establish the culture of customer care in the after-sales market. The after-sales market consists of the servicing and parts sales markets that arise after a customer has purchased a new vehicle. The WTOW campaign aimed at building trust between customers and the Toyota dealer, as well as reinforcing the idea that, when you service your Toyota at your Toyota dealer, then 'everything keeps going right' becomes a reality.

After-sales market structure[2]

There are four major competitors in the after-sales market. These are:
- manufacturers' franchise dealers
- independents (independent garages/workshops/service stations)
- fast fitment centres
- do-it-yourself enthusiasts.

In terms of numbers, the franchise dealer is outnumbered four to five times by independent garages.

Franchise dealers offer high service standards and the expertise particular to the manufacturer's products and replacement parts. The perception is that they are impersonal and expensive in their relationship with customers, compared with independents. Customers who do support franchise dealers do so mainly because they are reassured that their cars will be serviced by a reputable and knowledgeable organization, and that there are warranties and guarantees if anything should go wrong. They are therefore prepared to pay a premium for the peace of mind that franchise dealers are supposed to offer.

Independents, on the other hand, are perceived to offer the same product as franchise dealers (the service), but at a better price. Their advantage is that they are seen to be more personal in their approach, build a better relationship with their customers, and give them the impression that they won't be ripped off, as compared with franchise dealers.

For a number of motor manufacturers, roughly a third of new vehicle buyers do not bring their vehicle back for servicing within the first two years of purchase. After the second year this figure rises significantly to levels of 70 to 80%.

The promotional activity for after-sales for most motor manufacturers takes place at dealer level, using dealer motivational programmes and other promotional tools. These are very difficult to measure. Advertising expenditure for the service, parts, and accessories market as measured by MRA's Adindex for 1995, was estimated at R54 million. This would include advertising by the so-called independent dealers.

Advertising strategy: Toyota after-sales

Extensive qualitative research was undertaken towards the end of 1994. The methodology followed was four group discussions among white and black owners of Toyotas, exploring areas such as:
- current beliefs about and attitudes toward after-sales repairs
- attitudes toward Toyota dealers
- awareness/knowledge of 'full-service history' (FSH) concept
- Response to FSH concept after exposure.

It was found that in the minds of Toyota owners the desired end result – affordable costs and a trusting relationship with the Toyota dealer – seemed somewhat unrealistic and not likely to be achieved with any short-term actions.

As far as Toyota was concerned, it would be very difficult to bring down the cost of parts and servicing to the levels expected by the customer without sacrificing on important aspects such as quality, safety, and reliability. It would be feasible, however, to develop and nurture a trusting relationship with the customer, which would allow the dealers to address the cost issue in such a way that the customer could perceive the added value resulting from the use of genuine parts and Toyota quality service. Thus the premium paid by customers could be justified through the value being delivered to them.

Toyota's advertising agency, Saatchi Saatchi Klerck & Barrett, recommended that the WTOW process be redefined, accelerated, and intensified. This would invite customers to use the dealer and at the same time address their perceptions about the above issues and dealer credibility.

The challenge for Toyota and the agency, therefore, was twofold:
- To break through the negative attitude customers have toward franchise dealers and the product they offer, by providing a tangible benefit that is meaningful to customers and satisfies their real needs

- To promote the benefit in such a way that it would effectively position Toyota's after-sales efforts as trustworthy, professional, and caring. This should be strongly linked to the overall Toyota positioning of 'everything keeps going right'.

The campaign

The major benefit for the customer that needed to be communicated was the reassurance and value offered by the Toyota full-service history (FSH). A full-service history is the track record of the scheduled maintenance services for the vehicle, as tracked by the service book given to each customer.

The acceptance and relevance of the concept had been investigated in the qualitative research done in late 1994. The conclusion drawn from the research was that the FSH concept did have the potential to draw Toyota owners back to Toyota franchise dealers. The proviso to this, though, was that the concept had to be packaged in such a way that consumers would clearly understand its benefits, and could relate to it on both a rational and emotional level.

The FSH concept entailed the following:
- The vehicle is serviced by Toyota-trained technicians at the due time.
- Only genuine Toyota parts with a 12-month unlimited kilometres warranty are fitted, ensuring Toyota reliability and a higher resale value.

The agency recommendation was to use the generally undervalued and under-used concept of a Toyota FSH, to repackage it, and to aggressively promote it as something truly special and valuable to any Toyota owner. This would also differentiate the message and Toyota from the generic industry position of other manufacturers.

Campaign objective
- To paint a clear picture of a full-service history – exactly what it is and what it is not.
- To create firm expectations of real-term financial gain for customers through Toyota's full-service history.
- To convince Toyota owners that there are also short-term benefits of affordability and reliability to be gained from a full-service history.
- To brand and establish a Toyota FSH as a much-sought-after item when selling or buying a used Toyota.
- To assist in encouraging customer trust in Toyota dealerships through maintaining the 'caring feeling' established through the previous Welcome to our World campaign.

Target audience
Three target audiences were chosen at which the promotional effort could be aimed. The most important primary audience was the current Toyota owners.

The particular focus was on drivers/owners of any Toyota not older than 24 months. Many of these owners are at the point where they may not continue servicing their vehicles at Toyota dealers, possibly because they perceive such dealers as expensive, and there may not be high levels of trust. They may also not be aware of the importance of the Toyota full-service history, and by leaving the Toyota fold they could jeopardise the value of their vehicles.

A second primary audience was the Toyota franchise dealers themselves. The overall success of the whole campaign was dependent on the commitment and involvement of the whole franchise network. A lot of emphasis, therefore, had to be placed on getting the franchise network both motivated and committed.

A secondary audience considered for the campaign was used-car buyers. By targeting them, the campaign could help these potential customers by taking the guesswork out of a used-car purchase. The FSH concept ensured that they would have reliable motoring.

Creative strategy

It was clear that Toyota needed to make the concept of a FSH both effective and synonymous with Toyota. In other words, it had to be seen as Toyota's property. To achieve this aim, the concept had to be packaged in such a way that:
• It was clearly differentiated from the generic concept of a FSH.
• It allowed consumers to relate to it and clearly see the benefits for themselves.

An inspired creative leap led the agency to recommend naming the service history record the 'Book of Life'. The objective was to attach all the well-known and positive associations of the SA 'Book of Life' (ID) document to the Toyota Book of Life, thereby creating instant recognition and identification. The book-of-life concept is something with which all South Africans are familiar, and can relate to. Everyone knows that the Book of Life contains a person's life history, and that without it you have no way of proving who you are. This was the basis of the creative execution. Spontaneous associations about Toyota's 'Book of Life' that were reinforced and put into context by the campaign were:
• It is valuable; something you must look after very well.
• It is a form of security.
• It is non-discriminatory.

The idea is that it should be a special and treasured possession.

Media strategy

The total media budget for the campaign was R3 million. It should be emphasised that the target market and audiences for the campaign were very broad and, in effect, covered all South African motorists – and Toyota owners in particular. This indicated that a broad-based media strategy was called for. Television was selected

for reach and impact, as well as its ability to convey the emotional warmth needed to accurately position the creative concept as very special. The emphasis was to
convey the idea of peace-of-mind motoring and eventually a higher resale value
for your Toyota by ensuring you had your 'Book of Life' and FSH for your vehicle.
Television was supported by both print and radio advertising. Placements of
advertisements in these media were selected to match the profile of Toyota owners. This helped in the introduction and provision of the necessary information to
fully communicate the value and benefits of the Toyota 'Book of Life'.

Promotional support through dealer involvement

It was clear that the success of the campaign would be largely dependent on dealer involvement and support. The campaign concept was presented to dealers at a
national conference. Toyota also designed an incentive competition to run
throughout the duration of the campaign. This was based on the dealer's plans for
marketing the 'Book of Life' concept and to coincide with the national advertising by Toyota. The plans, along with an indication of the results, were handed in
at the end of the campaign period and the winners won a trip to the USA.

There were also a number of activities at dealer level. The dealership itself provided another opportunity to reach Toyota owners. The most important benefits
of regularly servicing at a Toyota dealership were highlighted on point-of-sale
(POS) material.

The old Toyota service book was redesigned to reflect the 'Book of Life' concept
as portrayed in the advertising. Educational posters and mobiles were also produced and put up in all high-traffic areas within the dealerships.

In addition, a Toyota 'Book of Life' leaflet was designed, informing new Toyota
owners of the importance of the FSH, and how the owner could achieve a better
resale value for his/her Toyota if it had the FSH.

A new invoice folder was designed in which the workshop could insert the
invoice after a service. In this folder the value of the Toyota 'Book of Life' was
again reinforced, with the objective of making the customer realise the value of
the service for which he/she had paid.

A menu pricing poster was produced to give dealers the opportunity to prove
that Toyota's prices are competitive. This poster was laminated and used to list
special prices offered on fitted shocks, brakes, exhausts, and the like, as is done on
a menu. Toyota Full-Service History boards were also designed to place on Toyotas
which carried a Toyota FSH in the used-car division of dealerships.

Dealers themselves also promoted the campaign by means of radio, print advertising, promotions, and incentives. The agency developed three radio spots that
allowed dealers to personalise the advertising to their own dealership and for use
on their regional stations. A dealer advertising kit was also supplied with example
print ads which dealers could personalise. There were also headlines, logos, and
advertising grid pages if they wanted to produce their own print advertisements.
These advertisements were placed mainly in the local or community papers.

The agency also assisted Toyota dealers in their media placements to ensure maximum impact and cost efficiency for the dealership media spend.

Results of the campaign

The results of the campaign were carefully tracked and a post-campaign evaluation was carried out. Toyota measured the performance of 82 of their 314 dealers. These 82 dealers represented 80% of total parts and service sales in the Toyota dealer network. It is important to note that no other marketing activities were taking place during the campaign period which could have influenced the results positively. In this way the effects of the campaign could be clearly measured.

The results clearly show significant increases in turnover during the campaign period, which can only be attributed to dealer commitment to the 'Book of Life' campaign.

In general, parts and service turnover, as well as labour hours sold, increased significantly from the levels previous to the campaign. A comparison with the same period the previous year shows the extent of the success of the promotion.[3]

Category of dealer	Service centre turnover % up or % down	Parts centre turnover % up or % down
Platinum	13,8%	9,0%
Gold	14,1%	14,2%
Silver	15,6%	10,2%
Category B	22,8%	2,3%
Category C	23,2%	12,7%
Category D	42,4%	56,0%

Table 8.1: Parts and service turnover – August–October 1995 vs. August–October 1994

Feedback from dealers themselves further supported the campaign and showed the success and excitement generated at dealer level. Many dealerships planned further parts and service campaigns on their own to keep the momentum going and to build on the success of the 'Book of Life' campaign.

In conclusion, the 'Book of Life' campaign successfully integrated all above-the-line and below-the-line activities to produce a cohesive campaign in both national consumer media and at dealer level. The creative execution of the 'Book of Life' formed the cornerstone of the whole campaign and was carried through in all elements of the communications mix. The concept succeeded in providing a sceptical market with a tangible benefit for supporting franchise dealers, added value to the service product, and overcame the perceptions that Toyota dealers were more expensive. Lastly, significant increases in both service centre and parts sales turnover provides hard proof of the success of the campaign. The campaign also won a silver award in the Advertising Performance Excellence Awards for 1996, as well as the Special Award for Strategic Thinking.

Everything still keeps going right

Toyota South Africa has just celebrated 25 years of market leadership. With R400 million dedicated to upgrading by Toyota dealers, the introduction of a wider product range, and, of course, the winning formula of consistently good after-sales service, Toyota is set to hold its market position. This leadership focus is neatly encapsulated in their change of slogan from 'Everything keeps going right' to 'Lead the way'.

References

1   This case study was written by Saatchi Saatchi Klerck & Barrett. Case study procured by Ricardo Machado.
2   Toyota SA.
3   Toyota SA.

9

MARKETING FEATURES:
ADVERTISING
BRANDING
COMMUNICATION
IMAGE
POSITIONING
RELATIONSHIP MARKETING

Foschini

A force to reckon with[1]

In just three years, Foschini has been transformed from a somewhat lacklustre chain store into a vital and major fashion force. Under the leadership of its managing director, Simon Bowley, Foschini has earned the respect of its customers, its critics and its competitors, attracting comment and compliments alike. Success is attributed to Foschini's barefaced review of its market perceptions and positioning and its quick and effective application of new principles, merchandise, store design and marketing communication.

As the Foschini Group's largest trading division, Foschini accounts for around 45% of the total turnover. Foschini has over 300 stores – including Donna-Claire and Fashion Express – throughout South Africa, Namibia and Botswana.

Brief history

Foschini was established in 1924 by George Rosenthal, an entrepreneur who had run a successful clothing venture in the West Indies before identifying that South Africa would be the best market to introduce 'American frocks and gowns at popular prices'. The first Foschini store was in Pritchard Street, Johannesburg and within months new stores were opened in Pretoria, Cape Town, Port Elizabeth and Durban. In 1926, after just two years in operation, Foschini had nine branches.

By 1928, Foschini was a household name across South Africa and in 1932, Rosenthal registered Foschini as a private company – Foschini Dresses (Pty) Ltd. In 1937 profits were so healthy that Foschini went public and the shares became as popular as the dresses.

In 1967, Foschini acquired the American Swiss Watch Company; in 1968, Markhams was incorporated and in 1969, Pages Stores was established. Foschini Limited then became the Foschini Group and the 1970s saw the group's massive expansion programme.

In a country where the political climate has changed drastically over the years, the Foschini Group has been as aware as any other retailer in South Africa of the need to embrace change in order to not only survive and move with the times but also to be at the cutting edge of fashion retailing.

Effecting change

Research showed that Foschini's image said very little about fashion and, if anything, was simply attracting customers who were seeking a bargain. Foschini had become a reactive retailer – in other words, it wasn't blazing a trail to new fashion heights or fulfilling its customers' needs by providing real choice at realistic prices. Change was essential if Foschini was to continue appealing to fashion-conscious South African women.

Research underpinned Foschini's review of its image in the market and helped build the foundation for a massive repositioning programme. National qualitative and quantitative research was conducted to define and understand Foschini's brand image in the market. The results revealed that a fashion store's image and brand perceptions have a major influence on where women in South Africa choose to shop. As Foschini did not have a clear brand personality nor one that was distinctive from its competitors, the task of repositioning and developing the new Foschini brand had to begin in earnest.

The customer

The starting point of all marketing strategies has to be ensuring that one has a very clear picture of the customer one is targeting.

Foschini's marketing director, Kathryn Sakalis, ensured that this was the case by doing an in-depth profile of Foschini's target customer. This customer definition painted a picture of the customer in a way that all of Foschini's staff could clearly visualise her. The definition included demographics such as age, income, education and occupation, but also spelled out her habits (e.g. what magazines she read, TV she watched, where she shopped), her life stage and very importantly, her fashion orientation.

The competitors

Research revealed exactly what customers' perceptions of all Foschini's major competitors were, their strengths and weaknesses and how Foschini was placed relative to these. Foschini then identified a distinct area in the market, which they could own and in which they could excel.

It should be noted that no one fashion store could ever hope to be a woman's only choice, as women enjoy shopping around. However, a store can obtain 'preferred provider' status i.e. a store where customers trust they will always be able to find something and where they will feel comfortable.

Although women tend to assess stores on a rational basis, the image of the store has a major influence in determining where they choose to shop.
Foschini's challenge was therefore to develop an image which women could relate to and which would attract them to Foschini before any of its competitors.

The brand strategy

A concise, easily understandable vision was developed, setting a direction that everyone in the company could follow.

Vision statement
To be the women's champion of easy-to-wear fashion.

In order to achieve this vision, Foschini must deliver:
- Products that are consistently good value and quality, easy-to-wear, mainstream fashion with flair.
- Service that is consistently warm, friendly, efficient and knowledgeable.

The Foschini brand proposition

Foschini understands women, their spirit, their differences and their individuality, their needs for multidimensional lifestyles, their aspirations and their budgets.

Foschini knows what women want from fashion and how to interpret this for them with flair.

Implementing the brand strategy

Once the strategy had been devised, every aspect of the business was re-examined to ensure that the offering would consistently meet expectations.

Culture

Andy Warhol once said, 'They say time changes things, but you actually have to change them yourself.'

In order to ensure that all the Foschini staff were motivated to consistently deliver their vision, Foschini's culture had to encourage the adoption of change; an ownership mentality and staff that were willing to be accountable and responsible.

Various HR initiatives were therefore launched; these included:

- A standardised performance management system, which encouraged open and honest feedback.
- A retail academy, which encouraged projects to be initiated from 'the bottom up'.

Merchandise

The product range was reassessed to ensure that not only was the offering good quality and value, but that it also catered for the various aspects of a woman's lifestyle in a way that reflected Foschini's own distinctive fashion flair.

Instore experience

An ambitious store upgrade programme was initiated, so that the customer's impressions were immediately arrested by a totally different image upon entering the store.

Attention was given to the entire shopping experience to ensure that each step was viewed through the eyes of the customer.

An extensive training programme was introduced to upgrade the service levels offered by the store staff. Linked to this was the research mechanism of mystery shopping to monitor the staff's progress against the goals set.

Communication

All aspects of the communication mix were reviewed.

Each element had to reflect the brand's stated personality of being:

- Feminine and sexy
- Friendly, approachable and sociable
- Confident and sincere

An important facet of the communication strategy is to give fashion advice in a non-challenging, tongue-in-cheek way. In other words, the women behind Foschini talk directly to their female customers about fashion and trends in a language that the customers can relate to. As Kathryn Sakalis, marketing director of Foschini explains: 'Giving advice – woman to woman – and using messages that have a touch of attitude, makes us more accessible while grasping the attention of our customers.'

Examples of this fun, sassy and confident mode of communication include lines such as . . .

> Your winter exercise programme:
> Shop. Shop. Shop.
> I would be modest. If only I wasn't so stunning.
> I do gorgeous for a living.
> My inner child is nagging for a shopping spree.
> A staple diet should consist of at least one new outfit a week.
> 'SMS' stands for 'so much shopping.

Important communication vehicles, which were utilised to communicate this new brand personality, included:
- TV
- magazines
- direct mailing of brochures to account customers
- loyalty programme for top customers
- website
- sponsorships (e.g. dressing TV presenters, Idols finalists)
- store windows – which capture the imagination of passers-by who now stop to check out what's inside.

Internal communication (within the organization) is as important as external communication – a comprehensive and ongoing internal communications programme ensures that everyone in Foschini is up to speed with all the new developments and that the key messages are not only understood and applied, but conveyed convincingly and consistently at every point of customer contact.

Corporate social investment

Foschini initiated and annually sponsors the Foschini Annual Design Awards. Through this Foschini invests in fashion education, in small business and in promoting entrepreneurial skills. Giving back to fashion in this way forms the cornerstone of Foschini's social responsibility programme. Entrants to the FAD Awards are tasked with designing a range of reality fashion items that contemporary South African women would love and want to wear; this objective is at the heart of Foschini's offering.

The winner of the student category is awarded a study bursary as well as an internship at Foschini. A significant cash prize is awarded to the overall winning entrepreneur and this package includes business skills and financial advice from Foschini.

Ongoing business strategy

The core principles of Foschini's offering are quality, value, femininity and accessibility. Backed by excellent service and convenient locations, Foschini's stores provide an environment conducive to a pleasant shopping experience offering an appropriate translation of mainstream fashion with a unique flair.

As the formula for Foschini's repositioning has been so successful after just three years, the strategy will be continued and strengthened, checked by constant evaluation of its relevance to South African women through regular research programmes.

Reference

1   This case study was written by Foschini and procured by Michael Cant.

10

MARKETING FEATURES:
ADVERTISING
BRANDING
COMMUNICATION
DIVERSIFICATION
GROWTH
PROMOTION
RETAILING
SOCIAL RESPONSIBILITY

Game

Playing the retailing game[1]

The roots of the highly successful Game brand – which today dominates the general merchandise retail discount sector in southern Africa – go way back to 1970, when the first store opened its doors in cramped premises in Smith Street, Durban, and rang up sales of just R78 000 in its first month of trading.

The Game name was born out of the founders' belief that shopping had become tedious and boring and needed to be turned into a fun experience. They conceptualised retailing as a 'game' and created in their store an environment in which customers could 'play'. They even carried the concept through to the various departments on the store floor, that is, 'Baby Game', 'Auto Game' and so forth.

Characterised by its shocking pink livery, in-your-face advertising and unprecedented low pricing, the brand found instant success with local consumers, while visitors to Durban carried the brand awareness back to their home towns, cities and provinces – to the extent that a call on Game became a 'must do' for those on a trip to Durban.

Essentially a KwaZulu-Natal retail phenomenon in its early years, the 'upstart' newcomer was initially treated with disdain by the then staid and conservative retail establishment, but it would not take long before traditional department store chains such as Ackermans, Greatermans, and OK Bazaars began to feel the sharp point of Game's fast growing competitive edge.

The Game brand grew steadily throughout the three decades of trading since its inception in 1970 – but particularly in the nineties – reaching into all spectrums of consumer society to become the household name in non-food retailing. In a nutshell, the typical Game customer was 'anybody with disposable income' and a yen for a different, price-beating shopping experience.

Exponential growth

Tracing the history of the burgeoning Game brand reveals an almost exponential growth that, in its most explosive phase, took the company from a turnover of R440 million in 1993 to over R2 billion in 1998 – growth that was driven by the inherent strength of the brand loyalty. Since then, following the acquisition of Game Stores by Massmart Holdings for R755 million, sales have risen to even greater heights.

The product range was – and remains – anchored in meeting the non-food requirements of the average South African, and now southern African, household. Housewares – including large and small appliances, plasticware and kitchenware – TV, hi-fi and other audio equipment, Manchester (linen), garden and outdoor products, hardware and DIY, home office automation, clothing and footwear are some of the core departments in Game stores.

Today, the Game banner flies proudly over 60 stores that form a trading footprint spanning all nine provinces of South Africa as well as Botswana, Namibia, Zambia, Mauritius, Uganda and Mozambique – an area that stretches vertically from Cape Town to Kampala and laterally from Oshakati and Windhoek in the west to Empangeni and Maputo on the eastern seaboard... and beyond to the Indian Ocean islands.

The unmitigated success of the Game store in Gaborone (Botswana) – which, in 1993, represented the discount chain's first foray beyond South Africa – coupled with consistent enthusiastic buying support from other neighbouring countries in close-to-border Game stores like Polokwane (Pietersburg) and Nelspruit, proved that there was great potential waiting to be unlocked in other African markets. This led to the opening of a further four cross-border Game stores before the arrival of the new millennium.

The continued implementation of a bold into-Africa growth strategy will roll the unique Game formula out into other African countries, thus further entrenching the Game brand on the Sub-Saharan retail landscape. The most recent opening was in Mozambique (at the end of 2004), while the next phase will include the establishment of stores in Nigeria and Tanzania.

This ongoing expansion clearly demonstrates management's confidence in the future of the brand and in its resilience to the shifting sands of consumer spending that have become synonymous with trading in Africa.

The only limiting factor on the momentum of the drive into the rest of Africa is the lack of retail property developments which measure up to the high standards demanded by Game for its trading outlets.

Key stepping stones in the successful marketing of the Game brand are attributed to the factors described below:

Building the brand's personality

The 'personality' of the Game brand – a fun, satisfying shopping experience highlighted by incredibly discounted prices across a massive range of goods on offer in friendly, breezy surroundings generally in single-level stores – has been crafted over the years by a dynamic marketing strategy.

A cornerstone of the personality has been a strong emphasis on bold in-store promotions which add pleasure and amusement to the shopping experience and continually reinforce the Game brand in the process. For example, 15 winners of one of Game's most recent promotions will take their partners on a dream, expenses-paid, holiday to Mauritius in 2005.

The Game brand personality, in its earlier years, contrasted sharply with the staid, blue-rinse, tea-and-cucumber-sandwiches approach of traditional department store retailing in multi-level ('going up') facilities – and it found virtually instant acceptance by a consumer market that was ripe for change.

Over the years, constant reformulation and innovation of the strategy has kept Game in step with, if not ahead of, changing patterns, rates and modes of consumer spending, thus ensuring that it continues to deliver value retailing – which is essentially offering the broadest range of merchandise, mainly for cash, at the lowest prices. This is the foundation of the trading philosophy of parent company Massmart Holdings.

Supported by a combination of sustained, forceful advertising and in-store promotions, a strong, top-of-mind brand awareness has been a key result of this process.

Defining the brand's signature

One of the most distinguished elements of the marketing strategy has been the 'signature' catchphrase 'You Always Win At Game' – now modified to 'Game, You Always Win' – which is constantly delivered into consumer households by way of promotions and print/television/radio advertising.

Consumer perception of the Game personality, embodied by this catchphrase, is underlined by the fact that the discount chain today has a customer base of over

20 million – calculated on the number of annual transactions currently being rung up at store tills.

The shocking magenta pink corporate colour introduced by the founders to attract consumer attention and reinforce the 'fun' shopping experience on offer has since been toned down somewhat but nevertheless remains a distinctive feature of the Game brand – finding expression everywhere from the brand logo to in-store signage, staff uniforms... all the way down to calling cards.

The core of Game's fine-tuned marketing strategy has been to constantly fortify brand awareness, relentlessly reinforcing the message that, at Game, you get a great deal more than you thought for a lot less than you think.

Driven home constantly, with many variations on the words, the message always remains the same: 'At Game you get the widest range of products at the lowest possible prices' and 'you get more for less'.

The success of the marketing strategy, and the competitive edge it has created, is reflected in the steadily increased flow of feet through the doors of Game stores over the past decade.

Yet another Game signature is the widely publicised trio of customer-friendly guarantees that, by ensuring 'no-risk' shopping, are unique in the market:

Price Guarantee

Found it cheaper anywhere else? Tell us and we will beat that price! We will not be undersold – if you've purchased any item from Game, and later find the same product for less elsewhere, we will refund more than the difference. If you intend purchasing from Game and find the same item elsewhere for less at the same time – tell us and we will beat that price!

Satisfaction Guarantee

Changed your mind? We will exchange your purchase or refund you! If you've changed your mind – bring it back in unused condition, in the original packaging, and we will either exchange it or refund you. Exceptions are indicated at point of purchase.

Service Guarantee

It's not working? Complete after-sales service satisfaction! We will have any item under warranty repaired for you. Should that take longer than three weeks, the item will be replaced or refunded. For warranty purposes, proof of purchase date is required. We also ensure ongoing service on any products bought from Game – even after the warranty expires. Costs will be kept to the minimum.

Brightly coloured in-store signage, as well as print and broadcast advertising, has conveyed these unbeatable guarantees to the Game customer base at large – helping to build up a brand loyalty that is today unshakeable in the southern African market for discounted general merchandise.

Replicating the winning formula

The optimum store layout, and the shopping ambience it provides, has been determined through careful and ongoing market research – both at home and abroad – ensuring, in the process, that Game outlets are world class.

The brand is ultimately represented by the store, which is why Game continually and uncompromisingly strives for store-on-store consistency that will keep the brand alive.

Store layouts are based on extensive information and statistics provided from Game's own extensive data base, as well as on knowledge gained from constant monitoring of international retail trends.

In stores which average around 4 500 square metres of trading area, space is allocated to departments based on projected sales and gross profits, as well as taking into account the requirements for customer flow, potential for impulse purchasing and serviced departments.

Wide aisles which flow through low profile, as well as two-and three-metre high, steel fixtures that showcase the merchandise are used extensively to create a shopping ambience characterised by bulk appeal, good product visibility and customer comfort.

In the past, the formula was meticulously replicated across all Game stores, irrespective of where they are located. This is still true in that in the general range of merchandise, the mix of departments, customer service levels, hygiene standards, security arrangements, lighting, fixtures and fittings Game stores present a uniform environment, which reassures the customer as to the quality which he or she has come to expect.

However, towards the end of 2004, Game introduced the first of a new-look generation of stores that it plans to weave into its nation-wide trading portfolio. Situated at Umhlanga just north of Durban in KwaZulu-Natal, Game Gateway opened its doors with a host of new features. The new features include unprecedented wide aisles – 2,8 metres compared with the standard 1,8 metres – and a bright and breezy lifestyle trading look, supported by enhanced product display, better colour co-ordination and improved signage. In addition, unlike existing Game stores, where access to glass-enclosed high-tech (audio-visual) areas has traditionally been controlled, Game Gateway offers a completely open-plan trading configuration in this department. Another first for the new store is a 155 square metre dedicated promotions area – bigger than in any other Game outlet.

Communicating with customers

The publication of high-impact mass-distribution product catalogues has proven to be an indispensable tool for communicating with existing and potential Game customers.

The full-colour tabloid and broadsheet weekly leaflets, featuring product photographs, information and pricing, have an average print-run of 3-million and consume more newsprint and other print paper than most of South Africa's largest national newspapers.

The leaflets are distributed into households across southern Africa as inserts in carefully-selected major daily newspapers and community publications. They are also placed in postboxes via 'knock and drop' manual distribution agents. With an average readership estimated at four per leaflet, this potent form of communication reaches over 10-million existing and potential Game customers a week and is clearly a big factor in the store chain's ongoing success.

Social investment

In line with its philosophy that it is incumbent upon business to be responsive to the problems and needs of communities in which it operates, Game runs an extensive, two-pronged social investment programme, which reaches into every town and city where it trades.

The programme is focused almost entirely on child education in disadvantaged communities. On a national level, Game's strong support of SOS Children's Villages and ongoing country-wide provision of wheelchairs to school-going children with physical disability are typical examples.

While Game's ongoing actions as a responsible corporate citizen have clearly made – and continue to make – a difference to the lives of those in need, an important by-product of the social investment programme has been the further strength it has added to the Game brand in terms of consumer perception and support.

The future looks bright

Driven by a young, highly skilled and dynamic management team, and supported by the resources of the R20-billion-plus sales-a-year Massmart Holdings group, of which it is a key operating component, the Game brand is well poised to take advantage of future growth opportunities – both from within its existing store base and in new markets yet to be penetrated in South Africa and countries elsewhere in Africa

It is a retail brand for which the future holds great promise.

Reference

1   Case study by Sharon Futter, Massdiscounters. Updated by Shelley Owen, Game. Case study procured by Michael Cant.

11

MARKETING FEATURES:

CORPORATE CULTURE

CUSTOMER SERVICE

DIVERSIFICATION

GROWTH

INTERNATIONAL MARKETING

SALES TRAINING

SOCIAL RESPONSIBILITY

Pep

Pep people make the difference[1]

A wholly-owned division in the Pepkor Group, Pep trades in five southern African countries through 1 010 stores and employs around 6 700 permanent employees. Another wholly-owned division of Pepkor, Pep Africa, also trades under the Pep banner as a separate business unit with 70 stores in three other countries. This case study only deals with the Pep division (1 010 stores).

In 2003, Pep reported record results with R3,3 billion turnover and an operating profit of R317 million.

Pep's ethos is to create a great company through great leadership. Through a combination of its people, a firm strategic focus and the right systems and processes, Pep believes it can increase turnover at a higher rate than costs; this, in turn, ensures an acceptable increase in operating profits. Over the last few years, Pep has shown a bigger increase in like-for-like sales and operating profit than any other South African clothing retailer. However, this was not always the case and Pep's current success is the culmination of a sustained five-year programme to turn itself around after facing a near disaster.

From humble beginnings

Pep's founder Renier van Rooyen had noticed that the poor and disenfranchised people in his home town of Upington in the Northern Cape badly needed durable clothing but could not afford what was available in the local stores. He believed he could provide dignity and respect by selling clothing cheaply – but not cheap clothing.

In July 1965, Pep Stores was registered as a company and in September of the same year, the head office moved from Upington to Albert Road, Woodstock in order to be closer to harbour facilities and the Western Cape market.

By 1970, the chain boasted 58 stores with an annual turnover of more than R7 million and during that same year, a new head office and distribution centre was opened in Kuils River, Western Cape to cater for a planned rapid expansion. On 28 April 1971, Pep Stores opened a record of nine new stores in one day.

This rapid growth continued apace until by 1980, Pep had 286 stores and by 1990 the chain was 853 strong. In 2000, there were 1 198 stores and turnover, which had been growing in tandem with the expansion, was R2,2 billion.

Pep in the past (when the Pep-tanic almost sank)

Before 1994, Pep's customers were disenfranchised, but after the first democratic elections in 1994, the mindset of these customers changed completely and Pep failed initially to keep up, being slow to react to this drastic change in attitudes.

In 1998 the then Pepkor CEO decided to bring in a management team to introduce a new leadership style at Pep. A new managing director, operations director and financial director were appointed, none of whom had any retail experience. The newly appointed director of logistics had no logistical experience. A big gamble involved total inexperience on the one side balanced on the other by youth, pragmatism, prudence, passion and a common vision. That common vision was that if every brain, every pair of hands, every heart and soul in the company could work together towards one common goal, then success would be achieved.

However, a major stumbling block had to be overcome first. Soon after the new management team started, it became alarmingly apparent that the company was fast heading for financial disaster. At the time, Pep Limited was a listed company and the financial director, who started two months after the managing director, had to issue a profit warning on his first day at Pep. Shortly afterwards, Pep was hit with a claim of R93 million plus penalties by the Receiver of Revenue because a clearing agent had defrauded the company over a number of years. The company was also burdened with old and unacceptable stock, which was warehoused in old and run-down stores, most of which were in poor trading locations. Although a tailor-made merchandising system should be at the core of any retail operation and despite past attempts to install such a system, Pep didn't have one. As the managing director, André Labuschaigne, stated at the time: 'Pep is like the Titanic. Only the Peptanic is already heading for an iceberg in a devastating storm.'

Major moves toward the turnaround

It was identified that the company needed to dissemble and re-assemble the ship, stay afloat, miss the iceberg and sail to successful shores – quite a challenging journey at the time. It was also apparent that there were no quick-fix solutions and that the company had to embark on a long-term strategy and one that could tackle and win small battles every day in order eventually to win the war ... and keep the peace in years to come.

A series of important processes was initiated to coincide with an internal Pep cultural revival. In order to gain a deep understanding of its customers, an inexperienced team of buyers was empowered to buy the products they believed in and to form strong, collaborative relationships with their most important suppliers. A focused approach was adopted to implement the first comprehensive basic merchandising system. Under an achievable plan, a list of arduous tasks was outlined and initiated, including changes to the store image, getting rid of old stock, closing 170 unprofitable stores and finding better locations for many of the stores.

A cultural revolution

The managing director knew that the only way the company could really succeed was through the hearts and minds of its people. As their involvement was integral to this cultural revival, all employees (Pep calls them Dynamos) were asked to come up with recommendations for a vision, mission, value system and basic strategic plan. A 'dream' was formulated to give guidance to the process: 'To all become Dynamos who enjoy our work. We are growing all the time to fulfil our potential. We are determined to become a world-class company, showing the best financial results in the retail industry. We'll have fun while doing so.' This ethos was key in the Pep turnaround.

Labuschaigne quoted van Rooyen at the time, saying: 'Ordinary people like us can do extraordinary things.'

PEP people

With Pep staff's full involvement and commitment, a new culture was born: 'Sikhula KunYe – we are growing together'. A vision, mission, value system and six-point strategic plan were formulated to provide the bedrock of the Sikhula KunYe culture throughout the company. The view of the leadership team was that everyone in the company should be empowered to make a meaningful difference within their sphere of responsibilities.

The most important outcome to emerge initially was the staff's positive attitude, particularly as they had previously been despondent. It then took over a year for the first positive financial results to come through. Everybody at Pep greets one another with a 'High 5' handshake, which reinforces the team spirit and the belief that it's the people who make the difference and create a successful company.

To operate a business based upon low cost requires acuity at every level of the company and as Pepkor's chairman, Christo Wiese adds: 'If you want to sell cheaply, you must operate cheaply'. This is why one of the Pep values is resourcefulness in cost savings and in finding ways of being more effective rather than simply throwing money at problems. The financial controls and business acumen of the broader leadership team ensures a responsible and conservative approach to dealing with hard-earned money. Performance driven systems and methodologies create a sense of urgency and excitement – critical factors in any retailing organization. Regular evaluations and continuous communication (through emails, an in-house journal, information sessions, booklets and leaflets on important topics, conventions and work groups) ensure that every leader is aware of his/her responsibility and every team member is a business partner.

The company is divided into around a thousand work groups that meet from time to time to brainstorm plans for cutting costs and red tape (Pep calls red tape 'Value Parasites'). These proposals are then moved up into the relevant structure and either implemented immediately or considered for wider implementation.

A BHAG (Big Hairy Audacious Goal) philosophy was also introduced, which involves each team forming and pursuing its goals. These goals are set against the background of knowledge that, while the competition will always be tough, Pep's efforts will be that much better than the competition's!

Officially...one of the best companies to work for

In the 2003 Deloitte & Touche Human Capital Corporation Survey of The Best Company to Work For in South Africa, Pep shot up the charts from its previous year's position at number 14 to become the tenth best company overall. In the retail sector, Pep is number one and for companies employing over 5 000 people, Pep is just one behind the leader in second position.

Pep retail offering

Pep was established on the principle of providing affordable clothing for everyone in South Africa. Today, the chain can still (and will continue to) claim, with confidence, that it sells its merchandise at the lowest prices of any retailer in the country. Pep's cause is 'to make it possible for everyone to look and feel good'!

Pep operates on a cash only basis, which obviates all credit risks. Because of this and the fact that the company keeps its margins to a minimum and has a low cost culture, Pep can maintain the lowest prices in the market. For those customers who would like to purchase items on credit, Pep operates an alternative system whereby the customer can 'lay-by' an item, which Pep then 'reserves' until the item has been paid off.

The chain was founded by Renier van Rooyen three decades ago when van Rooyen's philosophies, which still ring true today, were: 'treat our customers and our staff with dignity and respect'; 'ordinary people can do extraordinary things'; 'we don't sell cheap clothing, we sell clothing cheaply'.

Other achievements

PEP believes its biggest single achievement is the development of a unique culture of honesty, passion and resourcefulness amongst its staff. It is a lively culture in which fun is encouraged, especially when specific targets are achieved. The leadership team regards people as the biggest strategic core asset in creating the key competencies of the company. As General Patton once said: 'Show your people where to go, but not how to get there and you will be amazed with the results'. As Labuschaigne says: 'We've adopted this motto and we have been not only amazed but also delighted with what's happened'. Other achievements include:

- Pep is the biggest same brand store network in southern Africa.
- Pep was the first company in the world to sell prepaid airtime electronically through its own till points (1999).
- Pep won a national award for the best logistical system in South Africa (2001).
- Pep was voted one of the two best employers to work for in the large companies section (2003 Human Capital Corporation survey).
- Pep ranked one of the top four clothing retailing brands (2003 Markinor/*Sunday Times* survey).
- Pep recorded the highest like-for-like sales (one of the most important indicators in retailing) amongst all clothing retailers (2001 to 2004).
- Pep has recorded the highest growth in operating profits in the clothing retail industry in South Africa (2001 to 2004).
- Pep's in-store radio station – Feelgood FM – has the widest geographical reach of any radio station in South Africa.

Feeling good about Feelgood FM

At the end of 2003, Pep launched its in-store radio station – Feelgood FM. Available by satellite, all of Pep's stores in South Africa, Botswana, Namibia, Lesotho and Swaziland receive live daily programmes from some of South Africa's favourite presenters.

The future

Representing an investment of R121 million annually, the capital expenditure programme includes the upgrading and relocating of around 70 existing stores and the opening of a further 40 stores. The store-opening programme will lead to the creation of a minimum of 200 new jobs. Pep's investment in its people will continue, as will, no doubt, the number of people who now queue up to work for the company.

Labuschaigne concludes: 'A catastrophic and colossal retail disaster has been averted with few casualties. The Peptanic is now well on course to charter new waters in our quest to be a great retail force in Africa.'

It is the way in which the Pep people have embraced the company's culture and how this culture and the business have been integrated, that has steered the Pep ship safely into the new millennium. Supported by its advertising, PR and social responsibility campaigns, this culture will ensure Pep's future course on the route to growth and success.

Reference

1   Case study by Mariki Schwiebus at Pep; procured by Michael Cant.

12

Ford Motor Company of Southern Africa

History of a marketing success[1]

Ford Motor Company, the second largest motor manufacturer in the world, has been associated with South Africa for over 75 years. In 1911, a Ford agent was appointed in Cape Town and, by 1924, Ford had opened its plant in South Africa.

So began Ford's involvement in South Africa – an affair that was to flourish over many decades. Ford South Africa initially made Port Elizabeth its base, where it developed manufacturing facilities. The company rapidly increased its share of the South African vehicle market – by the late 1960s it commanded 28%. The company is currently the second largest motor manufacturer in southern Africa.

In 1985, Ford Motor Company merged with the automotive operations of Anglo American. Together they formed the South African Motor Corporation, better known as Samcor. At this stage, Ford faced enormous pressure from suppliers, customers, and the American nation to withdraw from South Africa because of apartheid. Three years later, this pressure had grown to such an extent that Ford disinvested from the country. However, Ford made it clear that it would return as soon as South Africa was deemed politically acceptable.

The re-entry of Ford occurred in 1994. In November that year, Ford Motor Company acquired 45% equity in Samcor from Anglo American and the employee trust fund.

In February 2000, the announcement was made that Ford would be increasing its investment in South Africa by taking a majority shareholding of 90% in Samcor. At the same time, Ford increased its shareholding in Ford Credit South Africa to 50%. During August 2000, Samcor was officially renamed the Ford Motor Company of Southern Africa.

Ford Motor Company recently purchased the remaining 10% and now owns 100% of the company.

1903	Ford Motor Company is incorporated. The first production car, the Model A, is sold and Arthur Youldon orders the first Ford for South Africa.
1908	The first Model T is introduced.
1915	The one millionth Ford car is built in the world.
1923	Model T Ford assembly in Port Elizabeth on Africa's first assembly line. 10 millionth Ford car built.
1979	Ford acquires a 25% interest in Mazda of Japan.
1984	Ford reaches a 13% market share in Europe and becomes the best-selling marque for the first time.
1988	Due to South Africa's apartheid legislation and after increasing pressure from suppliers and customers as well as a large portion of the American nation, Ford made the decision to disinvest from the country until such time as it was correct to return.
1990	Ford acquires Jaguar.
1994	After a six-year absence, Ford returns to South Africa after the first democratic elections. The deal is announced in November, following the purchase of a 45% stake in Samcor.
1995	Ford 2000 is launched. North American and European automotive operations merge into one global business, Ford Automotive Operations.
1996	The 250 millionth Ford is built. Mazda and Ford enter into a closer tie-up with Ford, increasing its equity share from 25% to 33,4%.
1998	Ford becomes first automaker to have its plants certified worldwide under the environmental standard ISO 14001. The Ford Focus is introduced in Europe and later wins European Car of the Year. Ford Fiesta wins South Africa's Car of The Year.
1999	The Focus wins the North American Car of the Year. Henry Ford named Businessman of The Century by *Fortune* magazine. The Model T is named Car of the Century. Ford acquires Volvo Car Corporation.
2000	Ford officially takes ownership of Land Rover from the BMW Group.
	Ford acquires over 90% of Samcor by buying Anglo American and employees' trust holdings.

Now a full international player, Samcor is renamed Ford Motor Company of Southern Africa.

2001	Ford acquires the remaining 10% and now owns 100% of the company.
2002	Following the announcement in 1999 that Ford Motor Company of Southern Africa's Port Elizabeth engine plant had been designated the sole supplier of a 1,3-litre RoCam engine to Ford plants around the world, the first shipment left during the first quarter of 2002.
2003	Ford Motor Company celebrates its 100th year and the Ford Motor Company of Southern Africa its 80th. Ford Motor Company of Southern Africa announces it has been selected as the manufacturing source for future vehicle and component export programmes. The initial export programme, a commercial vehicle with volumes of 2 700 per annum was set to commence in the third quarter of 2004. A passenger vehicle export programme with volumes of approximately 41 000 per annum; 30 000 for export begins in the first quarter of 2005.
2005	Ford Fiesta finalist for Car of the Year 2005.

Table 12.1: Ford milestones in the automotive market

We're back!

The marketing team of Ford Motor Company of Southern Africa had to spread the message that Ford was officially back in South Africa and that Samcor was now the Ford Motor Company of Southern Africa. This part of the marketing strategy was called the 'We're back!' message.

Ford tried to communicate this message to as many people as possible in the shortest possible space of time. It used a corporate advertising campaign, which included all primary media. Specific and separate strategies were developed for the different media. This included electronic (TV, radio, and Internet), newspapers (national, regional, city, and suburban and country press), and magazines (financial, motoring, trade, and others).

An important step in the marketing process was to make sure that the message communicated within South Africa was in keeping with that communicated in other parts of the world. This was the responsibility of Ford Motor Company's Corporate and Public Affairs division.

Building up to the actual announcement, a 'positive information' campaign was conducted through regular media releases. These releases were issued to build the image of Ford Motor Company in the minds of the respective target publics.

In addition to these media releases, an A3-size, full colour, glossy brochure was published and placed in all major national and selected regional print media announcing the new Ford Motor Company of Southern Africa and its trustmark brand portfolio, which includes: Ford, Mazda, Volvo, Jaguar, and Land Rover.

Ford took the pre-announcement to the media a step further than media releases and brochures. To effectively impress upon relevant media and create a lasting impression that Ford Motor Company had returned as a major and committed player, an influential group of South African journalists was invited to visit Ford in Dearborn, USA.

Once the media had spread the word, the public was ready for the big announcement. The official renaming of the company took place on 21 August 2000 at the Silverton facility and on 22 August 2000 at the Port Elizabeth facility. The function, primarily to reveal the name on the front of the building, was attended by the media, dealers, fleet owners, all employees and government officials, including the Minister of Trade and Industry, the Mayor of Greater Metropolitan Pretoria, as well as the US Ambassador to South Africa. Television newsrooms as well as influential publications were directly contacted prior to the media conference and were invited to attend the announcement and interview the relevant Ford executives.

While the media and the actual public announcement formed the biggest part of the message, the Company didn't forget about the importance of direct communication. To protect relationships and to ensure that important contacts were well informed, major fleet owners, rental companies and government departments were advised of developments through face-to-face communication, telephone calls, and written communication.

Ford Motor Company of Southern Africa: A corporate signature

Part of the 'We're back!' message was that Ford's return signified the company's trust, dedication, and commitment toward South Africa. This was the message that came across loud and clear in all corporate statements.

'Ford Motor Company's decision to increase its shareholding in Samcor and change the name to Ford Motor Company of Southern Africa reflects the confidence that the company feels in the potential of southern Africa as a growth platform,' Marcos S. Oliveira, chief executive officer and group managing director of Ford Motor Company of Southern Africa was quoted as saying at the time.

'The name Ford Motor Company of Southern Africa is our corporate signature. It reflects the foundation of trust that supports all of our brands, products, services and actions. It will also represent our core values, such as our commitment to leadership in customer satisfaction, safety, quality, corporate citizenship, and environmental responsibility,' he continued.

Lewis Booth, Ford Motor Company's president of Asia Pacific and Africa operations, said at the time that Ford's decision to increase its shareholding in Samcor reflected the company's confidence in South Africa as a growth platform. 'To demonstrate our commitment to South Africa and the surrounding regions, it is appropriate that Ford Motor Company should have a majority shareholding,' he said.

The marketing strategy had to convey the message that the change of the name of the company reflected Ford's confidence in the potential of South Africa's future economic growth and the good management of its social and political issues.

The marketing strategy

A well-formulated marketing and public affairs programme had to be implemented to maximise positive publicity for the company. At the same time, any potential negative perceptions by the respective target publics had to be minimised.

The marketing strategy had the following objectives:

- Elevating the status of the new Ford Motor Company of Southern Africa.
- Building trust in the Ford trust mark and brands.
- Building confidence in the other primary brands through the association with Ford South Africa.
- Creating significant excitement.
- Most importantly, addressing the question: 'Ford is back – so what?'

The Ford Focus

Ford had to convey the progressive 'We're back!' image but, at the same time, it needed to place a tangible value on this move. In other words, the previously mentioned 'So what?' question had to be answered. As a part of the strategy to answer this question, it was decided that the launch of the new company would be married to the launch of a significant new product.

When Ford designs a marketing strategy for a particular vehicle range, a bull's eye is used in order to ensure that the strategy is on target and in keeping with the positioning of the brand. Ford's bull's eye consists of three keywords: genuine, progressive, smart – also known as the DNA of the brand. These three words basically encapsulate what Ford means. Ford's marketing team, therefore, had to find a car that exemplified these characteristics. That product would be the Ford Focus.

There were two main reasons for marrying the two launches. In the first place, the two events were very close in date. The launch of Ford Motor Company of Southern Africa took place on 21 August 2000 and the launch of the Ford Focus on 1 September 2000.

However, the second reason was more important and was by far the overriding factor. Ford Motor Company needed a concrete example to the market of its return to South Africa. It was all very well to make the statement that Ford was back – but what did this mean to the general public in practice? It meant that the South African motoring public would have access to the very latest automotive technology in the world – and that was exactly what the Focus represented.

The Ford Focus proved to the customer that Ford's return to the country was more than just market puffery. The fact that the Focus had won the European and North American Car of the Year Awards gave the vehicle massive credibility. It was a visible substantiation of Ford's promise and conveyed the message that, thanks to Ford's return, this was the sort of technology that motorists could expect in the future.

This message was conveyed in the form of billboards, bearing a photograph of the new Ford Focus with the teaser slogan, 'The shape of things to come'. Billboards were erected in high-traffic locations – three in Johannesburg, two in Pretoria, and two in Durban. The billboards were erected long before the availability of the car. This was to create hype around Ford and its new image.

Through the billboards, Ford announced the Focus three months before it was available. The company's intention was to convey the message that this was a product that was worth waiting for.

Only six months after the first launch of the Focus did consumers see the Focus television advertisement. The Focus television advertisement was in sync with the Focus slogan 'DNA of tomorrow's cars'. Like the slogan, the television advertisement incorporated the successful heritage of the Ford Focus. Both the television advertisement and the slogan maintained that you had to have it in your genes to design and desire a car like the Focus.

As was mentioned before, the basic keywords of Ford's marketing are genuine, progressive, and smart. Focus followed on this with confident driving and smart design. Chief designer John Doughty's brief called for striking new edge design, driven by maximum practicality and versatility. 'We wanted a new look for the car, a dynamic design that boldly signalled an unmistakable step into the new millennium,' he said at the time.

With its progressive, adventurous, and dynamic image, the car was absolutely ideal to represent Ford's new image in this country.

Ford hits cyberspace

Each of the five brands marketed by the Ford Motor Company of Southern Africa has its own website. When the Company was renamed it launched its new corporate website: www.fordmotorcompany.co.za.

Ford Motor Company firmly believes in the strengths and opportunities offered by the Internet. 'This is because marketing on the Internet is often much more effective than print brochures and advertorials'.

The Ford Motor Company of Southern Africa Web page has the primary role of being an information source for the media and other parties interested in the new company and its products and services.

Ford, like other auto manufacturers, is aggressively pursuing online marketing. Last summer it shifted $100 million of its 2000 print budget, for instance, into media including the Web. It went live almost a year ago with ford.com and its online consumer-connect strategy, Ford Connections. It also signed on to two high-profile online strategic partnerships: One with women-focused iVillage, the other Digital Entertainment Network. David Ropes, director of Ford's corporate advertising and integrated marketing group, referred to this as the first sign of a Ford 'virtual mall'.

On a local front, it hit cyberspace in a big way, with two major websites – its corporate site and a site dedicated to the Focus (www.fordfocus.co.za).

Also, because the Company wanted a fresh, innovative campaign to assist in increasing the awareness of thousands of customers, as well as the general public, of the name change, they approached Independent Online (IOL) to help them achieve their goal.

Through a combination of banners, buttons, and up-to-date editorial information, IOL delivered a large number of qualified customers to the virtual showroom of the different Ford Motor Company of Southern Africa manufacturers.

The awareness campaign was devised by IOL's AdSolutions team and designed by IOL's creative department, IOL Interactive. A freestanding micro-website was developed to focus on the Ford Motor Company of Southern Africa's identity change as well as its various brands – Ford, Mazda, Volvo, Jaguar, and Land Rover.

The micro-website provided visitors with a wealth of information on the Samcor/Ford Motor Company of Southern Africa name change, as well as photographs of the official launch event, and included links to the websites for the company's various brands. The micro-website for IOL/Ford Motor Company of Southern Africa was hosted on IOL's servers and extensively promoted through banners and content panel campaigns in strategic IOL environments, including IOL Motoring.

Post-campaign analysis showed that the campaign was an overwhelming success. The banner and button campaign delivered a yield of 0,76% – or 1 303 clicks through to the Ford Motor Company of Southern Africa micro-site hosted on IOL. From there an extraordinary 42% (541 IOL users) clicked through to the various brands under the Ford Motor Company of Southern Africa umbrella (Ford, Mazda, Volvo, Jaguar, and Land Rover). The biggest winner was Volvo (12% of the clicks) followed by Ford (8,5%), and Landrover (8,89%). These statistics compare very favourably when looking at previous campaigns averaging a yield of 1% for standard banner advertising (468x60 banner ads only) promoting motoring brands.

Dave McKenzie, IOL Sales & Marketing Manager, summed up the campaign: 'In four weeks IOL delivered 541 qualified prospects to the online showrooms of the different brands. Communicating to targeted audiences within the IOL environment by pushing the relevant advertising messages through interesting and compelling information has proved a great success.'

What about the other primary brands?

Ford Motor Company of Southern Africa is the South African home of Ford, Mazda, Volvo, Jaguar, and Land Rover. Each brand is very distinctly positioned and each needs to be independently marketed to their respective target audiences. For each to succeed in its own right, brand integrity is paramount. This is in line with Ford Motor Company's worldwide philosophy in this respect.

Where the other brands were concerned, the marketing strategy had two objectives. The first was to educate the general public on Ford Motor Company's trust mark portfolio of brands approach. The second was to make sure that other primary brands (especially Mazda) did not suffer as a result of the increased focus on Ford with the Ford Motor Company announcement.

In order to prevent the other primary brands from suffering, television and print campaigns were launched by those brands at the same time as the Ford announcement. This campaign also assisted in offsetting attempts by competitor motor manufacturers to dilute Ford's announcement in the media.

The same strategy was applied at Ford dealers. Facilities and showrooms specifically needed attention. To focus on Ford alone could have harmed the dealers' efforts with Mazda, especially where the combined Ford/Mazda dealers were concerned. Through advertising agencies, a campaign was developed where the Ford and Mazda primary brands were positioned under the Ford trust mark. The Auto Africa 2000 Motor Show was also used to present all the primary brands under the Ford Trustmark as had already been done at the 1999 Detroit, Frankfurt, and Tokyo Motor Shows.

A new slogan for a new image

Powerful brands in the SA market like OK Bazaars, Edgars, Coca-Cola, and Ford have shown that brands can live on to provide wealth for current or new owners if they are not left for too long without the support of quality, service, distribution, and innovation.

Despite this, in South Africa, people tend to view Ford on a smaller scale, where globally it is one of the strongest and most recognised brands. This image also had to be created in South Africa.

In order to do this, a new progressive slogan had to be established. While 'Built Ford tough' is the slogan of Ford bakkies, Ford decided to retire its slogan of 15 years, 'Have you driven a Ford lately?' New television and print ads were planned to portray Ford's rich heritage as an automaker and to introduce a new tagline with the Ford name.

Executives familiar with the campaign process said that one spur to the change had been consumer tests which indicated that positive responses to 'Have you driven a Ford lately?' had plummeted to the 20% range after years of 50% readings.

At the time of printing, Ford was still busy with an ongoing strategy to find a new slogan for Ford passenger cars. This will be established after the results of current consumer research have been revealed. Irrespective of the results, however, is the fact that the slogan will be in the line of the 'can do spirit' and will play up the idea of the company being a family business all these years.

With the Focus and its new slogan, Ford is moving away from old positioning. The old positioning was not a conscious positioning, but one that came out of the sheer heritage of Ford. The new positioning of Ford is far more progressive.

Ford is trying to establish itself as an aspirational brand. Not aspirational in the premium segment, but aspirational because driving a Focus will generate peer approval. Ford is now also aiming at the female and black market, especially with a brand such as the Focus.

Ford's culture of caring

Ford has changed its outlook on business considerably over the past 100 years. When it first started trading, the emphasis was undeniably on business.

Henry Ford did not pioneer the modern assembly-line method of car manufacture to create jobs. He did it to make himself rich, which he most certainly did. In the process of making himself rich, he also created millions of new jobs in his own company and others who followed his methods. He sold 15 million of his first car, the Model T Ford, which, by making rapid travel affordable, changed the way we live.

What is fascinating is that, in the new assembly-line jobs he created, Ford, rapacious capitalist that he was, insisted on paying double the going wage rates. His theory was that well-paid workers were not only productive and willing but also themselves constituted a market for the very product they were manufacturing.

Today, an important part of Ford's marketing and brand positioning is establishing the perception that the Ford Motor Company of Southern Africa does more than just build and sell world-class cars. It had to be positioned as a company that has fostered a culture of caring and had to be seen as one of the foremost companies within the sphere of social responsibility.

In order to achieve this brand image, several campaigns are in place:

Ford's HIV/Aids awareness campaign

It had to be communicated to the public that the senior management of Ford Motor Company of Southern Africa has a sincere intent and commitment to execute a constructive HIV/Aids Action Plan.

In order to formulate such a plan, Ford Motor Company of Southern Africa utilised assistance and guidance from Ford Healthcare Management and entered into partnership with Ford, USAID, Centre for Disease Control Foundation in the USA, and NUMSA.

As far back as April 1999, Ford Motor Company of Southern Africa (then Samcor) had ensured maximum accessibility to free condoms. The popularity of this programme grew over time – the volume of condoms dispensed on-site has increased by 400%.

Ford Motor Company of Southern Africa also established a HIV/Aids steering committee, which meets monthly to discuss HIV/Aids problems and possible solutions. To support this project, a Ford Motor Company of Southern African Policy Statement on HIV/Aids was concluded and published.

While Ford did a lot for Aids awareness in the community, it focused strongly on Aids preventive programmes internally. The company appointed an HIV/Aids programme manager at the engine plant in Port Elizabeth and one for the assembly plant in Pretoria. To establish ongoing employee awareness training and counselling, 75 peer educators per location have been appointed and trained.

HIV/Aids awareness training has been delivered for all Ford Motor Company of Southern Africa employees. All operations in Pretoria and Port Elizabeth shut down for a two-hour training session. In addition to this, Ford Motor Company of Southern Africa hosted and funded an Aids awareness family day for employees and their families in both Pretoria and Port Elizabeth.

Ford also did an actuarial assessment of the impact of HIV/Aids on the company. This assessment covered projections in respect of medical cover, retirement benefits, employee absenteeism, productivity, staff turnover, recruitment, training factors, and loss of skills.

Other Aids preventive initiatives from Ford Motor Company include an HIV/Aids voluntary testing campaign, conducting ongoing HIV/Aids awareness training at the workplace and provision of educational materials at the workplace and during community events.

The company obtained recognition for its efforts when it received the CDC (Centers for Disease Control and Prevention) Organizational Award for a US-based company with an international presence during 2000. The Ford Motor Company of Southern Africa was the only company outside the USA to receive the award, which recognises the highly effective workplace programme it has put together and the contribution made by the company towards educating other employers in the area about HIV/Aids.

In 2000, the Company was awarded the Award for Corporate Excellence by the USA State Department. The award recognises the important role US businesses play abroad as good corporate citizens.

In January 2002 the FMCSA was awarded the US Secretary of State's Award for Corporate Excellence for the Company's HIV/AIDS programme. Of the over 60 nominations received in 2001, Ford was selected as the winner in the multinational category. The Secretary of State's Award for Corporate Excellence was established to recognise the important role US businesses play abroad as good corporate citizens. It highlights the Department's increasing role in business-related issues. Candidates for this award are nominated by the Chiefs of US Missions around the world.

During October 2002, the Company took another significant step in the fight against the Aids pandemic when it announced the formation of a company-funded, on-site Voluntary Counselling and Testing (VCT) programme.

The SOS Village programme

The SOS is a welfare organization that looks after neglected, orphaned, and abandoned children. In South Africa SOS has six branches. One of these is located near Ford Motor Company of Southern Africa, in Silverton, Pretoria.

The SOS provides a home, mother and family setting from childhood through to age eighteen when children are transferred to a SOS youth home. At the youth home, the post-adolescent youth co-habits a house with other SOS youth and learns to be independent. The youth homes are under constant supervision by the village management, and the youth themselves maintain constant contact with their adoptive mothers.

Ford Motor Company of Southern Africa and Ford Credit have adopted one of 15 houses in the Mamelodi Village. The house, which is now known as Ford Motor Company of Southern Africa-Ford Credit House, is home to ten children and an adoptive mother.

Ford got involved with SOS long before this particular village was even built. It was one of the donors that contributed funds for the building of the Village. After it was built, Ford Motor Company of Southern Africa donated funds annually for the upkeep of one of the 15 houses. Ford Motor Company of Southern Africa and Ford Credit contribute towards the purchasing of food and clothing and to pay school and medical fees. Several Company staff members have also donated items from their own homes and those given to them by suppliers and other business partners.

Ford's donation to Mozambique

US-based Ford Motor Company contributed over R600 000 in cash and in-kind donations to provide relief to the victims of the devastated African region of Mozambique, Zimbabwe, and Mpumalanga (South Africa) after torrential rains flooded villages and countrysides.

Ford Motor Company of Southern Africa and Ford Credit also donated four off-road vehicles, estimated to be valued at approximately R410 000, for transportation and emergency response purposes. Local Ford dealers, situated in the respective regions, offered to service the vehicles, free of charge, for a period of two years or 40 000 kilometres.

'As a company, we are privileged and delighted to be able to make this contribution towards easing the plight of desperate people in these flood-ravaged areas,' Marcos Oliveira, Group Managing Director of Ford Motor Company of Southern Africa, commented at the time.

A-Ford-Able Bike programme

In 2001, the Ford Motor Company, Japan and Ford Motor Company of Southern Africa (FMCSA) joined forces to provide bicycles to underprivileged communities in South Africa.

Volunteer employees from Ford Motor Company Hiroshima Operations gather together at the City of Hiroshima Bicycle impound lot in Nishi-ku Nicho-me to select abandoned bikes provided by the City of Hiroshima, prepare them for shipment, and then load over a hundred bikes into a 20-foot shipping container which is currently sent to South Africa.

A-Ford-Able Bikes is a community service project being undertaken by Ford volunteer employees with the cooperation from the City of Hiroshima, Safmarine, Mazda, and the SOS Children's Villages operation in South Africa, and Nittsu.

The first two shipments of bicycles were given free of charge to orphans who live in the six SOS Children's Villages located around South Africa. The orphans use them to transport themselves to school and for other pressing needs, like having fun.

Ford's image as a corporate environmentalist

Ford Motor Company enhanced its image as a corporate environmentalist on Earth Day, emphasising a commitment to reducing smog-forming emissions and its future plans to sell fuel-efficient hybrid vehicles. Ford was the exclusive sponsor of *Time* magazine's special Earth Day 2000 edition, which went to 30 million readers worldwide. Ford also sponsored a special concert in San Francisco on 15 April 2000 honouring the 'heroes for the planet' saluted in *Time's* Earth Day edition.

Company officials say that Ford's chairman, William Clay Ford jr., is a self-described 'lifelong environmentalist' and has pledged to make the company the industry leader in developing cleaner vehicles.

'Ford has made a pledge to provide ingenious environmental solutions that will position us as a leader in the automotive industry of the twenty-first century. Our actions, such as making all of our trucks in the United States low emissions vehicles, demonstrate that we care about preserving the environment for future generations,' said James C Schroer, Ford's vice-president of global marketing.

In keeping with this philosophy, both assembly plant facilities of the Ford Motor Company of Southern Africa in Pretoria and Port Elizabeth are ISO 14001 and TS 16949 compliant, which means that experts agree that the company is world-class in terms of environmental management. To emphasise this, a nature reserve was recently established at the rear of the Silverton assembly plant, which currently supports blesbok, impala and a variety of birdlife. Also, the company drives its environmental and conservations initiatives through the Mazda Wildlife Fund.

Currently celebrating its fourteenth year of operation, the Mazda Wildlife Fund has played a vital and constructive role within the conservation sector to help meet this challenge. The company realised that, to make a really meaningful contribution to the preservation of South Africa's precious natural heritage, its contribution had to be both substantial and sustained over the long term.

To date, the Fund has contributed around R15 million to assist major conservation projects with their transportation needs.

A consumer-driven company

One of Ford's core values is consumer satisfaction. This means that Ford had to position itself as a consumer-driven company, which meets customer requirements by setting the highest standards in technology, safety, and the environment. The message had to be spread that Ford's customer focus allows it to bring to South Africa innovative, wide-ranging products, and service opportunities from across the globe.

Ford is currently engaged in consumer research in order to fine-tune its strategies and to change negative perceptions.

Henry Ford's heritage – Into the future

Now, for the first time, Ford has a product line-up that looks similar, that communicates the same message and has the same intrinsic values. It is the first time Ford has a marketing offering that is complete.

While it is clear that Ford has given its image, its products and its positioning strategies a face-lift, the Ford heritage will remain. This is because the rich tradition is one of the Ford brand's strongest points.

No matter how progressive or new Ford's image and positioning will become, it will always boil down to Henry Ford's philosophy: 'I will build a motorcar for the great multitude. It will be constructed of the best materials. It will be so low in price that every person making a good salary will be able to own one.'

References

1   Case study written by Craig von Essen, General Manager, Communications & Government Affairs. Case study procured by Annekie Brink.

PART THREE

CONTEMPORARY CASES

Introduction

Part 3 contains a combination of cases retained and updated from the previous edition and new case studies. Most of these case studies concern companies which are recognisable to and popular with South African consumers, and which they may use on a daily or weekly basis. For instance, any given day one may buy a *Daily Sun* newspaper, while buying a breakfast bun at Butterfield, pick up lunch at Hot Dog Café or King Pie, book a flight with kulula.com and dine at any one of the food stores examined. As consumers of these companies' products and services, and as marketing students, it is interesting and instructive to analyse the path to success which these innovative companies have followed.

Many of the cases grouped in **Part 3: Contemporary cases**, such as kulula.com, *Daily Sun*, and Debonairs, have succeeded through niche marketing. To a large extent, these niches came into existence following South Africa's transformation to a democratic society after 1994. However, a case study such as Hot Dog Café demonstrates that the simple recognition of a business opportunity does not alone lead to success. As the chapters in **Part 1: Socio-economic parameters in South African retailing** illustrate, the consumer market in South Africa has become increasingly complex, diversified and demanding. In order to identify target markets and develop marketing strategies effectively, professional market research, accurate analysis, and careful auditing are necessary in order to save time, effort, and money and to ensure a success rather than risk a failure.

Many of these case studies demonstrate another exciting contemporary development, namely the emergence of a franchise culture in South Africa. Once again, this strategy needs to be undertaken in a controlled and regulated way, following SWOT analyses and with support from the franchisor.

It will be exciting to follow the progress, development and expansion of these companies in the years to come.

Daily Sun –
Circulating what consumers want[1]

Daily Sun was launched on 1 July 2002 into a seemingly crowded South African daily newspaper market. The rapid circulation success of the paper can be attributed to a combination of operational and strategic innovations, which includes credible market research, a unique editorial mix, innovative distribution and a fresh promotional approach. Within 15 months of its launch, the *Daily Sun* became the biggest daily newspaper in South Africa. The latest audited circulation figures (Jan–Mar 2004) of 284 000 copies per day puts the paper far ahead of established papers like *The Star* (165 000) and *Sowetan* (120 000). A national rollout strategy is currently underway and promises to add at least another 50 000 copies to the existing sales base.

The genesis of a people-centered newspaper

The *Daily Sun* concept is based on successful examples of similar newspaper products in the United Kingdom and Brazil. *The Sun* and *Mirror* gained widespread popularity in the course of significant political, social and economic changes in Britain. *Mirror*, for instance, championed the cause of returning World War II soldiers and their ailing families. Returning to their dilapidated, war-ravaged neighbourhoods after the war, soldiers fast discovered that the fruits of victory were rather bitter. Unemployment, food shortages and the mammoth task of reconstructing their lives were common experiences among the lower-middle classes in Britain shortly after the war. *Mirror* provided an opportune media platform for them to express their frustrations and to pressurise the government into action.

Almost thirty years later, the children of World War II veterans – now grown up – emerged as a dominant and viable market segment in the midst of political, social and economic challenges that were vastly different from those that their parents faced. *The Sun* identified this opportunity and fashioned its editorial stance in accordance with the lives of this new market segment. Readers of *The Sun*, enamoured by the politics of Margaret Thatcher, ultimately ensured her election and long reign as British prime minister.

In the Brazilian coastal city of Rio de Janeiro, a popular newspaper – *Extra* – was launched on the strength of a concerted government effort to improve the lot of Brazilian citizens through a range of economic, political and social reforms. The beneficiaries of these initiatives would form the target market for the new paper. Five years after a successful launch, *Extra* sells 350 000 copies per day and it is, by far, the biggest newspaper in Brazil.

The common success factors for *The Sun, Mirror* and *Extra* were:
- Selecting a large, viable and vibrant working-class market segment that promises to develop very rapidly into the leading middle-class sector of society.
- Designing a newspaper product that caters, very succinctly, for this select market in all respects e.g. price, editorial mix, distribution and character.
- Allowing the market to lead the product in all respects and reflecting the expressed needs and wants of the market.
- Embracing the issues that are important to the market and providing a loyal voice or platform for the market to express itself on a daily basis.

These are the key philosophical tenets of the *Daily Sun*. Dramatic changes in South African society were evident as early as the mid-70s. The combined effect of all the political, economic and social changes of the past 10 years contributed towards the creation of a unique South African market segment that is very similar to those discovered by the tabloid press in Britain and Brazil.

Emergence of the target market

The *Daily Sun* reader started to appear on South African marketing radar screens in the mid-to-late 80s. It was during this time that acclaimed social researcher Jos Kuper identified some 3-million black, urban adults (25–49 years) who are English-literate, reasonably educated and unusually positive in their outlook. Almost 10 years later, this segment has almost doubled in number and threatens to dominate all other social profiles in the country. They are the major beneficiaries of change in South Africa. The collective effort of government, business and NGOs all serve the interest of this group. Affirmative action, minimum wages, empowerment, the new Labour Relations Act, housing grants, education, job creation projects and a range of entrepreneurial opportunities are some of the benefits that accrued directly to this market over the past 10 years.

Apart from their demographic similarities, this group expressed its common dissatisfaction with existing sources of news by not buying or reading any of the existing newspapers with any measure of regularity. The existing press simply did not cater for its needs. When asked, respondents from this market indicated very strongly that they would support a newspaper that was written for them. On the strength of this information the *Daily Sun* was born.

A newspaper was designed that satisfied the expressed needs of the selected target market. The response was overwhelming! Starting with lows of 30–40 000 copies in July 2002, sales increased at a rate of 23% per month. By the end of March 2003, *Daily Sun* was selling an average of 184 000 copies per day and still growing at the same rate. The steady growth in Gauteng and the expansion to Kwazulu-Natal, Free State and Eastern Cape consistently delivers sales above 300 000 per day with notable highs above 350 000 copies on Monday, Thursday and Friday. Already the biggest daily newspaper in South Africa, *Daily Sun* might just become the highest selling daily newspaper in South Africa, ever.

The newspaper for a new market

Some 13-million urban adults comprise the *Daily Sun* target market throughout South Africa. They are English-literate, reasonably educated and fiercely patriotic. Respondents from this market indicated that they would support a newspaper that reflected and embraced their lives, hopes and dreams totally. On the strength of this information the *Daily Sun* was born. The paper is designed and sold with the articulated needs of the selected target market in mind.

LAUNCH THABA NCHU AUGUST 2003

Reader empowerment

South African newspaper sales have been in decline over the past decade. Daily newspapers like *The Star, Sowetan, Daily News, Cape Times* and others are struggling to maintain their readers. The *Daily Sun* targets a vast market of largely non-readers and a substantial amount of irregular newspaper readers. The aim is to turn them into regular readers of the *Daily Sun*. The astonishing growth in sales over the past nine months certainly suggests that *Daily Sun* is attracting a large number of people who did not read newspapers before. At least 60% of the *Daily Sun* buyers are new to the market. *Daily Sun* created a new family of very responsive readers in under nine months of publication. The existing editorial offering of news, sport, entertainment, lifestyle and education continues to attract and hold the attention of readers in the selected target market every weekday. The editorial, entertainment and educational value of the paper is widely acknowledged through its popularity in and around major city centres of South Africa. *Daily Sun* is, according to the readers, affordable, easily accessible, enabling and exciting to read.

Economic value added

Daily Sun is distributed through 13 000 outlets nationally. The conventional outlets include shops, chain stores, kiosks and street sellers and account for approximately half of all sales. A network of entrepreneurs who are predominantly black and previously unemployed sells the other half. The *Daily Sun* franchise network is a unique empowerment concept that affords franchise holders the opportunity to run their own small businesses by purchasing the paper at a discounted rate and selling it at a profit. A daily sale of 1 000 copies guarantees a gross monthly income of R10 000. After paying seller commissions and transport costs, the franchisee pockets at least R5 000. So far, most of the 80 franchise holders sell close to or more than 1 000 copies per day. Collectively, they employ over 1 000 street sellers.

Sipho Galela, for example, is in his mid-40s and lives on the East Rand with his wife and children. He currently sells an average of 6 000 *Daily Sun* papers per day in and around Thembisa on the East Rand. Sipho earns just over R50 000 per month. Within six months of working with the *Daily Sun* he was able to expand his network substantially, thereby increasing his income dramatically. Sipho is currently building an impressive new home for his family with the proceeds of his hard work. He was unemployed before he took up the opportunity that *Daily Sun* offered.

The numbers are growing. Prospective entrepreneurs, encouraged by the success of trailblazers like Sipho, are lining up for an opportunity to make a decent living and eventually prosper. *Daily Sun* will extend its franchise network to Kwazulu-Natal, Free State and Eastern Cape soon.

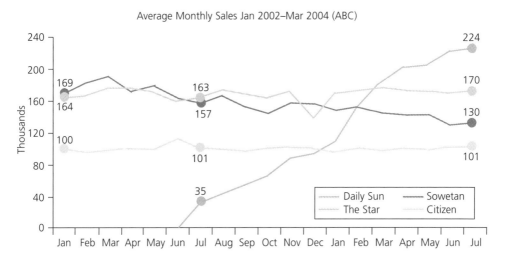

CIRCULATION SALES TREND

Average Monthly Sales Jan 2002–Mar 2004 (ABC)

Graph 13.1: Circulation sales trend: Average monthly sales Jan 2002–Mar 2004

Readership profile

The latest All Media Products Survey (AMPS) results show the following demographic profile of the *Daily Sun*:

Demographic	Number	% of Total
Readers	2 052 000	100%
Urban	1 580 000	77%
Black	2 011 000	98%
Age 25–49	1 457 000	71%
R2500+ Income	1 026 000	50%
LSM 4–6	1 354 000	66%
Literacy	2 052 000	100%
Female	821 000	40%
'Startup' Life stage	1 436 000	70%

Conclusion

The needs of the selected readership market inform the editorial concept, marketing plan, overall business plan and all the current operations of *Daily Sun*. The paper exposed a market segment that was largely neglected by other newspapers. In doing so, *Daily Sun* has added 12% to the overall daily newspaper readership pool in South Africa. *Daily Sun* promises to become the first truly national daily newspaper in the history of South Africa.

Daily circulation **235 386***
Closest daily rival **165 948***

Reference

1   Case study written by *Daily Sun* and procured by Michael du Toit.

Retail Park Stationers

David in a world of Goliaths[1]

Stationery supply is a business sector controlled by the biggest of giants, where the odds are against the survival of a small business in the industry, unless it is able to gain an advantage by, for instance, recognising a gap in the market left by the big players. Given this market environment, the fact that Retail Park Stationers went from zero to hero is surely a case of David conquering Goliath.

Background

Retail Park Stationers is situated in the Retail Park Shopping Centre opposite the gigantic Menlyn shopping complex in Pretoria. The store that became Retail Park Stationers was originally owned by one of the giants in the stationery industry. The failure of this original store terminated in a settlement offer by the fallen giant in the industry being made to the current owners.

New owners

The new owners were faced with the headache of recouping their investment in an industry giant that was no more. In order to do this they needed to meet the tremendous challenge of taking on a so-called corporate store with all its drawbacks and transforming it from a non-profitable business unit into a profitable venture.

The odds were stacked against the new owner:

- Stock items were in some cases under-supplied but – even worse – in most cases they were over-supplied due to the fact that stock purchases were controlled by a head office buyer with no insight into the unique requirements of this specific store.

- The staff complement should have been 50% less to justify sales. The corporate owners believed in quantity with a low remuneration base instead of fewer quality staff at a higher premium.
- A contract was in place with the South African Post Office for one of their Post Point branches on the premises – the rental 'for free'. This meant that there was a 110 square metre area of the shop space that produced no income.
- The shop space was huge in comparison with the turnover. A fact of life is that the huge corporate companies do get a lower rental from their big brother landlords and, in many instances, get lease contracts without marketing fee clauses. For a small businessman privileges like these do not exist.

The road to recovery

The first important factor to rectify was to establish the market potential for the shop by addressing the question 'Is this a small business?' The business strategies undertaken would depend on the business classification of Retail Park Stationers. If the decision was to go the small shop route, a lot of drastic steps had to be taken:

- Unwanted stock had to be reduced at great losses over the short term for the new owners.
- Staff had to be dismissed.
- The shop had to be relocated to a new shopping complex to obtain smaller premises. With this step one could get a lower rental bill but stand to lose firstly the Post Office on the premises (at that stage neither a plus nor a minus), as well as losing an already existing customer base.

The decision was not an easy one to take. To go smaller would have reduced the future risk to the new owners a lot. The opposite approach, of course the riskier one, had the potential to be so much more rewarding.

Retail Park Stationers sets out to compete with the giants

The first step was to take control of the stock in the shop. This included expanding in new fields of the industry such as computer consumables and catering for the rapidly growing office market in the east of Pretoria. The approach was not to move away from school stationery and bric-a-brac for the housewives of the area, but to utilise floor space more effectively in order to introduce extra lines, and through that approach to increase turnover density per square metre.

This called for new investments. Knowing the ironic fact that banks lend businesses money if they can prove they don't need it, the new owners had to go a different route and approach the suppliers to provide them with the same trade credit as the giants in the industry. At that stage the suppliers were still positive about the retail potential of their market and, despite the collapse of one of the retail chains at that stage, decided that newcomers in the market had proven business knowledge and should be given a fair opportunity. Although the terms were not as attractive as the ones given to the giants, Retail Park Stationers got the green light from the wholesale fraternity.

Stock was, however, not the only investment that had to be made. The business also needed a purchaser that knew the industry and could negotiate deals, special offers and favourable payment terms – essential helping factors during the first steps after a take-over. An individual who was expensive – but without a doubt the most knowledgeable buyer in the industry – was appointed. Although it was difficult in the beginning years to afford him, he later proved to be the best investment that was ever made in the business.

With the right stock in the shop the marketing of the business was so much easier.

The next step was to figure out how to turn the area taken up by the Post Office rent-free, into an advantage for the business. Although the layman will immediately be of the opinion that to have a Post Office on the premises can only be an advantage to the business, the opposite, however, is true as the area utilised by the Post Office is rent-free and the people it brings into proximity with the business are, in most cases, messengers from the surrounding businesses with no interest in buying any stationery.

Turn the negative into a positive with well-aimed marketing
The aim devised was to get more housewives in the area to utilise the Post Office. Accordingly, Retail Park Stationers started an advertising campaign on radio and in the printed media about the advantages of the Post Office on the premises for the community immediately around the Shopping Complex. Specific reference was made to the safe parking environment and the fact that people also had the opportunity to buy general stationery, or creative stock for hobbies such as decoupage and painting when using the Post Office.

This campaign quickly gained momentum and soon the Menlyn Post Office on the premises of Retail Park Stationery grew to be one of the busiest Post Points in the country, by far exceeding the number of transactions per day of many of the large Post Offices existing already for many years.

Expansion

Piggy-backing on the above success, a decision was also taken to further utilise unused floor space by allowing other entrepreneurs to take up space in the shop and provide further services to the growing amount of customers. A Kodak One-Hour lab was established in the shop contributing to the rental, but more importantly servicing the customer profile of the business.

It was proven in the past that one of the main causes of bankruptcy is the refusal of the infant entrepreneur to let others into the action at an early stage. The time to swallow private pride is when you are not forced to do so: diplomats call it negotiating from strength. It worked for Retail Park Stationers twice in a row – the top buyer in the industry was made part of the business and instead of taking focus away from the principal business, namely stationery, other entrepreneurs such as the Kodak One-Hour lab were brought into the wealth-creating efforts of the owners.

Renewing focus on the main business

With the majority of red flags neutralised, the owners had the opportunity to concentrate on their real core business, namely to be a dedicated stationery supplier to the surrounding offices, and scholars and students living in the area.

Dealing with the corporate customer

Customers who purchase more than R5 000 per month are categorised as corporate assets and dealing with them can be very complex at times. To obtain this business it is important to allow the customers to set the pace regarding their needs:

- Corporate customers need credit facilities as they do not want to be bothered every day by the completion of requisitions and cheques to be signed for insignificant amounts for the purchase of stationery.
- To be competitive, pricing needs to be handled in a very sensitive way as this corporate market is serviced by most of the real giants in the industry.
- Deliveries must be the responsibility of the retailer, right to the doorstep of the corporate customer and this requirement includes large deliveries as well as the R4,95 ruler or refill the boss quickly needs.
- Special stock not applicable to the general customer base of the shop is needed. For instance the corporate colours of your customer may be pink, meaning it needs all its stationery i.e. baskets, staplers, rulers, files in that specific colour. The customer will expect you to be able to supply that need all the time, regardless of the fact that your supplier may not manufacture that specific colour. Nevertheless, meeting such specific demands on the part of the corporate customer, is an area where the smaller stationery supplier can make its mark as the giants do not like to shop around in the trade to satisfy one customer.

To find this category of customers is not always so difficult, as the buyers in these companies are not very loyal to a specific supplier and react fairly well on direct mail shots introducing the business.

The real issue is to keep their loyalty and support and to provide them with what they need in the shortest time possible and at the most competitive price. Customers do not see the nice shop and friendly floor assistants as they will be dealing mostly by phone, fax or e-mail orders – they need to be provided with a knowledgeable staff member as permanent contact to reduce their frustrations.

In the beginning this type of relationship tends to be very turbulent as corporate buyers are usually very aggressive in their demands especially in the beginning phases of a relationship. Good public relations skills and a lot of patience are needed to take this category of customer to the level of permanence.

The reward is, however, worth the effort!

The home office and household stationery

This category can be described as the real bread-and-butter stuff of any stationery establishment.

The important factor here is that the giants in the industry have forgotten about this market. Firstly they have substituted the sales staff with closed circuit television cameras to look after security. The only human contact the small buyer of stationery experiences is when he/she arrives at the till points to pay.

At Retail Park Stationers the decision was to develop the staff to be first-class sales people who can assist customers before they walk out of the shop highly frustrated when they do not manage to find a certain item.

This customer needs to be supplied with good advice and a quality product and, as a result, the majority of them do not mind paying a few cents more for an item. Personal service has become a bit of a novelty in the retail stationery trade but it is an ingredient that is absolutely necessary in the arsenal of a small businessman if he wants to compete with the giants.

In this category, marketing can be spread between advertising in the printed media, regional radio advertising and in store promotions. However, the real advantage here is the word-of-mouth advertisement that the happy customer will do for free.

Back to school

'Back to school' is the magic time in the industry, but also it is also the time that one needs to pay a lot of attention to one's enemies, as they are the first to discover one's mistakes.

The small business stationer needs to be absolutely sure of the needs of the different schools in the area and to keep on assessing what kind of products and brand names are bought during the year by school children. It is important to keep a register of these items to avoid running out of stock during 'back to school' time.

An easy approach, but so difficult to keep up in practice.

In the past the giants of the industry flooded the market during this time of year with advertising, stock and specials, but had no sales staff to assist when very irritated parents doing the grudge purchase of the year, walked into their shops.

The sales strategy to follow is to be sympathetic towards the parents' complaints and to be friendly in assisting them. That way the customers leave the store with a smile on their faces even though they are walking out with a bag of stationery prescribed by the schools, 50% of which they will never use.

The most important aspect to remember when competing with the giants is that the giants can't hear the customers' specific requests and appreciative comments and therefore lose out on implementing customer service-oriented strategies to their advantage.

Summary
The case of Retail Park Stationers shows how a small business can compete effectively with the giants of the industry through effective marketing strategies: well-focused stock management, procuring favourable dealings with suppliers, sharing business with other entrepreneurs, original and specific campaigns to attract customers, building good relationships with corporate customers, being able to rely on word-of-mouth, and providing good customer service during peak times. The combination of these strategies allowed a David to compete on an equal footing with the Goliaths of the stationery industry.

Reference

1   Case study written by Johan van Zyl and procured by Michael Cant.

PricewaterhouseCoopers

When two giants merge[1]

PricewaterhouseCoopers is the world's largest professional services firm, and was formed on 1 July 1998 by the global merger of professional services firms Price Waterhouse (PW) and Coopers & Lybrand (C&L). Bringing together two large organizations has been a formidable effort involving the commitment of all PricewaterhouseCoopers people.

The challenge

The decision to merge these two organizations was based on many factors, the most overriding of which was the need to move ahead of the competition – a move that was facilitated by the size and geographical spread of the merged firm, and the expanded global range of services that it would be able to provide to its clients in all sectors of the economy. However, this was to present many unique challenges.

Once the merger was announced in September 1997, word went out to partners around the world to prepare for a vote by November 30. Part of the preparation toward that vote involved what might well have seemed a deluge of necessary communications explaining the benefits of the merger and what the integration of the predecessor firms would mean for PW and C&L partners and staff. Another element of this massive effort was the organization and deployment of global roadshows to provide information about the merger and address questions directly.

Once these challenges had been overcome, next came a myriad of detail. What would the management structure be like? How would appointments shape up? What legal and tax issues would need to be resolved? What about governance and matters such as recruiting, benefits, and other harmonisation efforts?

At times the challenge seemed overwhelming. But through the willing efforts of thousands of people in both legacy firms, PricewaterhouseCoopers was launched on 1 July 1998 as planned.

Tackling the challenge

After the launch, an entirely new set of issues took precedence. Pricewaterhouse-Coopers met them head on. Collocation (that is, mixing and mingling people from the legacy firms throughout the firm's now-shared offices) was carried out. Plans were made to fuel a massive recruitment effort – nearly 50 000 people per year. And the firm succeeded in cross-integrating service teams to ensure that clients received the full benefit of the expertise, talents, and resources of the merged organization.

Today, PricewaterhouseCoopers comprises a global network operating in 144 countries, with 122 000 partners and staff. The firm has a significant presence in every major market, both established and emerging, which makes it a global powerhouse with an unmatched ability to serve global, national and local clients. Locally, PricewaterhouseCoopers is the major player in South Africa, employing in excess of 3 500 people in 26 offices.

Vision and mission

PricewaterhouseCoopers' vision is to be the world's leading professional services organization, thereby solving complex business problems for top-tier clients in global, national, and local markets.

Values

PricewaterhouseCoopers' values are practical – they are about how the firm delivers its brand.

Belonging to the PricewaterhouseCoopers community means sharing a common emphasis on delivering value to the firm's clients. When Price Waterhouse and Coopers & Lybrand came together to form PricewaterhouseCoopers, it was evident that the organizations shared many values – for example integrity, devotion to client service, and excellence. But it became evident that these values needed to be supplemented by additional values such as speed and innovation. And they couldn't simply be for the short term. PricewaterhouseCoopers needed values to serve it through major and unpredictable changes in its business and in the marketplace.

To ensure that it developed values that would serve this purpose, PricewaterhouseCoopers analysed the various value statements that both legacy firms had produced over the preceding five to six years across geographies, service lines, and firms. The values teams also asked the Global Leadership Team and the Global Oversight Board to identify which of these values were important. Based on this analysis and input, three core values (Leadership, Teamwork and Excellence) and nine supporting values were identified. While it is important to identify core values, it is equally important to communicate, promote, and reinforce them throughout the firm's business. It is a daunting challenge, but staff need to live and breathe these values. The values guide staff's behaviour, in adaptation to meeting new business challenges, while staff make an effort to assess their actions in terms of the firm's values.

Code of Conduct

To broaden and deepen PricewaterhouseCoopers' commitment to integrity, a shared global Code of Conduct was developed, piloted in South Africa, and distributed to all members of the firm. This Code of Conduct comprises of a set of principles that articulates how PricewaterhouseCoopers expects its people to behave in conducting business. The Code is inextricably intertwined with PricewaterhouseCoopers' business strategy and vision, and places a heavy emphasis on its values and protection of its reputation.

Although all of PricewaterhouseCoopers' people understand that no code is a substitute for individual responsibility, judgement, and accountability, the Code offers a broad range of guidance about standards of integrity and business conduct. It specifically addresses issues such as behaviour by employees, the firm's obligations as a responsible corporate citizen, upholding the Pricewaterhouse-Coopers name, and respect for clients and colleagues. In essence, the Code guides the way in which PricewaterhouseCoopers' people live and work.

But abiding by the company values and following the Code of Conduct is not just an internal exercise. The PricewaterhouseCoopers values have a significant impact on how the firm presents itself to the marketplace through its brand. PricewaterhouseCoopers shows the world who it is through how staff behave with clients and with each other, and by the quality of service they deliver. The firm's values determine the behaviour of its people, and that behaviour makes up about 85% of the PricewaterhouseCoopers brand.

Brand

A brand can be seen as a name, term, sign, symbol or any other feature that identifies one seller's goods or service as distinct from those of other sellers. The PricewaterhouseCoopers brand is in many ways the most precious business asset owned by the firm. The brand was carefully developed by dedicated brand teams to be powerful and unique in the field of professional services firms and is carefully monitored, managed and regulated.

Given that the PricewaterhouseCoopers organization was born of a dream – a vision of what the newly merged organization could become and achieve, the firm's brand strategy will always be a work in progress, shaped by time and the changing marketplace. What is certain is that it has been very much about establishing an organization decisively different from the stereotypical image of an accounting firm. It is about establishing a new reality for professional services, a new professional services model.

The decision to launch a brand strategy for the new PricewaterhouseCoopers was based in part on research that showed that the business community and general public do not perceive compelling enough differences between and among the 'Big Five' accounting forms. Although the merger has made Pricewaterhouse-Coopers the leader in terms of global size, resources and reach, the marketplace has indicated that these qualities are not enough to set it apart. Instead it is the PricewaterhouseCooper brand that dramatically differentiates the company from the rest.

The cornerstones of the PricewaterhouseCoopers brand

The PricewaterhouseCoopers brand is founded on the integration of three concepts: People, Knowledge, and Worlds, and the power of the brand only reaches its full potential when these elements come together.

Simply put, the firm distinguishes itself through the extraordinary talents of its people, sharing and expanding their knowledge with clients and others, within the many worlds in which they and their clients are at home.

Connected Thinking

A brand needs to be positioned in the market so that it can occupy a distinct and valued place in the consumer's mind relative to other brands, and then this distinctiveness must be communicated through marketing efforts. Positioning depends on a perceived image of tangible or intangible features. The importance of positioning can be understood by recognising that consumers create a perceptual space in their minds for all the brands they might consider. A perceptual space is how one brand is seen in any number of dimensions, such as quality, taste, price or social display value, in relation to those same dimensions in other brands.

The firm's new positioning statement is **Connected Thinking**. The statement evolves from the firm's value-creating efforts: PricewaterhouseCoopers applies its industry knowledge and professional expertise to identify, report, protect, realise and create value for its clients and their stakeholders. The strength of this value proposition is based on the breadth and depth of the firm's client relationships. Networks are built around clients to provide them with PricewaterhouseCoopers' collective knowledge and resources. The firm's international network, experience, industry knowledge and business understanding are used to build trust and create value for clients – this is called **Connected Thinking**.

Connected Thinking is the standard of excellence that distinguishes PricewaterhouseCoopers in the marketplace and supports its strategic growth as it moves forward. It articulates what PricewaterhouseCoopers does and what it can accomplish when it performs at its very best – when its breadth of service, depth of expertise and geographic coverage are leveraged to serve clients' needs.

Connected Thinking is about:

- Making connections that matter.
- Understanding the connections that make different businesses and industries work.
- Working together to bring world-class thinking to clients.
- Stretching each other to bring new perspectives that challenge the basis of existing thoughts and solutions.

Information technology

With regard to information technology, PricewaterhouseCoopers aims to make use of fully integrated global technology that links its people, wherever in the world they are. Whether they are in one of the firm's offices, at a client site on the other side of the world, or in a hotel, PricewaterhouseCoopers people expect seamless access to data, tools, and support. Global Technology Solutions (GTS) make this a reality. Partners and staff have global Internet and intranet access, and use Lotus Notes databases for daily communication purposes. Exciting new tools facilitate knowledge management, on which the firm's products and services are based.

Communications

The communications infrastructure, channels, networks, visual identity standards, branding, spokespeople, and policies that permit PricewaterhouseCoopers to function as an integrated whole have been rapidly developed.

From day one, staff have been communicating with one another worldwide, with clients and prospective clients, with the media, with allied businesses, with job applicants, and with other stakeholders in the enterprise. This has enabled PricewaterhouseCoopers to build relationships, establish the firm's brand and provide its stakeholders with the service that they have come to expect.

New frontiers

Web-based communications play a rapidly growing role in Pricewaterhouse-Coopers' programmes to provide greater value to clients and link the firm's 122 000 people worldwide. Two critical components in this effort are the

PricewaterhouseCoopers global website and the firm's intranet, KnowledgeCurve. Clients want online information of real value: issues; news and analysis; insights into trends; management ideas they can put to work. The firm's practice leaders require a strong recruiting section and flexible information design; and they want to originate and own their practice units' content. The PricewaterhouseCoopers website enables the firm to provide these value-adding services.

Internal marketing

KnowledgeCurve, PricewaterhouseCoopers' global intranet, provides the up-to-date information essential to world-class client service. Connecting staff to people, data and ideas, and furnishing a powerful global platform for sharing knowledge, KnowledgeCurve underscores the value of belonging to the world's leading professional services organization. KnowledgeCurve keeps Pricewaterhouse-Coopers' professionals current on client events, industry trends and competitive issues, lets them stay on top of breaking business news, allows them to locate and quickly tap the firm's worldwide expertise, and brings peers together to share ideas and information.

Media and public relations

Today PricewaterhouseCoopers is continuously building a global public relations network in order to leverage good news, manage negative news, and ensure that clients are represented fairly and accurately in the media. Another critically important task is to establish the firm's partners in the media as thought leaders on business and economic trends that affect clients. PricewaterhouseCoopers' network is driven by a shared set of standards, policies, and procedures – and an ongoing global dialogue on how best to accomplish the organization's shared aims.

Print

Print still matters, even in the new world of e-communications. The development of print media and a visual identity system that gives a vital and unique appearance to everything PricewaterhouseCoopers does is essential in making the brand manifest in everything the firm does.

A look ahead

A much-quoted statistic is that 70% of corporate mergers and acquisitions fail to achieve their objectives or deliver the expected value to shareholders. Certain external commentators view PricewaterhouseCoopers' merger as possibly the most difficult business transaction ever attempted. A brief look at what the firm has had to manage and how it has coped may help to explain their view. The complexity faced from the outset was awesome – for example, having to attain regulatory approval in most jurisdictions around the world, merging separate firms in over 120 countries, and ensuring the operation of merged IT networks from day one. Doing the deal was in many ways the easy part. The phase that PricewaterhouseCoopers is in now, integrating the organization successfully across all of its dimensions is a far more challenging – and ongoing – task.

References

1   Case study written by Denise Diesel, Senior Marketing Manager, PricewaterhouseCoopers and Laurie Snyman, Manager, Communication, PricewaterhouseCoopers. Case study procured by Annekie Brink.

16

Branding through publicity: Labour Movement Solidarity[1]

> The crucial step is getting the brand name (and what it stands for) into the mind of the consumer. You can't build a brand if you can't win the battle for the mind – Al & Laura Ries.

Solidarity, with its approximately 130 000 members, is the oldest and largest independent trade union in South Africa. The trade union emerged from the old Mine Workers' Union that was founded approximately 100 years ago. After the political changes of 1994 the Mine Workers' Union, as a brand, found itself in an existential crisis. One reason was the fact that it recalled memories of a defunct political order, and in the second place the trade union was no longer confined to the mining industry, which means that the brand no longer reflected the trade union's reality. In 2001 the leadership came to the risky conclusion that the trade union's branding had to be changed, and that this change was to include a change of name. The trade union would in future be known as Solidarity.

One of the challenges facing the leadership was to find the most effective way of establishing the brand. A failed branding process would have had disastrous consequences for the trade union. A choice had to be made between a comprehensive advertising campaign and a comprehensive publicity campaign to establish the brand. The latter option carried the day – partly because there was no budget for a multi-million rand advertising campaign and partly because of the belief that publicity carries more weight, since a third person communicates it. The leadership also had faith in the trade union's ability as a socio-political institution to generate continued publicity. Today Solidarity is one of the South

Africa's most successful publicity achievements, with approximately 2 000 publicity mentions during the first seven months of 2004. The union's membership grew with 20 000 members from 2001. Publicity for the sake of publicity, however, is not enough.

Without back office support (in the form of systems, service levels, research, policy development, product improvement) for the front office publicity (media liaison, news angles, media relations, creativity), publicity becomes mere propaganda that is neither sustainable nor credible. The trade union's final challenge is to turn publicity into sales. Publicity builds brands, but publicity does not sell. Membership of the trade union is a commodity for sale, but in the absence of store shelves the sales effort has to create sales channels. Advertising is employed only in the sales process, and then not conventional advertising but direct marketing. Virtual sales channels on the Internet and a call-in centre have been established to support the sales channels. In other words, the advertising is not brand advertising, but sales advertising. The greatest challenge here is to align the back office support, the front office publicity and the sales effort.

Branding, therefore, is a holistic function of the entire organization. A brand is more than just a name: it is a sub-culture. Every employee plays a part in the branding process. Publicity popularises the brand, but without an effective organizational culture from which the brand emanates, and an effective sales effort, publicity is fruitless.

The Solidarity process may be represented as follows:

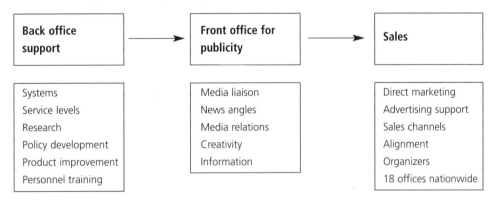

This article shall focus on publicity as a means of building a brand and the reasons for Solidarity's choice of publicity over advertising to build and maintain its brand. In other words, we shall look at the front office publicity process.

Branding through publicity

Solidarity's views on branding were strongly influenced by the branding philosophy of Al and Laura Ries, as contained in the books *The Fall of Advertising & the*

Rise of PR and *The 22 Immutable Laws of Branding*. The basic premise is that brands are created by publicity, and not by advertising.

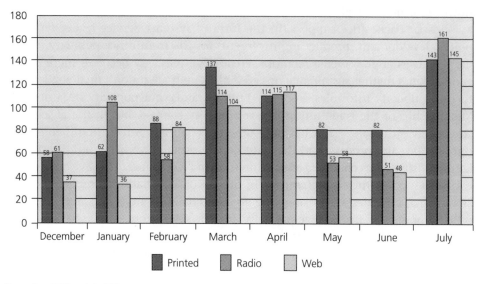

December 2003 to July 2004

Value: R 20 740 000

Graph 16.1: Solidarity's publicity hits for 2004

The publicity decision was based on the following considerations:

Publicity is credible

Advertising lacks credibility because it is the self-serving utterance of the company. Publicity is believable because it is conveyed by a third person. Today, in the information age, consumers cannot rely on their personal experience only. They need the corroboration of a third party, and media institutions are the most credible third parties communicating with the masses. The purpose of publicity is to get 'mind share' for the brand in the heads of consumers. Solidarity requires the publicity process to create, in the minds of consumers, a need for protection in the workplace and Solidarity must be put forward as a credible means of supplying this need. Publicity is not, in other words, a mere exercise in communications, but a branding effort.

Publicity expands influence

Publicity establishes one as a market leader and expands one's influence. In Solidarity's case it strengthens the negotiating power of the trade union, which reinforces the protection brand. The trade union's position as an established, credible role player in South Africa facilitates interaction with a variety of role players across a wide spectrum, which in turn creates new opportunities for publicity and builds the brand.

Publicity creates publicity

Publicity processes are mutually supportive, resulting in an exponential growth in publicity. The more publicity the easier, and – ironically, the cheaper – it becomes per publication. Solidarity has the competitive edge of being a multi-industry trade union, which ensures publicity across a wide front.

Advertising is expensive

Advertising is an expensive undertaking. Establishing a new brand costs millions of rands.

Solidarity, as a member organization, simply does not have the money it takes to establish a brand. Although strongly supported by publicity, ABSA could spend millions to establish itself as a new brand. Apart from being the better process, publicity is also more effective.

Advertising follows publicity and is functional

Advertising follows publicity and has to carry on the theme of the publicity. It was only after three years following the launch of the new brand that Solidarity began a functional advertising programme.

The aim of the advertising is not to build the brand and not to defend the brand, but tough direct marketing. Branding creates 'mind share', sales create market share.

Critical success factors

The following factors were critical for the success of Solidarity's publicity programme:

Position of the head of publicity

A publicity chief cannot be a communications official. Solidarity took care to make the head of publicity a part of the management team and someone who plays a critical role in the trade union's strategic positioning. The head of publicity does not merely communicate the decisions of the top management – he is part of that decision-making.

Personal relationship

A good relationship with journalists is as important as the news itself. A publicity chief must have a sense of balance in relationships. Journalists do not want to feel that they are under moral pressure to publish a story, but they do appreciate a good relationship with their sources. And remember: it is foolish to pick fights with people who order their ink by the drum and their paper by the kilometre.

Be news-orientated

The organization must be news-orientated. Everybody in Solidarity has a head for news. Many front-page stories pass unnoticed over many a company's desks every day, simply because not everybody is news-orientated.

Speed

For those who wish to invest in real estate the most important consideration is 'location, location, location'. For Solidarity's publicity team it is 'speed, speed, speed'. Solidarity decided on guerrilla publicity, with the emphasis on mobility, accuracy and speed. The person who is positioned as head of publicity has sway over speed.

Know your basics

Although Solidarity believes in guerrilla publicity rather than conventional publicity, the basics of publicity remain important. One must be able to, for instance, identify a news angle, draw up a media statement, communicate effectively, relate to journalists, and abide by the unwritten rules of publicity ethics.

Creativity

Creative publicity is the determining factor in whether or not a story is carried. The publicity person must find a news angle that is of interest to the reader. It often happens that the visual aspect determines whether or not a story is used.

Substance

In the long term credibility is determined by substance. Solidarity subscribes to all web news services to ensure timely and correct information. A researcher identifies trends so that the right things may be said at the right times and a research panel investigates relevant subjects and produces in-depth reports. If the communication is to deal with Iscor's retrenchments, studies on shareholder fundamentalism are produced. If the subject is affirmative action, international comparisons are sought. If one is writing on sustainable development, a green paper on the balance between production and conservation is put forward.

The major test of the trade union's publicity achievements now lies with its recently announced direct sales programme. If the back office, front office and sales programmes are successfully aligned a further exponential growth curve may be expected.

Reference

1   Case study written by Solidarity and procured by Michael Cant.

17

MARKETING FEATURES:
BRANDING
ENTREPRENEURSHIP/ SMALL BUSINESS
FRANCHISING
LOCATION
NICHE MARKETING

Debonairs Pizza

Background[1]

Debonairs Pizza, founded in September 1991, was the brainchild of university students Craig Mackenzie and Andrew Harvey. Having seen the success of the pizza delivery industry in the USA, Mackenzie realised that this market in South Africa was, at that time, undeveloped.

On exploring the opportunities and discussing their proposed pizza delivery service, they were met with a great deal of scepticism back home. The standard reaction was that South Africans do not eat pizza and that free delivery would never be economically viable. Effective delivery would be impossible due to security risks. Homes and businesses were barricaded and protected by various levels of security. Regardless of this negative sentiment they believed in their idea and started the business with their army savings, which was a sum total of approximately R6 000.

Pizza and pizza delivery around the world generally conveyed either an Italian or American image. Either theme was typically casual and informal. One of the first points of differentiation was Debonairs Pizza's smart image. From the outset the credo was 'we get them to you smartly'. This was later adapted to the current 'we deliver smartly'.

The name had to encompass this objective and during a digs brainstorm session, one of their university buddies came up with the name Debonair by paging through the Oxford dictionary. The single word encompassed the smart, suave image the new entrepreneurs were looking for. Hence the birth of Debonairs Pizza. From the first night, the delivery team were clad in the signature bowties and tux shirts.

The beginning

The business was started in Pietermaritzburg where the two were studying as full-time students. Mackenzie was a Bsc Agric student whilst Harvey was studying law. Mackenzie's brother owned a Spar supermarket in the town. The Spar housed a typical supermarket bakery, which was positioned at the back of the outlet, and fortunately had a separate back entrance. Since the main objective of the business was home delivery they used the bakery after hours and had no shop front at all. Space was limited within the bakery and the only storage facilities available were the space on top of the oven and a small domestic fridge. The balance of the stock and other important elements such as the computer POS system were carried in daily.

Early marketing

Early marketing initiatives and the strategy from the start was to create a customer database. The advantage of having a customer database was that they knew where the customer lived, what their favourite products were, the spend per head and the ordering patterns. As a result of the lack of high street exposure the need for pamphlet drops in the form of informative menus was soon recognised. 'Thank you for trying us' cards were sent out after the first night thanking customers for their patronage and offering an attractive special to encourage repeat business.

This was exceptionally well received as database marketing was limited at this time. Information such as the top 50 customers could be used to reward frequent usage. It is generally easier to get your existing customers to purchase more rather than luring new ones.

Free delivery

Another differentiating feature was the idea of 'free' delivery. Although costly, the convenience element and the resultant volumes formed a critical role in the success of the business model. The culture of relationship marketing was nurtured as part of the fabric of the business.

The first night of trading resulted in a total of eight pizzas ordered and delivered to suitably impressed friends around town. The next night a small pamphlet drop and more obliging friends resulted in a considerable increase in sales. From that day on, Debonairs Pizza's deliveries grew exponentially. The increased volumes in the confined space of the bakery caused many operational headaches and a team scurrying around desperate to deliver on their promise of 'getting them to you smartly'.

Franchising

It very soon became evident that bigger, dedicated premises were required in order to sustain the growth. It was decided at that point that the pizza take-away market was equally attractive. Hence an outlet that had good exposure and passing traffic was located in Commercial Road, Pietermaritzburg.

As a result of the lack of capital, payment terms were negotiated with suppliers for 30–60 days. Fortunately, due to the nature of the business being cash and the exceptional growth, the initial commitments were met. The combination of the growing delivery trade and the more cost-effective take-away business created a robust business model.

The first outlet was simple in layout but an attempt was made to convey the smart image to match the vision in every sense. The resounding success of the first outlet resulted in a great deal of interest by many. Due to the lack of capital for a company store rollout the obvious expansion path was the relatively less capital-intensive franchising route.

When the next outlet opened in Nedbank Plaza in Pietermaritzburg, it was feared that this outlet would cannibalise the existing business. However, as a result of the increased exposure and the enhanced marketing fund, the original store continued growing unabated, while the second store became equally strong.

The first truly serious franchise enquiry was from school friends, Derek Ross and Peter Bateman. They opened the first outlet in Brickhill road in Durban. Peter and Derek went on to open more very successful outlets.

The expansion trail led to Gauteng where varsity colleagues, Graeme Morrison and Iain Clark opened the first outlet in the region. Graeme Morrison has recently been appointed the Managing Director of Debonairs Pizza.

Steers KZN

After Mackenzie and Harvey had opened 14 outlets, including two in Johannesburg, it became evident that considerable investment needed to be made to support a national franchise base.

The young entrepreneurs were approached by the licence holders of Steers KZN, who were interested in this new expanding business. The businesses merged and Mackenzie and Harvey became part of the Steers KZN management team, incorporating the Debonairs Pizza brand. This merger gave the brand access to an established supply chain, a developed administrative infrastructure and general franchise support, as well as bolstering the management expertise. One of the partners who became a key player in the brand and held the position of Marketing Director was Trevor Edwards.

World-class interior design company, Enterprise IG was commissioned to revise the corporate image and interiors. With a modern, sophisticated image, a proven business model and an experienced support team – the rollout began.

The larger, more formal structure frustrated Harvey and at this point he decided to pursue other business ventures. Mackenzie moved to Gauteng in 1997 as Managing Director of the brand to steer what was soon to become one of the most sought-after franchise investments in the country.

For the next two years Mackenzie and his lean team with the assistance of the Steers infrastructure opened an outlet every seven days around the country and in Africa. The brand was fast becoming a household name and a shining example in the industry.

With the rapid growth, control was critical and a philosophy of zero tolerance with regard to operational standards was adopted. Simply, operational excellence had to go without saying. The worst possible investment ever to be made is to invest in advertising if the customer is going to receive a bad product experience.

This operational excellence was attained and then monitored and measured by introducing tools such as production flows, portion control, simplified training aids and team motivation such as quiz road shows and annual Pizza Olympics. These activities were important for the teams working in the outlets to bond and feel part of the bigger picture.

Franchise consultants were given responsibility of a maximum of 12 stores each and besides monitoring the operational standards via an objective and effective new evaluation tool, they obtained income statements from all franchisees and benchmarked these to allow for effective feedback to franchisees on the entire business systems.

Store turnovers were growing with the aggressive locality-based marketing campaigns and the brands' increased visibility in the marketplace.

Public relations

Considering the limited budgets and the lack of means to run effective above-the-line campaigns, an aggressive PR programme was undertaken. Due to the fact that stores were now popping up everywhere, the strategy was to hold opening parties for important outlets e.g.: the 50th, 75th, 100th etc. Celebrity guest and industry figureheads as well as local members of the community were invited to grand opening parties.

Debonairs was constantly in industry magazines as well as in regional and national newspapers in order to keep the brand top of mind. Franchisee enquiries were endless.

Media

In the early days, relationship and database marketing and the sporadic use of radio were effectively used to build the brand and create very loyal customers. It was, however, evident that to maximise the sales and take the business to a new level it was necessary to utilise television. The biggest challenge was that the budgets as they stood would not allow for a meaningful television campaign. Mackenzie and marketing director Edwards embarked on a road show proposing the plans to go on to TV. A prerequisite for achieving this ambitious goal with only 50 stores in the system was to convince franchisees to pay an additional 1% to the marketing fund, which was matched by the franchisor, for a period of approximately six months. With 100% buy-in, the ad was in production. This first-ever Debonairs Pizza TV ad catapulted the business forward. It resulted in a spike in system-wide sales of 40% after which a new sales plateau was set at this higher level.

Product innovation was vital at this point so Mackenzie and team made annual pilgrimages to the Pizza Conventions around the world to keep abreast of trends.

Market research conducted indicated that two or more people generally share pizzas. Hence the introduction of the 'on the double' special – two pizzas at a price point. The local consumer welcomed this offer, which was used extensively worldwide. This product offer was coupled with packaging innovation and saw the introduction of the double box housing two pizzas. The entire package was nothing short of Debonairs' innovation!

Around this time, Dominoes Pizza, the world's largest pizza delivery company made a grand entry into the South African market. Pizza Hut had approximately 35 outlets and was threatening to expand aggressively throughout the country. The lack of adaptation of the product offering and the systems to the local South African environment, as well as the onslaught of Debonairs Pizza's aggressive roll-out and marketing efforts, contributed to the closure and exit of both of these multinational pizza brands.

Locality marketing

In order to ensure that the database and relationship marketing were constantly carried out, certain tools and measurements were implemented. Locality and relationship marketing are very powerful tools but can allow for inconsistent messages to be sent out with outlets going off on their own tangents. The introduction of locality marketing kits proved to be most useful. Each franchisee was given a kit of standard ideas, such as 'pop a balloon' competitions, generic posters, school fund raising projects etc. Each franchisee was encouraged to spend a further 1% of his turnover (over and above the marketing royalty) to market and promote his store in his community. Pamphlet drops worked very well for the brand and a spike in sales could be seen on the day a drop was carried out.

Another successful locality marketing drive was 'cold canvassing'. This activity encourages franchisees and managers to walk around their neighbourhoods meeting the people. A few businesses are targeted every day with the objective of making those people your friends and encouraging use of the brand. Samples or vouchers are used to make the introduction easier. This relatively low cost exercise works incredibly well with your new base of friends now dedicated to the brand.

A daily locality marketing plan ensures that all stores are on track with their locality marketing and this is closely tied to the daily turnover budget. The objective being that if it appears that you are not going to make your turnover budget today – get out to the robots and drop pamphlets.

Success

In 1998 Debonairs Pizza was awarded the prestigious industry award of Franchisor of the year by FASA (Franchising Association of Southern Africa). Not bad for a brand only seven years old!

In 1999 Debonairs Pizza won the FASA Brand Builder of the year award. At this point the brand was ranked amongst the top 10 in the country and had experienced growth of more than 203% a year.

In 2000 Debonairs Pizza was once again awarded the FASA Franchisor of the year award.

In 2001 Debonairs again won FASA Brand Builder of the year.

Key success factors of the brand

1. Franchisee profitability
2. Marketing-driven
3. Delightful experience (internal and external)
4. Technology/Innovation
5. Swift and sustainable growth

Similar awards achieved include:
- 2003 Best Pizza Leisure Options – Readers Choice Awards – Best of Johannesburg.
- 2002 Best Pizza Leisure Options – Readers Choice Awards – Best of Johannesburg.
- 2001 Best Pizza Leisure Options – Readers Choice Awards – Best of Johannesburg.
- 2001 Finalist FASA franchisor of the year.
- 2000 Best Pizza Leisure Options – Readers Choice Awards – Best of Johannesburg.
- 1999 Best Pizza Leisure Options – Readers Choice Awards – Best of Johannesburg.
- 1999 Silver Assegai Award for Direct Marketing.
- 1998 nominee for FASA brand builder of the year.
- 1998 *Financial Mail* Apex Awards. Bronze for Advertising Effectiveness and Special Award for Best Campaign on a limited budget.
- 1998 Nominee for IMM Marketing organization of the year.
- 1998 Voted Best Pizza in Cape Town – *Saturday Argus*.

Other awards include:
- Radio 702 'Best pizza in Gauteng' award.
- *Fast Food and Family Restaurant* magazine's 'Number one pizza in South Africa' award.

Mackenzie and his Steers KZN colleagues sold out to Steers Holdings in 1998 but Mackenzie continued to run the brand until 2001.

Looking ahead

Craig Mackenzie and his partner Wayne Duncan have formed a retail and franchising company – Retsol Pty Ltd, which specialises in the development of concepts, brand ownership, and in outsourcing management of brands. Mackenzie is now the Managing Director of Ola Milky Lane and Juicy Lucy which are managed by Retsol Pty Ltd on behalf of Ola SA who hold the trade marks. Ola Milky Lane has been re-branded and the new upbeat brand is back on the radar screen. The brand re-appeared on television in November 2004, the first time in 10 years. For more marketing successes, watch Ola Milky Lane and Juicy Lucy.

Reference

1   Case study written by Debonairs and procured by Michael Cant.

18

MARKETING FEATURES:

BRANDING

COMMUNICATION

CONSUMER BEHAVIOUR

ENTREPRENEURSHIP

FRANCHISING

NICHE MARKETING

QUALITY

RESEARCH

Hot Dog Café – Fast food's top dog

Facts about hot dogs[1]

There are three icons of the fast food industry that are recognised the world over: the hamburger, the pizza and the hot dog. There are some that say that in the United States, the hot dog gives the hamburger a run for its money as the most popular fast food – especially over holiday periods and during key sporting events. The National Hot Dog and Sausage Council in the USA issues the most amazing facts and figures about hot dogs – from the fact that 5 502 are eaten every second of the day, a whopping 19 billion annually, to the fact that children prefer hot dogs to hamburgers and ice-cream, and mustard remains the hottest topping, with children preferring ketchup.

Concept of 'fast' in fast food

Fast Food is essentially food not only prepared and served quickly but consumed by a public that wants food on the move. As life becomes more frenetic and fast-paced, the convenience of fast food keeps on improving and concepts are developed to cater for every kind of consumer – from the person who wants to sit down in a fast food restaurant to have a quick meal…to the person who pops into a fast food outlet to order food 'to go'…to the person moving between meetings or shopping who feels peckish and will stop at a vending cart to buy that 'pick-me-up' snack.

Why fast food is famous

There are thousands of food concepts around the world that are popular, but what makes a food item famous? If asked to make word associations with foods like hamburgers, pizza, ice-cream, and coffee, the food stores McDonald's, Steers, Debonairs Pizza, OLA Milky Lane, or Seattle Coffee Company will be most likely to spring to mind. The reason for this is that all these famous foods have been made super-famous through franchising. And even though it's the hamburger, hot dog or pizza that becomes the universal fast food icon, it's the business mechanism behind the product that drives its success. Not only must a fast food meal be of consistent quality – whether it's purchased in Bloemfontein or Beijing, but in order for that product to conform to those exact standards, each and every franchise operator in that company must run his business in exactly the same way – from the way he cooks the burger or hot dog…to the way he greets his customer… to the brand image he projects.

It is the Franchisor, in this case Hot Dog Café, who:
- is the originator of the idea and develops it into a viable business,
- develops the concept, the brand and the goodwill,
- duplicates his concept in order to grow the business and build the brand,
- supplies the business structure, the training and on-going support; and
- continues to expand the franchise to the benefit of all involved.

To those who invest in a Hot Dog Café, the turn-key franchise offers the franchisee the following:
- The opportunity to go into business 'for yourself but not by yourself'.
- A successful formula based on uniform standards, operational methods and marketing guidelines.
- A support system that will help the franchisee be successful.
- A blueprint on how to succeed in an independent business.

Revolutionising the hot dog market

No other franchised fast food company has been able to perfect not one, but three different concepts to fit every retail opportunity and every consumer's taste whilst setting the benchmark for future vending opportunities. The rollout of Hot Dog Café's three unique concepts in fast food concepts includes:

The Hot Dog Café Diner

A traditional shop concept found indoors in mall environments, designed and built to mimic the typical retro diner of the 1930s whilst incorporating the most advanced technology that aids in fast and efficient delivery of quality products under meticulously hygienic conditions.

The classic Hot Dog Café theme is reflected throughout, with compact, bright, clean, user-friendly equipment and fittings, including powerful branding, retro tables and chairs and hand-etched murals. The size of the diner can vary, from 18 m² to 30 m², which makes it suitable for high volume foot traffic location.

The futuristic E-Diner concept

Designed to fulfil the need for a high quality, strongly branded, semi-permanent retail concept, the futuristic E-Diner is designed with the most advanced technology in mind and is state-of-the-art. With its modern design and appeal, the E-Diner retails that classic diner theme and projects a compact, bright, user-friendly fast food outlet with customised equipment and fittings, including powerful branding and striking features.

The size of the E-Diner is 12 m² , which makes it suitable for just about any location and is not dictated to by services such as water, drainage or even electricity. Ideal for the African scenario, the concept has all the luxuries, image and ability of a traditional fast food outlet with the flexibility of the perfect location, energy-wise consumption, and true quick convenience shopping and low overhead structures of the vending sector. See below.

The Hot Dog Café support office concept

The Hot Dog Café cart concept, available as an option to the diner or as a Support Office concept includes six carts, inflatables, six Dog Walkers (sling trays) with supporting mechanisms that allow a franchisee to develop a designated area thereby creating a sustainable and profitable business. Carts are easily transported, extremely versatile and require minimal floor-space. The ultra-hygienic, fully insulated, 100% stainless steel unit can be used at special events, filling station forecourts, strip malls, cinema complexes, beach parking lots or practically any high-traffic location. Each cart is equipped with a branded umbrella, a menu board and signage on both sides. Giant inflatables or flags further increase awareness to the cart site and drive impulse sales. Two hundred hot dogs can be prepared from a fully stocked cart per day without having to restock.

The Hot Dog Café Dog Walker

Although not franchised out on its own, this unit is designed to support the Diner, E-Diner and Support Office and is only available to current franchisees to utilise around their outlet. A world first, the Dog Walker, with its fully insulated sling tray, is designed to enable the vendor to prepare a hot dog in the presence of a customer thus assuring freshness and maximum appeal. Its lightweight and insulated design keeps the sausages hot for up to two hours and the unit has condiment holders to store packets, sauces and serviettes. Its rounded edges allow for easy cleaning, ensuring optimum hygiene. The Dog Walker has been successfully deployed at sporting events, promotional events and in high traffic areas.

Hot Dog Café in South Africa

Winning the FASA (Franchise Association of Southern Africa) Newcomer Franchisor of the Year Award in 2003 put Hot Dog Café on the map.

In the South African context, Hot Dog Café has the distinct advantage of having the potential to create a franchise culture not only within the group but in the fast food franchise milieu. Not satisfied with their over 100 outlets, Hot Dog Café revolutionised the franchising industry with the launch of the futuristic E-Diner concept as an empowerment and employment option for the previously disadvantaged. The E-Diner, which was planned to be 'exceptional, easy, express, energy-efficient, enjoyable and exclusive', is an innovative combination of the popular in-store Diner concept with the flexibility of the stand-alone Carts providing a unique, almost risk-free opportunity for the informal sector, entrepreneur and former employee. Due to the semi-permanent nature of the E-Diner, favourable leases negotiated with landlords and low-risk investment structure, the concept offers an unprecedented level of security in a traditionally high-risk industry. As the leader in its market sector, Hot Dog Café has made its mark and has great potential for expansion in all sectors of the community.

The early days...a flash of success and a rash of mistakes!

Established in 1998, the Hot Dog Café concept was introduced by Johannes Booysen who realised the opportunity of starting a hot dog vending business in South Africa that would deliver a quality product based on the good, wholesome, traditional values that gave the hot dog cult status way back in 1936. Although sausages (and hot dogs) were a popular food, usually prepared at home or served at outdoor functions, no one had managed to turn them into a viable fast food brand, sold from vending carts, with innovative sauces and a distinctive brand identity.

Starting with a few carts, the concept soon proved so popular and profitable that Johannes Booysen decided to open the first Hot Dog Café Diner. The Diner did more than triple the turnover of the cart in the same location and soon there were around seven diners and 20 vending carts. But, as with all businesses where growth is not planned in meticulous detail and expansion controlled by systems, the owners' attempt to franchise was just not working. Firstly they had never planned to franchise; they had no knowledge of how franchising worked and they certainly weren't prepared for the expansion that goes with franchising a concept. In a typical case-book study of how not to succeed in franchising they encountered all the classic problems:

- Short-sightedness as to the long-term implications of starting a fast-food brand, with very little thought put into laying a solid business foundation for the future development of the concept and the brand.
- Little concept of site selection and simply taking any site offered without doing the necessary research into the demographics of an area.
- With very few controls in the administration of the business, there were continual stock problems and crippling financial problems, coupled with acute cash flow problems.
- Although still a fledgling franchise company, it lacked the support structures so crucial to making a success of a franchise business. With the head office not operating optimally, there was little hope that the franchisees would get any of the real support they needed to effectively grow their own businesses.
- Whilst the quality of the product remained of a high standard and customer service was maintained throughout the group, this alone could not sustain a franchise that did not have a sound base and a business strategy for future growth and expansion.

The second wave: Analysis, auditing and action!

Faced with the proposition that the business either sink or swim and wanting it to swim, the directors of Hot Dog Café called in the person who had the one thing they lacked: experience in running a franchise. Derek Smith, an accountant who specialised in guiding small businesses through rapid growth phases, was the man who could not only make Hot Dog Café swim, but if he had his way, he could make it surf the oceans! Initially, his task was to plug the holes, crisis manage and keep the boat afloat. His second task was to bring in a team with experience – from operations to marketing, and then came the difficult task of re-grouping, strategising and analysing.

Firstly, the directors established the fundamentals about their concept:

1. They knew there was a niche market in value-for-money quality products. As opposed to most fast food concepts whose offerings were in a higher price bracket, they would ensure they catered to a wider market and could achieve higher volume sales.
2. The hot dog product was flexible enough and easy enough to prepare to allow it to be marketed and distributed in various innovative ways – from a standard food-hall outlet to an outdoor diner, from a vendor cart to a dog walker.
3. The hot dog business had to be established not simply as a business opportunity but as a business format franchise backed by a strong brand and a comprehensive business blueprint. The only way the franchising of the concept would work was if everything was stringently controlled – from design to branding; from product quality to service levels; from financial controls to product development.
4. They knew they had a concept that would allow them to become the number one brand – not only in the fast food arena but, in the long term, in a myriad of other service areas – from convenience goods to consumer services such as basic services and healthcare.

The market analysis[3]

The second step was to conduct a market survey to establish who their market consisted of and what they thought of Hot Dog Café. Additional factors in the survey included establishing the category of fast food hot dogs fall into and the identity of the competitors. Interestingly enough, hog dogs were highly rated along with other food items categorised as 'quick food' such as a drive-thru McDonald's or a pie. The survey was divided into those who had tried a Hot Dog Café product and those who had never tried one. The results established the following critical factors:

Users
- 20% of customers were new customers.
- 98% of those who'd tried a Hot Dog Café hot dog said they would come back for more.

Non-users
- 78% asked 'What is Hot Dog Café?'
- 29% just didn't like hot dogs.

This analysis posed some interesting challenges:

1. With 98% of customers saying they would come back for more, it was an achievable goal to work on growing the 20% that were new customers. After all, if that high a percentage of new customers would come back time and again (as did the 98%) then Hot Dog Café was on a winning streak!
2. Counter-balancing that was the figure of 78% who had no idea who Hot Dog Café was. As the survey tackled both users and non-users, this was not necessarily because they didn't notice Hot Dog Café, but more likely because Hot Dog Café was just not in their area yet. That indicated that there was an urgent need for the group to achieve critical mass through franchise expansion.
3. There was scope to educate on taste. If 29% said they didn't like hot dogs, then it was necessary to find out why. Was it because consumers distrusted what was inside the hot dog? Had they tasted other hot dogs but not Hot Dog Café hot dogs? Did a general public perception exist that all hot dogs were of the low quality, blood red vienna type that contained everything except meat?

The franchisor development initiative

Armed with these statistics, management set about doing an analysis of their own company structure – to see where they were weak and where they could improve. To this end, they worked in conjunction with Namac Trust, who, together with leading franchise specialists Franchising Plus,[4] undertook an intensive audit of the company to test the viability of the franchise. The results concluded, amongst other things, that:

*   Hot Dog Café did not have a clear vision for their vending carts/E-Diners. They did not have data on their ideal site, the geographical area or the ideal micro location within a shopping centre. Site selection occurred on a reactive rather than a pro-active basis.
*   The administration systems at head office needed to be tightened with respect to royalty payments, their franchisees' turnovers, and general tax payments.
*   Although achieving critical mass was crucial to the success of the franchise, it had to do so by focusing on one small geographical area at a time. The advice was to conquer one town or area; to become established in Pretoria for instance, and then move onto other areas. In this way, they were not taking a shot-gun approach but rather saturating one area, winning over the consumer, establishing a brand, then moving onto the next area.
*   Ongoing training needed to be implemented in areas such as customer care and service levels.
*   On a marketing basis there needed to be a clear definition of the customer profile as well as a clear positioning statement.
*   Although the Hot Dog Café brand was trade-marked, it was found to be too generic and would not be inclusive of a wider product range.

In order to assess whether the Hot Dog Café had long-term potential as a franchise brand Franchising Plus required Hot Dog Café to answer certain critical questions.

Does the business operate in a large growing market?

Within fast food concepts, the most appealing aspect is its convenience. The fact that Hot Dog Café could provide their offering in a short space of time and at the convenient, easy-to-access sites (which the E-Diner and carts offer), gave it the edge.

Is the growth in the market sustainable?

As franchising relies on the franchisor establishing a solid support structure that will sustain a large number of franchisees, the concept has to be sustainable and not just a passing fad. Hot Dog Café in developing the Support Office was mindful of this sustainability as franchising a single cart would not have made economic sense either to the franchisee or the franchisor. The concept of the Support Office with its multiple carts and infrastructure could, in theory, provide a sustainable business for a franchisee. With statistics showing that many franchise concepts founder within three years, Hot Dog Café's six-year track record showed they indeed had market sustainability.

Can the product demand a price premium?

Although on the surface one might think 'a hot dog is a hot dog, is a hot dog' the success of Hot Dog Café depends largely on upholding their 'quality' policy on their hot dogs. Hot dog sausages, in general, come in many quality categories – and as it is a processed product, the content of the sausage can be very suspect. One of the most important obstacles Hot Dog Café had to overcome was the perception that a hot dog is unhealthy 'junk' food, with the sausage having low meat content and being filled with artificial flavourings and bulk fillers. The public needed to be constantly educated on the 'quality' aspect of a Hot Dog Café sausage – what it contained and the effort spent to ensure the production of a hot dog of the highest quality. The pricing reflected the quality of the product although again the consumer needed to be educated to this fact. The challenge in the years to come and with Hot Dog Café venturing into the mass market was to ascertain whether the price premium applied to all market sectors or whether the lower-income areas would need to be given a lower-price product – although this could not be done at the expense of quality.

Does the franchisor have access to sufficient capital?

Hot Dog Café, in its early days, was guilty of not doing its homework before embarking via the franchise route. The research, development and rollout of the concept needed to be strictly controlled and planned. The setting up of a franchise requires a large amount of initial capital to fund research and development, not only of the product line, but also of the brand, the support structures and the marketing. It then needs to have a healthy bottom-line balance to sustain the growth within the franchise and make provision for the support structures that need to be continually added in order to service an ever-growing pool of franchisees.

Does the potential exist to establish a brand?
The hot dog fast food market in South Africa is still a fledgling industry with in fact only two major players in the industry. It makes establishing the Hot Dog brand that much easier if the franchise expands from a sound base. Hot Dog Café had succeeded in establishing itself as the leader in its sector, building up a loyal customer base and offering both a high quality product as well as a recognisable brand. The audit did however pick up on the exclusivity of the Hot Dog Café brand which limits the range of products on offer and which could limit the expansion of the vending concept from including other offerings based on the same business format.

Is there a substantial barrier to entry?
In vending, especially where the set-up costs are not as high as in other fixed fast food outlets, there is a risk of the concept being easily copied. However, if one considers the wave of vending carts that were prolific in the early nineties, it is clear that only those with sound support structures survived. In the mid-nineties, at the height of South's Africa's transformation when there was a relaxing of trade and health restrictions, entrepreneurs thought they could make a fortune or supplement their income by investing in a trailer cart and selling all sorts of fast food offerings. What many of them didn't factor in was that selling a hot dog or a doughnut was not as simple an exercise as they thought. There needed to be a sound infrastructure and in order to be successful, the operator had to sustain his concept, build on it and make it grow. It certainly wasn't a part-time Saturday side-line. Consequently, within a few months all of the newly-appeared vending carts disappeared from the streets. Hot Dog Café, with its structured approach, certainly has the competitive advantage and although there might be others who venture into the same arena, Hot Dog Café is, in fact, streets ahead of the competition.

Will the development costs give a satisfactory return on investment?
This question relates back to the flash-in-the-pan vending craze of the nineties. Operating one cart will not make anyone a millionaire. And within the franchise context, with its system of set-up costs and royalty structures, franchising one cart to an individual also does not make financial sense. Although in theory, Africa's answer to the proliferation of sidewalk hawkers would be to franchise them, in practice it cannot work on an individual operator basis. Hot Dog Café Support Office model, which incorporates six vending carts and dog walkers, would certainly give a return on investment to the franchisee with the franchisor being able to exercise control and benefit from the success of his franchisee.

Is it possible to grow a franchise culture within the organization?

Hot Dog Café has good potential to develop franchise culture. With its strong ethical standards and sound franchise principles, Hot Dog Café can pave the way for the future of franchised vending in South Africa. By simply leading by example and showing the consumers how vending should be done, Hot Dog Café can play a pivotal role in transforming the informal vending sector into a vibrant, efficient and well-run sector – not only in the food sector but in all types of convenience and service sectors.

Does the concept have staying power?

With Hot Dog Café's long term strategy and commitment to the success of the venture, their concept certainly has staying power and will be a leader in its field. All the surveys and analysis point to one clear factor: done the right way, with the correct systems in place, and given the opportunities that abound in the vending fast food sector, Hot Dog Café can become the number one brand of the future.

The brand analysis – the bull's eye of the brand

To end the trilogy of analysis, the management of Hot Dog Café looked at the one aspect that is synonymous with franchising world-wide – the BRAND! Brand expectation in today's commercial world is paramount:

For consumers, brand offers the following advantages:
- The brand is one clear way to differentiate one product from a similar product.
- The unspoken pact: once they buy into a brand, they will show unflinching loyalty as long as the brand delivers and continues to deliver.
- Images, values and reasons to buy.
- The process of choice.

For the franchisers, brand performs the following functions:
- Guarantees the legal monopoly of one owner.
- Ensures consumers that they are buying goods or services of a consistent quality.
- Has become the most effective way their product is chosen.
- Offers convenience, excellent service and value for money.

Taking some of the world's most famous brands as examples, Hot Dog Café set about entrenching the brand identity and cementing the ethics and ethos that would forever be the mainstay of the franchise. The signature slogan 'EXPECT THE BEST encompasses everything that Hog Dog Café stands for and is complemented by the strong Hot Dog logo complete with Hot Dog graphic. The brand slogan and logo help create the brand image, which performs the following functions:
- It consolidates everything the brand aspires to and is meaningful to all target markets.

- To the consumer it emphasises the message of consistency in quality, service and taste.
- It reminds staff that 'only the best will do' and 'we expect the best from one another'.
- It inspires the franchise family to operate in accordance with the values established.

From the bull's eye of the brand it became clear that Hot Dog Café was uniquely positioned to take ownership of the following core brand proposition: **Taste, Quality, Convenience, Value for Money. Every Time.**

Inherent in that proposition were the fundamental elements of a good product and a sustainable brand. It reinforced the essence of the brand: Tasty, honest-to-goodness traditional values or to use the Hot Dog Café strap-line **Traditional value on a roll.** Not only does that strap-line refer to the product but it implies that the company has traditional values of honesty, integrity and care whilst alluding to the core business of being fast food 'on the go' from a franchise company that is going places.

Hot Dog Café – The new wave

As a result of the intense scrutiny of Hot Dog Café business strategy, consumer profile and branding, the growth of the Hot Dog Café brand has been sure and steady. Currently the brand has over 19 Diners, 28 Wild Bean Cafes and over 55 Carts operating in Gauteng, KwaZulu Natal and Western Cape. By the end of 2005 Hot Dog Café expects a 50% growth in outlets countrywide.

From the onset, Hot Dog Café established itself as a unique, fast, user-friendly, mess-free, 'on the go' fast food operation. Its success is due to its adherence to:
- providing the most efficient service;
- providing the fastest, friendliest, tastiest, freshest food 'on the go';
- maintaining the consistency, quality and value of Hot Dog Café for customers countrywide; and
- updating and using the most advanced technology to facilitate the best returns for the franchisee and his business.

In early 2003, the Hot Dog Café management re-assessed their original business plan – taking into account industry trends, market movements, economy changes and political influences. A sharp escalation in food prices prompted them to make the conscious decision of going for quality rather than for price. Always mindful of their 'expect the best' motto, they set out to find key suppliers (for their products as well as for packaging and services) who would be with them for the long haul and provide both quality and reasonable pricing. In the franchising context, suppliers play a critical role in the success of the concept – without their support the franchise is simply an operational framework.

Once all the crucial elements of the business were set, the management of Hot Dog Café embarked on a spot of lateral thinking on ways to expand the business to include the emerging market and the demands of the broader consumer. Their assessment showed a glaring gap – and a wonderful opportunity! They needed to expand in a different direction – tap into new markets and create new opportunities.

Their 16 fixed sites were well-established but the concept of permanent shops and diners as a whole had limited growth potential. Mindful that the fast food industry is a cut-throat industry that takes no prisoners – where set-up costs are high, sites often don't give the returns expected and the consumer can be fickle – moving from one new fad to another at the drop of a hat. This was not where Hot Dog Café saw its long-term future and always at the back of its mind was the fact that unlike other fast food concepts which had to have fixed premises to ensure quality, it had an easy-to-set-up-and-serve commodity that could work equally well on a fixed site or a movable site, like the cart of a Dog Walker. As long as the brand could be upheld, the quality remained the same and the service was optimum, there were great opportunities to infiltrate countless new markets.

With that idea in mind, the E-Diner – a well-appointed kiosk that is the perfect combination of the regular fast food outlet and a flexible vending arena – was born. Given the restrictions of a permanent outlet with its risk factors, site selection difficulties, and the fact that in a fixed outlet an investor immediately loses up to 70% of his capital value if the site is not successful, the E-Diner proved to have following advantages:

- Lower costs.
- It was the perfect middle ground between a fixed diner and a cart.
- The market was ready for it and wanted it.
- It offered a semi-permanent site with the option of moving if the site was not right.
- Although, as with anything, investing in a diner could not guarantee success, it certainly could reduce the risks.

Once the perfect prototype had been formulated it proved to be a winner.

Product development/ quality control

Although franchised fast food concepts are successful because they sell the consumer an experience that often goes beyond just the food, a good product remains the foundation to any food concept and Hot Dog Café has made making the best quality hot dog their number one mission. Every product that Hot Dog Café offers meets the most stringent quality controls, so that taste, consistency and freshness are never sacrificed. In keeping with the Hot Dog Café philosophy of 'Expect the Best', the menus have been developed to offer the customer the best variation of the original hot dogs and accompaniments that complement each taste sensation.

Using top suppliers of products and services is a must to ensure on-going synergy and consistent quality in a fast food range. Hot Dog Café has entered into long-term relationship with all its suppliers to maintain superior quality and first rate services to ensure long-term success.

Branding and marketing

The challenge that Hot Dog Café faced in making the concept a successful franchise brand lay in its branding and marketing. Unlike most fast food franchises that are found only in upmarket malls and high streets, where marketing the brand and upholding standards is a standard operation, the Hot Dog Café many-tiered concepts offered a harder challenge.

The Diner concept was easy enough. Modelled on the typical Retro Diner of the 1930s, complete with hand-etched murals, retro tables and chairs and sophisticated brand identification, the Hot Dog Café in areas like Caesars, Gauteng, Canal Walk, Western Cape, Northgate, Cresta and East Rand Mall in Gauteng, are among the best examples of high-tech design and sophisticated branding.

The E-Diner offered a different challenge. How to get that same high-tech look and feel in a unit that is semi-permanent and is often placed in parking areas and on sports fields was quite a challenge. In addition, it had to not only look good and maintain the Hot Dog Café standards but it had to incorporate the most advanced technology with user-friendly components whilst incorporating the logistics of water, drainage and even electricity. The result is a revolutionary unit that is functional yet appealing and with a strong brand identification.

On another level, the Hot Dog Café Cart, which was based on the original American version, had to undergo subtle changes to allow more versatility in the harsh South African conditions. It had to be functional and appealing; hygienic yet inviting. A combination of stainless steel ensures optimum cleanliness whilst striking branding on both sides ensures impulse buying and confidence from the consumer. A cheerful, uniformed staff member serves from a well laid-out serving surface under a red and white branded umbrella. And to add that fun appeal and entice consumers from afar, giant inflatables of the Hot Dog Eating Giant ensure that those 200 hot dogs are sold within hours.

Throughout Hot Dog Café the brand remains paramount – whether it be in the retro finish of the Diner counters, the branded umbrellas on the carts, the sleek look of the Dog Walker or the neat appearance of the uniformed staff. Marketing a brand in such diverse outlets is not an easy task but with a pro-active marketing strategy and strong conformity, Hot Dog Café has succeeded in bringing the brand to the people – wherever they are – on the street corner, in the mall, on the sports field, the garage forecourt or on the beach.

Support services

In any franchise the support services offered by the franchisor are an essential ingredient in making a concept work. Without the persistent support and control standards imposed on the franchisees, most franchised outlets would drop their guard, slip on standards and let down the brand. The beauty of franchising is that every possible area of the business format is part of the back-up service that each franchisee receives on an almost daily basis. From distribution to accounting, from marketing to merchandising, the helping hand of the franchisor is always extended. Hot Dog Café is no exception and its main support office has been developed to incorporate all services essential to developing and maintaining a first-class franchise. Hot Dog Café oversees the following disciplines to ensure that the franchisees receive nothing but the best franchise support system in the following areas:

- Administration.
- Warehousing.
- Distribution.
- Marketing.
- Project Management.
- Store Design.
- Training.
- Operations.
- Product Development.
- Equipment Development.
- Concept Development.
- Site Selection.

Future strategies

The versatility of the hot dog concept has allowed the management of Hot Dog Café to look at a range of options for expansion that would cover as wide a spectrum of the population as possible. The current economic and political climate is conducive to growth and expansion and we are lucky to have a government that has been exceptionally pro-active in initiating far-reaching projects that will ultimately stimulate the economy and ensure sustainable growth. The small business sector (SME) has been receiving particular attention as our unemployment rate remains a concern and the bulk of the previously disadvantaged sector (PDI), despite having higher qualifications, cannot get into business for themselves due to the infrastructure costs being too high and the fact that the initial capital requirement creates a barrier to entry for many. There is no question that South Africa is desperate for an affordable mechanism and a structured, practical way to train entrepreneurs and bring them into the SME sector.

Government's role

Government has certainly put its weight behind assisting the small business sector (SMEs) to thrive and contribute to the economic development of the country. Various government funding agencies, under the auspices of the Department of Trade and Industry, have injected millions of rands to help get initiatives off the ground. In 2004:
- Umsobomvu Youth Fund gave out R61,9 million worth of funding.
- Khula put up R700 million worth of guarantees, creating one million jobs.
- Ntsika provided training for 35 000 start-ups and helped 626 SMEs win R87 million worth of tenders.

These agencies, however, have in the past worked in isolation from one another and government is working towards combining these funding agencies to form a cohesive service that will facilitate entrepreneurs starting their own businesses. The combined agencies will offer a one-stop service in centres around the country offering guarantees for loans, information and mentoring.

The private sector's role

In the wake of government's restructuring of its funding agencies, an appeal has also been made to the private sector to do their bit in mentoring entrepreneurs and small businesses and to provide the business opportunities that will help bring young entrepreneurs onto the formal business platform. On the cards are incentives ranging from tax breaks to points towards BEE compliance to companies who play a part in stimulating that sector.

Franchising, within this growth scenario, has an important role to play. It has been acknowledged as the one business format that can easily be adapted to suit many socio-economic climates and provides the best business foundation for creating entrepreneurs, skills transfer and in job creation.

Two ground-breaking surveys,[5] conducted on behalf of FRAIN (Franchise Advice & Information Network), an arm of NAMAC TRUST, by Franchising Plus, looked at two progressive initiatives to empowering entrepreneurs and creating workable business models:
- **Tandem franchising:** This involves implementing a mentoring and financing programme for new franchisees from previously disadvantaged backgrounds using informal, on-the-job training as well as financing on a joint-venture structure.
- **Social franchising:** This is a mechanism for service delivery to communities that harnesses the principles of franchising and makes them work for the benefit of social rather than commercial goals.

With initiatives like the Banking Charter forcing the lending community to look at making funding more accessible to the man in the street, and with international players like the African Development Bank launching a funding initiative for Africa, the door has been opened by government legislation and good intent to stimulate entrepreneurship through preferential financing options.

Hot Dog Café believes that it has both the franchise mechanisms in place and the ideal business opportunities to link in with government's SME proposals. It has developed, in the E-Diner, the ideal business opportunity for the SME market and by formalising vending options, it has developed what is undoubtedly the most progressive business option for the future of franchising on the African continent. Hot Dog Café is one of the few franchise companies in South Africa that has all the elements critical to creating true empowerment through the creation of emerging entrepreneurs who have access not only to funding initiatives, but who will reap the benefits of skills transfer and job creation in business opportunities that are both affordable and accessible.

While the franchise fraternity is always eager to assist the emerging market to get into franchising, it is often impeded by the large corporations and landlords who maintain prohibitively high rentals and won't adapt their operations to include the small business sectors. Strip malls, hyperstore sites and mall parking areas are ideal sites for the establishment of emerging franchise businesses. What is needed is the buy-ins from the wholesalers, large retailers and hyperstores who could easily sponsor PDI entrepreneurs in getting operating sites on their properties.

Career opportunities for graduates

These exciting initiatives also create career opportunities for students studying entrepreneurship, business and marketing. Hot Dog Café offers graduates:

- A learnership programme through Hot Dog Café with SETA accreditation.
- On-site training.
- Academic and business training.
- The opportunity to work through the ranks to manager and then onto franchisee.
- Assistance in financing one's own franchise.
- The benefit of a two-year learnership contract.
- The benefit of a 12-month mentoring programme by the franchisors.

Conclusion

Hot Dog Café has encountered and worked through all the classic problems involved in franchising. Careful and focused research enabled this company to establish the parameters of the hot dog market and the resulting analysis revealed the areas to be developed and strategies to be followed. Professional auditing allowed the directors of Hot Dog Café to re-evaluate the company's managerial and operational structure and finally focused on the brand analysis, the key to maintaining a successful franchise. The systematic and controlled approach toward product development and quality control, branding and marketing and the franchise support services which followed from the auditing process enabled Hot Dog Café to not only succeed in the franchise market but also to open up the way for future franchise opportunities and the development of a franchise culture in South Africa.

References

1   This case study was compiled by Giuli Osso of GO Communications for Hot Dog Café. Case study procured by Michael Cant.
2   www.gracechurchlexingon.org/hot_dog_facts.htm
3   Market research information taken from the Hot Dog Café Exit Interview Research – July 2003 – prepared by The Marketta Group.
4   Information taken from the Hot Dog Café Report, prepared by Franchising Plus.
5   Social Franchising & Tandem Franchising, commissioned by NAMAC TRUST's FRAIN (Franchise Advice and Information Network). Studies undertaken by Anita du Toit of Franchising Plus cc.

19

MARKETING FEATURES:
BRANDING
COMPETITION
IMAGE
LOW-COST STRATEGY
POSITIONING
SERVICES MARKETING
SLOGANS

kulula.com –
A value-based competitor
in the South African
airline market

Introduction[1]

An interesting development in the South African airline industry was the intro-
duction of kulula.com, a low-fares airline, which forms part of the Comair/ British
Airways group. Comair Limited started in 1946 and signed a franchise with British
Airways in 1997 to use the British Airways brand name in South and southern
Africa. Currently the Comair/British Airways group flies between Johannesburg,
Cape Town, Durban, Port Elizabeth, Lusaka, Harare, Windhoek and Victoria Falls.
The directors of Comair realised in that there was a gap in the market for a low-
fares airline, especially after the demise of various airlines catering for this

segment such as Sun Air. Kulula.com was introduced in August 2001 with a limited number of flights daily between Johannesburg and Cape Town. Passengers suddenly had a drastically cheaper option to fly between Johannesburg, Cape Town and Durban. Airfares of R400 per one-way trip between Johannesburg and Cape Town rocked the established airlines such as South African Airways, starting a price war with customers being the main beneficiaries.

The mission of kulula.com

Kulula.com's mission statement is not the run-of-the-mill statement that you find in the annual report of most companies. It reflects something of the corporate culture of the airline. The mission statement is irreverent and humourous reflecting the image of a down-to-earth company. The mission of kulula.com reads as follows:

Mission statement of kulula.com

To our superhero customers and staff we dream of being:

- The easiest around – this means we must constantly provide the easiest way to book, the easiest way to pay, and above all, be the easiest to afford.
- Simple – we don't complicate things. We don't use high-and-mighty language and overly wordy descriptions. We get to the point and that's that.
- Totally honest – this means we tell it like it is. We're not shy of being straight and down-to-earth. There is no bullshit. There are no hidden costs. What you see is what you get.
- Great fun – we help people lighten up. Smiles and jokes are free. We always want to be genuinely friendly and provide the right environment for our staff's natural talent to shine.
- Safe and professional – at no time is our dedication compromised. Our most important principle is 'safety first'.
- Inspirational – wherever possible, we provide our staff with the best opportunities to develop their skills, and take their abilities to new heights in the service of our customers.

Today we are an airline, tomorrow, who knows? Nothing is impossible. But wherever our customers see the kulula.com brand, they can expect these values.[1]

Services offered by kulula.com

Kulula.com offers two services to its customers: flights between the major destinations in South Africa and car rental. The logo of kulula.com flights includes the slogan 'Now anyone can fly', thereby appealing to the widest possible target market. The kulula.com/cars service was launched in August 2002. The two services complement one another. When passengers buy a return air ticket from kulula.com they may also rent a car at R165 per day (including unlimited mileage, standard insurance waivers, airport surcharge and VAT). Kulula.com also offers a reasonably-priced shuttle service to and from the airport.

Competition in the low-fares market

At the beginning of 2004 a new competitor entered the South African market with the promise of the same low prices as kulula.com. This entry contributed to the general overcapacity problem of the market, which some observers say will only be solved by the bankruptcy of one or more of the airlines. Despite that, kulula.com launched the acquisition of four McDonnel-Douglas 82 airplanes in January 2004 with an up to 30% slash in fares to the destinations Cape Town, Port Elizabeth, George and Durban. The executive director of kulula.com, Novick explained the 30% cheaper rates (e.g. the airfare between Johannesburg and Durban is R199 one-way) as due to the savings on the new airplanes, which are 30% cheaper to operate than the older Boeings 737-300s.[2]

The role of price elasticity of demand

The fundamental theory of price elasticity of demand provides an economic explanation why passengers are interested in flying with kulula.com and why kulula.com is in a position to charge these low fares. The price elasticity of demand refers to the percentage change in the quantity demanded from a change in the price.[3] If a decline of 50% in the price results in an increase in demand of 100%, we say that the price is elastic within the price range. This is the price principle being followed by kulula.com in its assault on the South African market.

What is further of interest is the fact that kulula.com is following the same strategy as some of the now famous European and American airlines such as Ryanair and Southwest Airlines.[4] These two airlines are following a powerful combination of low airfares and good service to win the hearts and minds of passengers and can be described as value-based players in the airline industry.

Value-based players' competitive edge[5]

The power of value-based companies are centred in two areas, namely having a cost advantage in the airline industry and in the relentless way in which this cost advantage is pursued while their second strength is based on the potency of the shift in consumer perceptions regarding the quality of the service that they offer. These two aspects will now be discussed in greater detail:

Cost advantage

Ryanair, for instance, charges lower fares by departing from lower-cost airports (e.g. departing from Gerona which is 60km from Barcelona while the national carriers departs from the Barcelona city airport), utilising aircraft more optimally by flying them more hours a day, keeping labour cost low, distributing tickets online and providing no in-flight frills. In South Africa the trend of utilising secondary airports is still in its infancy with Lanseria now being positioned as an alternative to Johannesburg airport. The financial and operational performance of Ryanair during the period 1998 to 2002 is depicted in Table 19.1 below:

Finance

Year	2002	2001	2000	1999	1998
Net profit (US dollars, in millions)	134,84	94,86	74,72	61,18	52,35
Net margin	24,09%	21,43%	19,59%	19,25%	19,63%

Operational statistics

Passengers (in millions)	11,1	7,4	5,5	4,9	4,0
Passenger load factor	81,2%	71%	67%	71,5%	72%

Table 19.1: Financial and operational performance of Ryanair[6]

Table 19.1 clearly shows the increase in net profit during the period, which is based on economies of scale with an increase in passengers and an increasing passenger load factor being the major reasons for the improvement.

Novick, the CEO of kulula.com states that they 'sweat the assets (airplanes)' flying six sectors a day on the route Johannesburg to Cape Town utilising the planes 12 to 14 hours a day.[7] Kulula.com furthermore does not have additional services that cost money such as frequent-flyer programmes, offering meals onboard, preseating customers and paying commission to travel agents and tour operators. Southwest airlines in the USA is following the same approach and the cost advantage of Southwest Airlines is explained in the excerpt below.

The cost advantage of Southwest Airlines[8]

Low costs have given Southwest Airlines in the USA the competitive advantage of having the America's lowest fares. This advantage has created a phenomenon known in the airline industry as the 'Southwest effect'. Airports served by Southwest have lower average fares than those that are not because competitors feel compelled to match Southwest's fares.

A shift in the quality perceptions that they offer

Although passengers flying with Ryanair cannot reserve seats in advance, the quality gap between Ryanair and British Airways (the official UK carrier) is perceived to be narrow, regarding aspects such as service, convenience and the buying experience. Similarly, in South Africa Novick, CEO of kulula.com, states that safety standards are non-negotiable and that kulula has a strong customer base and a strong brand.[9] Kulula.com also won the ACSA-Airports Company's award for best domestic airline in 2002 strengthening the positive quality perception of customers.

Value-based airlines attract large numbers of passengers with the winning combination of low prices and 'good enough' quality. With the large number of passengers these airlines obtain economies of scale, which translates into superior productivity increases, something which is unattainable by traditional airlines. Graph 19.1 below indicates the lower cost per available seat mile of Ryanair and Southwest, which is Ryanair's business model counterpart in the USA.

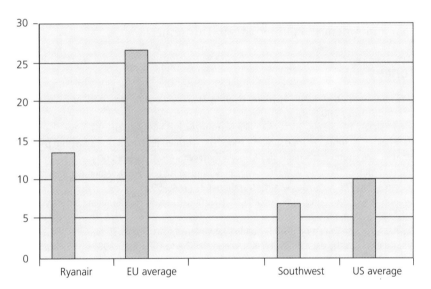

Graph 19.1: Cost per available seat mile of Ryanair and Southwest Airlines (2002 – in American cents)

As can been seen both Southwest and Ryanair have a major advantage regarding cost-per-available-seat-mile (in both instances more than 30%). With this saving they can offer the cheapest possible fares, thereby generating above-average customer loyalty as well as profitability, which in turn generates a virtuous cycle whereby the company can charge even lower fares, open up more routes, and stimulate even more traffic.

Another reason for the success of Southwest lies in the treatment of the personnel of the airline.[10] Management believes that when employees are treated well, they will treat customers well, creating a beneficial situation for all stake-holders. This does not mean that the personnel get fat pay cheques. In fact, Southwest Airlines wages are generally lower that those of competitors but the company sweetens the deal by making stock options available to employees, enabling them to benefit from the airlines' financial success. What further endears Southwest to its employees is a no-layoff policy, even in the darkest days after September 11 (the bombing of the World Trade Centre in the USA). Kulula.com is following the same approach as Southwest Airlines in as far as it keeps employees happy by giving them the freedom to perform their jobs to the best of their abilities.

Summary

The aviation industry in South Africa was for decades monopolised by the state carrier South African Airways. The earlier introduction of no-frill airlines was not a success for various factors. However, it would seem that the most recent cut-price airlines are providing more stringent competition to the state carrier and other national carriers. Only time will tell if kulula.com will be as successful as its European and American counterparts in this respect.

References

1   Case study written by Johan Strydom. Http://www.kulula.com/airkiosk/MN/info/mission.htm. Date accessed: 11 July 2004.
2   *Business Day*, 19 January 2004. Air-price war breaks out as kulula slashes prices.
3   Mansfield, E & Yohe, G. 2000. *Micro Economics*. 10th edition. New York: Norton, p 128.
4   What makes southwest airlines fly? Knowledge@Wharton, 23 April 2003.
5   Information based on Frank, RJ, George, JP & Narasimhan, L. 2004. When competitors deliver more for less. *The McKinsey Quarterly*, number 1, pp 49-59.
6   Gimeno, J, Cool, K, Fung, H & Buccella, A. 07/2003-5124. European airline industry: Ryanair in 2003. INSEAD, p 11.
7   *Business Day*, 17 December 2003. Kulula's new planes to cut costs 30%.
8   What makes southwest airlines fly? Knowledge@Wharton. 23 April 2003.
9   *Business Day*, op. cit.
10 Knowledge@Wharton, op. cit.

Promac Paints (Pty) Ltd

History[1]

Vaughan Prost and Stephen Reinecke founded Promac Paints in 1992. Vaughan Prost had spent some time in the paint raw materials supply industry, and felt that the entry into the paint industry, and in particular, the decorative paint sector of the industry, was a natural progression. There were more than 400 registered paint manufacturers at the time, so cost of entry into the market was relatively low. When Stephen Reinecke, a life-long friend, joined Vaughan, he brought with him quality assurance management as well as production and planning experience. Soon, out of meagre beginnings, Promac Paints took shape.

Our Quality Spreads Further

Basic market research was conducted and they decided to target the building trade, in the greater Pretoria area. Vaughan took advantage of the blossoming building and golf course estates in that target area and began developing the product range in accordance with the requirements of the Building and Painting Contractors Association.

Initially production was limited to small batches of primarily water-based products and limited solvent borne enamels, that is, PVAs and enamels.

Overall production was limited to what Stephen, and one helper, could produce, which Vaughan sold on a personal and intimate basis the next day.

Marketing strategy

The marketing strategy followed by the company was simple, straightforward and effective. Vaughan would target building development sites and then saturate the area with posters, technical data sheets and business cards. His persistence, together with his initial prognosis of the local paints market, provided Promac Paints with its first Perceived Use Value (PUV). The aim was to provide unmatched technical and customer service to its small customer base by offering excellent technical support, as well as advice to customers, coupled with good quality paint at reasonable prices. This strategy formed the foundation for future success of the company. Armed with good technical expertise, two half-ton bakkies, and endless energy, the intrepid entrepreneurs provided good technical advice, quality products and a 24-hour door-to-door delivery service, at competitive prices. This differentiated Promac from its competitors and made it possible to target the markets effectively. The competitors followed a more conservative approach and marketed their products through hardware and building supply outlets.

From a zero base the sales and reputation of Promac Paints grew exponentially and the company boasted a turnover of R240 000 in its first year of operation. A small profit was achieved and on the basis of sound financial control and monitoring the cash flow on a daily basis, profits were reinvested into the expansion of the company. The staff was expanded to include a production assistant and an administrative clerk and capital expenditure included the expansion of the delivery fleet by 50%, from two half-ton bakkies, to three.

The marketing strategy adopted by the company now extended beyond the concentration on building and painting contractors to include retail paints stores in greater Pretoria. Promac Paint products began to appear in hardware and paint chain stores, supported by promotional material in the form of technical data sheets, sign writing, and colour charts. It also heralded the beginning of the market segmentation policy of the company in the decorative paint market. New markets resulted in the introduction of new products and packaging and sales increased proportionately, resulting in the turnover reaching R1 200 000 in the second year of operation. Promac Paints boasted a gross profit margin of 48%.

In line with their employment policy, Geraldine Harris was appointed to oversee the administration and financial responsibilities of the company and with meticulous control of costs, expenses and cash flow, the company entered its third year of operation with optimistic sales objectives and increasing turnover by a massive 60%. Turnover reached R3 000 000 in 1994. Promac Paints who had entered the paint market hesitantly two years previously, had begun to establish a reputation in its chosen marketing sector and territory and was ready to make meaningful strides into an extremely competitive environment.

Growth stage

Our quality spreads further

During 1995 and 1996 equally satisfying results were recorded with turnover doubling on a compounded basis. Penetration into the market segments previously dominated by the two market leaders, Plascon and Dulux, emphasised the successful implementation of Promac Paints' strategy and also heralded the beginning of the next growth phase of the fledgling company. Although Plascon and Dulux were national players with significant advertising budgets, Promac began making headway by affording better service, delivery and increased margins on its products.

Production had by this time increased to unmanageable levels and a new production facility was acquired with sufficient space to accommodate the next decade of production, as well as office accommodation for the rising staff complement. The Promac image now took on a more corporate hue with a newly launched Promac Paints logo and a strategic theme of '**Our Quality spreads further**'.

The partners, Vaughan and Stephen, now concentrated on re-evaluating and improving the Four Ps.

- **Product:** On the product side of the business, expansion was necessary and the quality had to be reinforced and sustained. This led to the appointment of many specialists from the paint industry. Both partners realised the importance of consistent quality and technical support and accordingly a well-qualified and experienced technical manager was appointed. The incumbent was not only well-qualified but had work published in the journal of the prestigious Oil and Colour Chemist Association, as well as having presented a number of related papers to the OCCA. He set about consolidating and improving the existing product range in line with customer and market demand.

- **Place:** The place was extensively strategised, with consideration given to ego-boosting national distribution, but sanity and good basic business sense prevailed and Promac decided to concentrate on the local decorative market. Promac chose to pursue a policy of concentrating on its immediate market and to acquire a dominant share in it.

- **Price:** In terms of price, the company aimed to provide quality products at prices that satisfied the perceived value for money criterion demanded by the customer base. Promac also identified an opportunity of affording retailers improved margin levels, compared with the more inflexible and market dominating competitors.

- **Promotion:** Promac now found itself pre-occupied with the fourth 'P', promotion. The meagre beginnings of posters, technical data sheets and business cards, which had been so successful in past years, were now reviewed and expanded, culminating in a more balanced regional promotional campaign incorporating local newspaper advertising, radio support for sales promotions, outdoor signage and public relations exercises.

And further...

The historic levels of exponential growth of the company continued and as the new millennium dawned, Promac Paints had established itself firmly in the decorative paint industry. In terms of market share, Promac was firmly in sixth spot in the decorative paint league tables. Corporate promotional material described the company as providing a range of decorative paints to fulfil all the requirements of the market with relation to cement, plaster and brick, pre-fabricated cement, wood and steel coatings. The range is supported by user-friendly product data sheets, on-line technical support, through an active, user-friendly website and a colour tinting system, affording a range of colours similar to those promoted by its major competitors. A number of its contracted outlets are supplied with state-of-the-art company-owned colour tinting carousels and shakers (used to mix the paint when customers want specific colours). All retail outlets are offered up-to-date point-of-sale material (POS), that promotes Promac products.

And further... into the future

Promac Paints has become one of the most progressive and fastest growing surface coatings manufacturers in South Africa. Promac Paints stockists are widespread throughout the Gauteng province, Mpumalanga, Northern Province and Free State. Since 60% of South Africa's Gross Domestic Product is generated in the Gauteng and surrounding areas, this was the area where Promac Paints decided to concentrate its market penetration and strategic growth in the immediate future. In order to facilitate this strategic growth the company decided to expand its investment base with the appointment of Deryck Spence and Robert Frazer as directors and shareholders of the company. Deryck brought 35 years of experience in the retail oil industry as well as experience in strategic change processes both locally and abroad. Robert had 40 years of corporate experience in the building and earth-moving industry. The arrival of these two new directors and shareholders was extremely complementary to the company as it now had a management team in place that was balanced with youth and experience.

The historic growth of the company, in the opinion of the founders, has been as a result of the synergy between research and technology, product specification and by the choice of people employed by the company. The blend of cost-efficient and effective manufacturing processes has resulted in quality products designed to solve customers' problems, both simple and complex, and to anticipate future demands and expectations. Promac's product range therefore includes many different and unique products, developed to satisfy customers in the many different market segments in which Promac Paints operates.

In line with its Strategic Plan Promac moved into a new phase of growth in 2001. A new production facility was built to cope with the increased demands of the market in terms of capacity and to extend the quality standards that the company has set for itself. In terms of marketing, the image of the company was upgraded, both from a visual and strategic viewpoint. The company's product range was upgraded and expanded by means of a series of quality enhancers to meet and exceed the expectations of the marketplace. These expectations are manifested in many important areas and criteria. Promac introduced an innovative customer educational system within its packaging and promotional material, enabling end users the ability to choose a product on the basis of how long they want the paint to last. By way of example, all of Promac's products have been divided into a Quality Band System. Gold Band products represent ten years' life expectancy, Silver Band products represent five years' life or more and Blue Band products represent a paint life of up to three years. This innovation prompted Plascon to introduce the 'seven year paint' in retaliation. In addition, and in line with customers' expectations, Promac introduced a series of icons, which also afforded easy reference to consumers. Pack decorations and promotional material indicate which quality enhancers are in the paint that they are purchasing, for example, whether the paint is perfumed, scrubbable or stain resistant, UV resistant, chip-or-scratch resistant, alkali-or-mould/algae-resistant, lead-free or water resistant. This information is easily accessible and does not necessitate delving through piles of technical data. The Promac pack range has been totally upgraded in line with the new corporate image to accommodate both the Quality Band system as well and the product enhancement icons.

Promac also expanded its re-endorsement regarding its quest for quality improvement with the successful achievement of the SABS ISO 9001: 2000 quality accreditation in January 2003. In addition, in order to conform to the aspirations and ethics of the Coating Industry, Promac became an executive member of the South African Paint Manufacturers Association (SAPMA) and has played an active role in the pursuit of improving quality and trading standards within the industry and the all important task of protecting the consumer. In 2004 Deryck Spence, a Director and shareholder of Promac Paints, became Chairman of the SAPMA, confirming Promac's 'coming of age' and taking its rightful place in the coatings industry.

In its published Marketing Strategy Statement of Intent, Promac Paints describes these intentions as follows:

Promac Paints is committed to significantly increasing its market share in the southern African market over the next five years. This will be achieved by the supply of quality products that satisfy both customers' present needs and will meet and exceed their future expectations. In order to achieve these objectives, Promac Paints will:

- Gain market share through the development of a structured pricing policy and by pursuing continuous improvement programmes and margin protection solutions, without compromising quality.

- By understanding the current needs of our customers intimately, as well as their goals, objectives and strategies, so that we can provide solutions that satisfy and anticipate our customers' requirements.
- By accepting no compromise in our quest to provide outstanding customer service, by becoming customer-driven, both internally and externally and by monitoring our progress with regular customer performance measurement programmes.
- By implementing Human Resources Programmes to ensure management development and improvement of critical skills.

Through the achievement of our goals, we will establish Promac Paints as a company with whom employees, customers, suppliers and other service providers are proud to be associated, whilst achieving acceptable financial returns.

The future of Promac Paints

Promac Paints has enjoyed significant growth since it was founded in 1992. The growth, sometimes too fast, created new challenges for the management of the company. These challenges have been turned into opportunities and the company has accordingly enjoyed a period of consolidation in preparing for the next growth phase. Databases have been updated, management systems and information technology hardware and programs upgraded. Ever-conscious of the importance of Perceived Use Value and the role that service and delivery plays in the business mix, Promac paid an emotional farewell to its company-owned fleet of delivery vehicles, and contracted a logistical specialist company to improve the all-important task of servicing the ever-growing customer list. The company has also been engaged in an exercise of upgrading the product mix of its product range to the higher quality end of the market and confronting the major players in the industry on their erstwhile 'high ground'.

Still determined to maintain the dominance in the historical Pretoria arena, Promac has concentrated its efforts in expanding its marketing influence into the Johannesburg, Witwatersrand, and Vaal Triangle arena. This has been achieved with the successfully concluded contractual negotiations with the Kings Group of outlets. The Kings Group has projected the Promac range of products as its own house brand and has further improved the promotional draw of the company by entering into rewarding joint advertising campaigns which have brought the Promac Paints brand into this lucrative marketing area. Market research and customer relationship studies have indicated ever-increasing spontaneous awareness of the Promac Brand in these areas and more importantly, sales have shown similar trends, which augur well for the future. Increased brand awareness has also resulted in an increased volume of enquiries from other market segments in the greater Johannesburg area.

The most important marketing thrust by Promac, into the future and in pursuit of eventual national distribution, has been the introduction of the 'Paint

Logix' Initiative. The Paint Logix Initiative is based on the identification of experienced professional businessmen around the country, to whom the concept of a dedicated and exclusive Promac Paint outlet is franchised. Cognisant of channel conflicts in the marketplace, the Paint Logix Initiative has been carefully planned and implemented to obviate these conflicts. The success to date of the project has reinforced the Perceived Use Values (PUVs) of the quality of both product and service, together with the professionalism in the project's implementation and the exclusiveness of its design and concept. The Paint Logix Initiative, like Promac Paints itself is based on the all-important cornerstones of success:

- choosing the correct operators and partners; and
- training these operators and partners in the principles upon which Promac has built its business and reputation: high quality products, availability and customer service.

Although the Paint Logix Initiative is in its infancy in terms of introduction into the marketplace, the successes of the initiative are already starting to take on acceptance and popularity on a national basis and in neighbouring countries. The strategy adopted in this initiative is to continue expanding Promac's influence in the greater Gauteng marketing areas, whilst building a sustainable national distribution network for the future. This initiative clearly places Promac in the national distribution amphitheatre and is the biggest expansion project ever attempted before. It truly lives up to the strategic theme of the company: 'Our quality spreads further'.

Reference

1   Case study written by Promac Paints (Pty) Ltd. Case study procured by Michael Cant.

21

MARKETING FEATURES:

BRANDING

DISTRIBUTION

FRANCHISING

LEGISLATION

LOCATION

MARKETING CONCEPT/ PHILOSOPHY

RATIONALISATION

SALES TRAINING

Butterfield

Backgound history to the bread industry[1]

Government control

Until 1991 the baking industry was controlled by the government, specifically the Wheat Board, and the bread price was subsidised. The basic aims of the system of control as introduced in 1941 were firstly to promote stability in the industry through a purposeful policy of rationalisation, and secondly to keep the price of bread as low as possible, thus placing the staple foodstuff within reach of the lower income groups. The subsidies allowed bread plants to develop their infrastructure on healthy margins and guaranteed volumes. Governmental control over the baking industry also covered licensing, contents, quality and price.

"you'll be back for more"

Role players in the baking industry

The major role players in the industry can be divided into plant bakeries (usually situated in industrial areas and fully automated with low labour) and independent bakeries, which compass many different forms of business, for example super-market bakeries. The South African milling industry, of which +/- 80% is con-trolled by three major players, namely Pioneer (Sasko and Bokomo), Tiger and Genfoods (BB Cereals and Premier Milling), was deregulated in 1996. These same companies also own their own bakeries, for example Sasko, supplying the major-ity of bread produced. However, prior to the milling industry deregulation, the baking industry was deregulated, in 1992, with major ramifications within that industry. The discontinuation of subsidies meant that macro bread plants faced enormous overhead and distribution costs, which inflated the price of the prod-uct. With deregulation the major role players entering the bread baking market were the supermarket chains, which started to bake a portion of the bread they sold. Initially, in-store supermarket bakeries competed price wise, because baking takes place within existing overhead structures; however, the in-store bakeries often could not afford experienced qualified bakers, and because of limited volume turnover, they could not guarantee hot bread any time of day. The advantages of bulk buying also escaped them. From 1996 however the number of independent bakeries increased, including the retail chains, as well as a variety of decentralised convenience stores, garage C stores, a variety of small individual bakeries and the two recognised bread baking franchise groups, AIB and Butterfield. The develop-ment of these independents all contributed to the number of plant bakeries reducing to less than 70 in July 2001. Graph 21.1 shows how the deregulation of the milling and baking industry over the span of a few years enabled the independent bakeries steadily to gain on the plant bakeries.

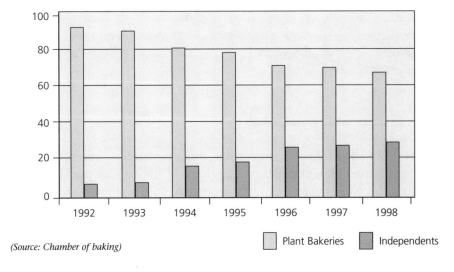

(Source: Chamber of baking)

Graph 21.1: Growth of the independent bakery sector since deregulation

The reduction of plant bakeries led to one single important fact and that is that in order for the plants to still compete in the same marketplace as the other role players, they had to adjust the specification, appearance and marketing channels of their product.

Market share within the bread industry

In 1999 it was estimated that a total of +/- 2,3 million tons of wheat was milled in South Africa, equating to 1,84 million tons of flour. Of this figure approximately 55% would have been consumed by the bread industry. Current bread production in South Africa is no less than 7 million loaves per day, of which approximately 30 to 35% is now produced by the independent bakery sector. This sector has grown from just 3% market share in 1993 to a present 35%. Indeed, in some metropolitan areas such as greater Durban, independent market share is estimated to be closer to 50% of the total market.

At present the bread industry wholesales its products to various sectors as detailed below, estimated wholesale turnover being +/- R10 billion per annum.

Category	1993 % Market share	1998 % Market share	2003 % Market share
Hypermarkets	3,5	5	5
Supermarkets	6	9	11
Superettes	1	2	4
Forecourt/Convenience store	1	3	10
Butterfield	0	2	6
AIB	0	2	4
General trade (urban)	35	22	15
General trade (township)	38	40	35
Catering/food service	3,5	6	9
Contract/tender (prisons/hospitals)	7	6	4
Industrial (mining)	5	3	2

Table 21.1: Market share within the bread industry

To date, apart from ad hoc discount structures, there has been no attempt to facilitate or recognise the different needs/requirements of the various market sectors within the industry. Most bakeries produce more than 95% of their product in two varieties (white and brown 700 gram sandwich loaves) and then deliver these products using their own brand names, and indeed delivery times, to various outlets. Different market sectors and/or customers'/consumers' requirements do not figure at all.

The larger part of all bread being produced by the independent bakery sector today has a net weight of less than 600 grams. Legislation was also introduced in 2000 to allow for the selling of lighter bread due to consumer demand. This has resulted in plant bakeries having no other choice but to move their production parameters in a direction where the bulk of the market exists and this very fact opens the gap wide for the supply of freshly baked bread and other baked goods, under a recognised national brand name, in conveniently located retail nodes. This is in essence the justification for the growth in the first four categories per the table above.

Dual market targeting – Butterfield

In Table 21.1, the top four categories service the retail market exclusively and the bottom five the wholesale market only. There is only one role player that has a very special strategic position in that it targets both. This bakery is Butterfield, whose business plan is devised around the fact that the market is moving towards convenience but also the fact that the larger part of the market is still being serviced by the wholesale-only baking industry.

In addition to offering customers convenience, Butterfield has also developed a unique product experience in the selling of its bread. Bakeries are designed and constructed in such a way that production takes place in full view of the customer base. The highest operational standards constitute the foundation of the concept of hourly, freshly baked, wholesome, affordable bread, offered through decentralised franchised bakeries. South Africa's burgeoning consumer market is changing rapidly in line with international trends. Worldwide there is a move towards the small convenience store away from traditional, impersonal bulk-buying outlets.

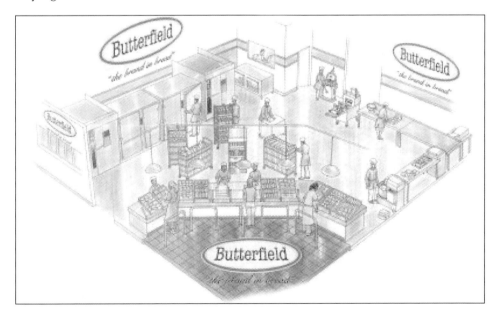

Product range

A factor in the company's growth is that its activities are centred on the staple and not a fad. Bread production itself is the core of the Butterfield product range, contributing 72% of turnover. The confectionery section that adds value to the brand is responsible for the rest of the 28% turnover. The bread range included traditional loaves in white, brown or whole-wheat, as well as a selection of health, rye and French loaves. The confectionery range includes croissants, Chelsea buns, scones, hot cross buns and doughnuts. Aimed at the lunchtime trade, vegetarian and ham-based pizza slices are also available.

Butterfield has also been able to compete with the wholesale-only baking industry through maintaining a broad consumer base. The consumer base as far as bread and other baked goods are concerned is very diversified due to the vast social and cultural differences that are so evident in the South African market. Butterfield had to differentiate in its concepts so that all segments of the consumer base can be targeted. It is for this reason that Butterfield offers a variety of bakery formats in order to cater for variations in the product, location, visual appeal, all tailored to the specific target market.

Target market

As much as 90% of Butterfield's customer base is made up of low-income commuters who do not have the time for breakfast at home. It is this market segment, made up of average wage earners, for which Butterfield primarily caters. Traditionally, Butterfield has catered for LSM 1–5.

	Population	Respondents	% Population
LSM 1	3 003 000	1 049	10,2
LSM 2	4 221 000	1 784	14,3
LSM 3	4 149 000	2 326	14,0
LSM 4	4 066 000	2 760	13,7
LSM 5	3 703 000	3 301	12,5
LSM 6	3 716 000	4 533	12,6
LSM 7	1 886 000	2 989	6,4
LSM 8	1 705 000	3 305	5,8
LSM 9	1 666 000	3 586	5,6
LSM 10	1 469 000	3 383	5,0

Source SAARF 2003B

Table 21.2: Population in each LSM group as in 2003

From the above graph, it is clear that the biggest market segment falls into the LSM 1–6 levels representing 77,3% of the population. It is thus in this market that Butterfield has established its brand.

The products are of excellent quality but with a low gross profit. High volumes need to be sold in order to make a profit.

Site selection

The selection of sites for the outlets is crucial to their success. The stores are located in high-density pedestrian commuter areas such as train stations, taxi ranks and industrial townships. Proof of Butterfield's good timing with the launch of this corner store concept in bakeries is the fact that since it was launched in 1997 with a pilot store in Pretoria, 102 bakeries have opened.

Butterfield needed to place its bakeries in high foot count areas to be profitable. These areas just happened to be close to taxi ranks and train stations.

Butterfield is now present in every major city and a number of towns in South Africa and new stores are currently opening up at a rate of three a month. Depending on the size of the store, a bakery can cost anything from R400 000 to R1 200 000 *(prices as per publication date)*. Of this amount, Butterfield insists that the interested party has to put down a third of the total cost in cash. Financing can be arranged for the balance.

Plant bakeries have always taken the bread to the people; Butterfield has taken the bakery to the people, thus ensuring that everybody can now take home freshly baked warm bread. Plant bakeries bake masses of bread at a central location and then deliver the loaves to cafés and quick-stop shops for the consumer to purchase there. Examples of these are Sasco, Blue Ribbon and Albany. To date virtually all Butterfield bakeries have been established on or near high density commuting pedestrian centres both in metropolitan and rural areas aimed at the economically active C and D income earnings consumer categories.

Butterfield outlets are located where the consumers are. This obviously involves understanding the consumer. The black working consumer generally does not eat breakfast at home but on the move – hence the correct placement of outlets near stations and taxi ranks. The biggest concern of a Butterfield bakery is that it cannot serve its clients quickly enough. It is not uncommon to see a queue extending, outside the shop and around the corner. The outlets already open are spread over the country and the table below indicates their locations.

Swaziland	Botswana	Northern Cape	Western Cape
Mbabane 1	Mogoditshane – Gaborone	Kimberley	Riversdal
Mbabane 2	Broadhurst – Gaborone	Kathu	
	Maru-a-Pula – Gaborone		
	Francistown		
	Jwaneng		

Eastern Cape	Kwazulu-Natal	North West	Free State
Port Elizabeth	Albert St Dbn	Mafikeng	Welkom
King William's Town	West St Dbn	Zeerust	Kroonstad
Uitenhage	Port Shepstone	Brits	Virginia
East London	Pinetown		Sasolburg
	Richards Bay		Parys
	Workshop Dbn		Klerksdorp
	Empangeni		Potchefstroom

Gauteng			Mpumalanga	Northern Province
Alberton	Hillbrow Jhb	Commissioner St	Ermelo	Potgietersrus
Anderson St Jhb	Metro Mall Jhb	Bree St	Bosbokrand	Thohoyandou
Bara City Soweto	Pretorius St Pta	Biccard St	Standerton	Pietersburg
Carletonville	Prinsloo St Pta	Roodepoort	Bethal	Sibasa
Cross Roads	Sebokeng	Randfontein	Bronkhorstspruit	Louis Trichardt
Dairy Mall Pta	Small Street Mall	Kempton Park	Kwagga Plaza	Tzaneen I
Daveyton	South Gate	Dunswart	Hazyview	Tzaneen II
DTI Campus Pta	Springs	Benoni CBD	Secunda	Giyani
Du Toit St Ptal	Tembisa	East Lynne	Marble Hall	Hammanskraal
Dube Soweto	Van der Walt St	Eersterus 1	Nelspruit	Phalaborwa
Fordsburg Jhb	Vanderbijl Park	Eersterus 2	Thulamahashe	Nylstroom
Gandhi Square	Vereeniging	Sunnyside	Jane Furse	Duiwelskloof
Jhb	Wynberg	Schoeman St		Hazyview
	Yeoville	Bosman St		

It is clear from the above that the outlets are widely spread over the country and some SADCC countries.

Butterfield formats
The conventional B480 and B240 bakeries
Since the introduction of the Butterfield concept to the retail industry, virtually all bakeries have been directed to the working, lower-income-class consumer. Bakeries are all situated in high-density commuter nodes and offer a range of products suited to the needs of its passing trade. The base product is bread but also on offer is a wide range of morning goods such as Chelsea buns, scones, raisin loaves, various rolls and other sweet confectionery that meets the needs of the market in which a specific bakery is located. These bakeries are equipped to bake up to 8 000 loaves per day and most of them also cater for a fair amount of whole-sale trade.

The B120 bakery

As far as visual appearance and product ranges are concerned, the B120 bakery is identical to the conventional B240 and B480 bakeries. The difference being that it is a much smaller bakery and its application will typically be where there is a need for a bakery in a remote location where the potential market is smaller than is the case with the larger bakeries. The B120 also has perfect application where a bakery may be erected inside an institution where a captured market exists as far as possible bread sales are concerned, e.g. large factories and mine canteens.

The B60 bakery

The most important and also obvious feature of the B60 bakery is that it is approximately half the size of the B120 bakery. This bakery will offer the full range of Butterfield confectionary products, as well as certain add-on products such as soft drinks. No bread will be baked in the B60 bakery. However, freshly baked bread supplied by the nearest Butterfield bakery, will also be offered as part of the range of goods.

Where the B120 bakery's market is to a large extent directed towards the low and middle-income groups of consumers, the B60 bakery's market may be focused towards the middle-to-high-income consumers. These bakeries will suit the medium to upmarket shopping centres. The B60 bakery will focus more on confectionary than on supplying bread as a basic consumer commodity. Confectionary generally has a higher profit margin than bread, a factor that will enhance this bakery format's profitability.

Success

The combination of capturing both the retail and the wholesale market, servicing a diverse consumer base, and ensuring maximum effectiveness in site selection has ensured Butterfield's success. Since 1997 Butterfield has grown from zero to 100 stores of which the majority are concentrated in Gauteng. Measured in terms of the investment that this represents in such a short space of time, this is an achievement that is probably unmatched by other South African franchise companies.

The group already boasts an investment of more than R50 million, a turnover exceeding R160 million per annum and flour consumption of 2 400 tons a month.

Over and above its achievements with regard to its bakery franchising, Butterfield has attained remarkable achievements in less than four years of existence.

Butterfield has, since its establishment, consistently won awards for the quality of its stands at exhibitions.

3 September '98	EXSA award at BIZ	Bronze award in Stand Excellence
4 September '98	International Franchise and Business opp. Expo	Most innovative stand award
19 October '98	FASA full member F98/0306	
26 March '99	International Franchise Expo	Most innovative stand award
9 July '99	KZN Franchise Expo	Best stand award
6 August '99	Cape Franchise Expo	Merit award for highly Commended stand
11 September '99	International Franchise Expo	Best large stand award
8 October '99	Institute of Marketing Management	Marketing award in recognition of outstanding achievement in marketing
26 October '99	FASA	Finalist for the award of excellence
26 October '99	FASA	Newcomer Franchisor of the year
24 March '00	International Franchise Expo	Winner Best stand award
16 October '00	FASA	Finalist – Franchisor of the year
11 October '01	FASA	Leading developer for emerging entrepreneurs
11 October '01	FASA	Finalist Franchisor of the year
19 October '01	IMM	Marketing organization of the year – Large Company
26 October '01	BIZ Expo	Best stand award
31 Augustus '02	BIZ Expo	Best stand award
30 September '02	FASA	Finalist – Franchisor of the year
30 September '02	FASA	Finalist – Leading developer for emerging entrepreneurs
30 September '02	FASA	Finalist – Brand Builder of the year
September '03	FASA	Finalist – Franchisor of the year
September '03	FASA	Winner – Leading developer of emerging entrepreneurs
May '04	International Franchise Expo	Winner Best stand award

Table 21.3: Butterfield list of awards

Future brand positioning

As one the few brands in South Africa that continues to grow through targeting lower-income customers, Butterfield has demonstrated that all customers, irrespective of income, seek value and the promise that brands offer. Targeting the low end of the market has shown that low-income customers also seek quality and service, but that convenience, satisfying their everyday needs and price are important drivers for their support.

Brand positioning to the lower-income market is rewarded when customers' needs are understood and their support is just as valued as that of higher-income customers. Future growth will be achieved through growth in distribution, product variety and customer retention. But more importantly, by offering a superior quality product recognised by all income groups in the market.

Above-the-line vs. below-the-line

Distribution is key to any commodity with low customer involvement. While a customer will travel and research extensively when buying a vehicle and even quality clothes, availability and convenience are the cornerstone for achieving volume with an everyday product like bread.

Therefore, although many brands are tempted to advertise above-the-line to reach larger audiences and to give prestige to a brand, advertising bread above-the-line can only be done when such distribution has been achieved. It is unlikely that most customers will ever travel to a specific outlet to buy a Butterfield product only (like they may do for quality clothes), therefore focus should be to understand how mediums can best be used to assist in distribution growth and to grow the brand either in-store or in very specific geographical areas.

Butterfield, through experience, realised that an effective marketing approach is not necessarily an above-the-line campaign to increase sales and growth. The below-the-line approach can also be successfully implemented through various activities such as promotions and point-of-sales materials in the stores e.g. loyalty cards etc. In addition to the above, it is important to understand the business processes; how staff interact with customers and the role that staff play in the customer experience of the brand.

In essence, the emphasis should be on bringing new customers to stores, but also on understanding the store experience so that staff and the company can deliver what the advertising promises the customers.

Expansion – Butterfield in Africa

Butterfield is expanding into Africa, as there are vast growth opportunities beyond South Africa's borders. A presence in Nigeria was established in 2002. It is envisaged that the outlets in Nigeria will be less directed at competing with existing bakeries. They will rather be aimed at the more upper-income consumers. The product mix will be aimed at a 50:50 spread between bread and confectionery products.

In neighbouring states the complete Ruto basic baking mix is sent to the bakery but in more distant destinations, only concentrate will be sent and locally milled flour will be used, under strict control. The concentrate is part of the success of the franchise and must be bought from the specified supplier, Ruto Mills.

Butterfield empowerment drives

First drive (Bakeries owned and operated by black individuals)

Over the last 24 months Butterfield Holdings has embarked on a conscious black empowerment drive in order to equip previously disadvantaged individuals with the business system, skills and hardware to work towards their own upliftment and to create their own wealth within an economically sustainable business environment.

The larger part of the target market of Butterfield is amongst the lower income groups and more specifically in rural areas where freshly baked goods are not as readily available as in the metropolitan areas. Taking this target market into consideration, Butterfield empowered its first historically disadvantaged franchisee in October 2000. By September 2002, 18% of its franchisees were from a previously disadvantaged background operating and owning bakeries in areas where they reside. By May 2003 this figure was exceeded 30%.

Large amounts of money were spent on the upgrading of training facilities and support systems in order to be able to develop the business skills of its franchisees to a level where they could take charge of their own sustainable businesses.

Butterfield Holdings is particularly proud of its black franchisees with regard to all aspects of implementing the business system and managing their businesses.

These bakeries were all set up and are competing in the retail trade environment. With the cooperation of governmental and parastatal institutions, enormously exciting empowerment opportunities can be unlocked through introducing the concept of institutional bakeries, which could be established through utilising the Butterfield business operating system.

Second Drive

There are many government, semi-government and private organizations that deal with and award bread supply contracts to various institutions and feeding schemes, e.g. prisons, hospitals and schools. These circumstances provide excellent opportunities for successful public-private partnerships between such organizations and Butterfield Holdings.

The current supply of bread to these institutions is predominantly done through plant bakeries in the vicinity of these institutions. The establishment of a bakery, operating through the Butterfield business system, in the midst of the community where these institutions are situated, creates a unique opportunity.

This will enable members of the community, by owning and operating this type of bakery and by contracting with the institution for the supply of bread, to create employment and wealth as well as furthering the process of transferring skills in the art of baking. This is a major step towards creating self-sufficiency and through the production and supply of various freshly baked goods to themselves, the standard of living is not only increased, but wealth is retained within the community.

The diagram below illustrates the interaction and the role of each of the partners in this enormously exciting empowerment opportunity

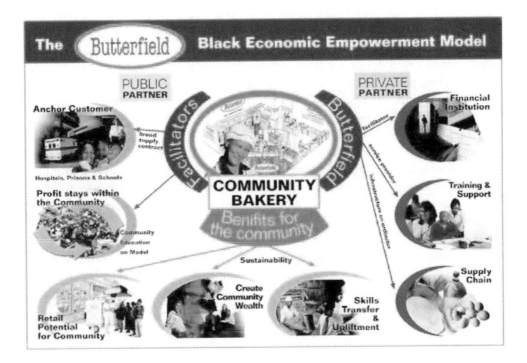

In conclusion it can be said that all the drivers in the Butterfield BEE model are directed firstly towards being most competitive in the bread baking industry and secondly to applying this business system towards creating sustainable black empowerment business opportunities.

Marketing

Marketing at Butterfield is threefold.

1   To sell bakeries

The majority of our bakeries have been sold through word-of-mouth. The first two bakeries were company-owned. Directors owned the next two, thereafter the Directors' friends and after that their family and friends.

The following corporate avenues promote the selling of new franchises:
- Exhibition Shows such as 'Biz' and 'International Franchise Exhibition'
- Editorials in various business magazines, e.g. *Start and Manage Your Own Business* and *Succeed Magazine*
- Advertising in various business magazines.

2   To improve the relationship between the holding company and the franchisees

The main objective of any marketing strategy in a company is not only to improve sales but also to improve profitability. Butterfield has adopted the principles from *Relationship marketing* by Ian Gordon. It was realised that it would be beneficial for the franchisees if the marketing department and the QCs (Quality Controllers) could develop a closer relationship with the franchisees. Butterfield has therefore prioritised the following goals:

- To manage customer profitability and to own the processes by which customer profitability is planned, delivered and improved. To this end, Butterfield has its own online business management system. The system has proved to be so effective that when properly administered, the shortage of even one loaf of bread or any quantity of raw material will be noticed immediately. Should a bakery's turnover not be as it should be, the marketing department will make an evaluation and help with point-of-sale material, wholesale, or assist in various promotions to improve the sales.
- To improve the favourability with which the franchisees see all aspects of the company, including its services, value creation, people and the brand.
- To increase communication Butterfield publishes a weekly newsletter on its website. The newsletter contains important information such as new products, marketing trends and changes in the industry to name but a few. Franchisees are encouraged to insert their own articles, ideas and suggestions in this newsletter. This streamlines the communication process and creates brand loyalty.
- To ensure that the Holdings Company is organized around its franchisees and to motivate franchisees to be actively involved in their bakeries, franchisees are taught from the beginning that they are in business for themselves and not by themselves. Franchisees know that the combined efforts of all personnel at Holdings and of themselves are of value to all.
- Performance measurement and reward systems reflect the importance of the relationship as an asset. A prize-giving at the end of each calendar year is the highlight for both the franchisor and the franchisee. Recognition in the following categories is granted: 'Brand builder of the year', 'Newcomer of the year', 'Franchisee of the year' and 'Most loaves baked'.

3   To lend assistance in marketing between the franchisee and customer (consumer)

Although stipulated in the original franchisee/franchisor contract, prior to 2000, no marketing royalties were collected. In 2000 a marketing fund was established. A National Marketing Committee was elected by the franchisees consisting of franchisees to represent the group. The committee has the following aims:

- To increase the amount that each individual customer spends per purchase (Rand per foot).

- To improve the mindset of the customer concerning the bakeries.
- To improve brand visibility and brand awareness.
- To motivate all franchisees to use the correct printed packaging, as this is the cheapest and most effective way of marketing and creating brand awareness.
- To attract new customers to the bakeries.
- To assist in the upkeep of customer satisfaction levels.

All of the above can be achieved by implementing the marketing principles (4Ps):
- **Price:** The aim of the business is not to undercut the prices of other bakeries in the areas Butterfield trades in, but to educate customers with regard to the quality and freshness of Butterfield products at a reasonable price.
- **Place/Distribution:** Ensuring that bakeries are placed strategically thereby guaranteeing availability. Where Butterfield has distribution channels in place it encourages the franchisees to deliver frequently and always to be on time.
- **Product:** Butterfield has always prided itself on selling quality products: great emphasis is placed on selling fresh products that look appetising to passers-by. A survey is done in all areas to establish which products the consumer would prefer in a particular area.
- **Promotions:** Through the newsletter, the *Breadline,* regular competitions or promotions are introduced. Promotional material is sent to all the bakeries to be handed out, e.g. calendars, rulers or posters.

In addition, Butterfield has a marketing department at head office which provides the following support:
- Assistance with any promotion or competition a franchisee would like to have on his/her own accord.
- Advice on local marketing initiatives.
- Assistance with artwork if franchisees wish to print their own.
- Supply of new ideas on improving turnover.
- Advice on retailing.
- Awareness creation when a bakery opens in a new area.
- Re-launches when a bakery is sold or taken over by new management.

Successful franchising

To establish Butterfield as a brand, management decided to go the franchise route. Franchising remains the best operational structure suited to the execution of the Butterfield business plan and brand-building programme. It is a fact that franchising is a convenient and marketable way of introducing a new concept to the public.

The advantage of the business format of franchising, as well as the positive sentiment of financial institutions toward small to medium enterprises, also favours the expansion of the concept. We now move towards the key areas explaining the specific factors contributing to the exceptional growth of Butterfield as business system and trade mark.

With experience gained through setting up their already successful King Pie franchises, the initiators of Butterfield have researched and formulated the fresh bread concept and successfully introduced it to the market through the pilot bakery in the central business district of Pretoria. Central to the success of the franchise is a total commitment to standards introduced and maintained by the franchisor. With the expert direction of franchisor management, every aspect of the Butterfield franchise operation has been tried, tested and proven, from the supply of raw material and the intricate production process, to the presentation and marketing of the brand.

Franchisor involvement

The most important duties of the franchisor can be described as follows:

1 Marketing and upholding the trade mark, through the application of funds accumulated by the marketing royalty.
2 Design of outlets to concept specification. Detailed specifications, in line with modern technology and trends, to meet all applicable requirements. This is what extensive research and experience in the fast food and bakery trade has revealed.
3 Defining and implementing the Butterfield business system into the franchisee's operation.
4 Continual back-up support in all areas of operations and administration.
5 Central negotiations with all relevant suppliers facilitated by bulk ordering.
6 Butterfield's flour suppliers contribute towards the maintenance of certain essential services for which the franchisee would have been liable. Currently, the group receives a contribution of 2,5% on all flour supplied by the official flour supplier/s. This contribution is used for the following:
   • A technical equipment maintenance team that is responsible for on-going preventative maintenance in all Butterfield Bakeries.
   • The subsidising of a labour consultant team that is responsible for all labour-related matters of the entire Butterfield group. Services include appointment and contractual issues, union negotiations, dismissal hearings, and CCMA representation.
   • Ongoing contribution towards various marketing-related expenses that are not covered by the official marketing fund of the group.
   • Maintenance and running expenses of the Butterfield training centre, not only for the initial training of new franchisees, but also for the periodic refresher and business management courses.

Butterfield Operational Control System (BOCS)

To ensure that the franchisee's profits are as high as possible, Butterfield developed an interactive website-based operational control system that assists the franchisee in controlling profits and making strategic decisions regarding his business. A team of skilled business consultants assists the franchisee in all aspects of his business through analysis, technical advice and ongoing training.

The Butterfield Operational Control System was specifically designed to control stock (raw materials vs. production output) and for the reconciliation of cash, stock, production and sales.

It is important to know that the movement or stock usage produced the required number of products, and that these products were actually sold, and if sold, that the correct amount of cash was processed through the cash register. Variations need to be analysed and verified daily.

The program also involved a basic accounting system, whereby the information contained on the bank statement can be entered in a cashbook. This information is then transferred to an income statement. From all this information a monthly VAT report is calculated as well as various other useful reports, e.g. monthly sales analysis, monthly management account, and a staff wage register, which calculates the exact wage a staff member should receive after all necessary deductions have been made.

The system is a discipline-based one, and requires the user (franchisee) to complete a specified daily routine every day. From this input useful management reports, such as financials, variance, stock and cash management, are generated.

Training: The National Skills Development Strategy

Because of the standardisation of Butterfield recipes and the simplification of ingredients, the skill required to become a baker is a matter of a three-day training process.

The Butterfield Group has taken very active steps to align itself with the Government's NSDS and is in the process of establishing the structures to throw its full weight behind the NSDS.

Butterfield currently has over 200 previously unemployed learners on the NQF2 Craft Baking of Fermented Goods Learnership and six previously unemployed Learners on the NQF Food Service Supervisory Management Learnership. The group has enrolled 30 currently employed learners on the Craft Baking Learnership. Butterfield is also busy aligning its Training Centre with the requirements of the FoodBev SETA and aims to have provisional accreditation as Training Provider by June 2004. The group is training several of its staff members as Assessors, Moderators, Skills Development Facilitators and Education Training and Development Practitioners.

Competition

Competition in the marketplace is anyone who sells bread including:
- Plant bakeries (Albany, Sasko).
- Self-baking shops (All shops with their own ovens).

- Fast food outlets (products for the lunch time trade also supplied).
- Supermarkets.

Bread is a commodity which is very difficult to brand. Butterfield has done the following to try and create brand loyalty:
- Created uniformity within the bakeries, including packaging and range of products.
- Concentrated on the service provided to all customers and promoted word of mouth.
- Ensured quality and freshness the whole day every day.
- Got involved in community projects.

Butterfield is not only branding a loaf of bread, but a concept and a mindset.

Suppliers

Being a franchise company, Butterfield is able to negotiate prices on a national basis as it can order in large volumes. Butterfield insists that franchisees use specified products that have been tried and tested to ensure uniformity and consistency.

Butterfield shares a distribution company with King Pie. This company serves as a one-stop shop selling everything from cleaning products to the raw material used, and also uniforms.

Flour is a crucial element in all products and Butterfield insists that all the bakeries only buy from one supplier, namely Ruto Mills. Sampling is done at the mills on a regular basis since baking is such a delicate process and inconsistency in flour will lead to inconsistency in the products.

Financial support

In the past it has been extremely difficult for previously disadvantaged persons to obtain loans for the purpose of starting a new business. Fortunately concerted efforts by government and other financing agencies are now starting to bear fruit. In the new, more favourable climate, Butterfield Holdings has been able to set up an infrastructure that will streamline the financing of loans for previously disadvantaged persons who wish to enter the bakery industry as independent bakers.

Conclusion

Butterfield has realised that it takes more than luck to make a business grow. It takes dedication, hard work and an understanding of the market you serve.

To succeed you need to concentrate on the basics first. This includes a great, reliable product, excellent customer service, teamwork and dedication from all involved.

The case study has demonstrated how a forward-thinking marketing strategy enabled Butterfield to grasp the opportunity of targeting both retail and wholesale markets. The careful monitoring of the franchising programme has permitted further expansion, while the investment in black empowerment and social development has further entrenched the Butterfield brand name in the South African landscape.

References

1   Information taken from the following sources:
     Butterfield website: www.butterfield.co.za
     South African Advertising and Research Foundation: www.saarf.co.za
     Online science magazine: www.scienceinafrica.co.za
     Butterfield prospectus.
     This case study was compiled by Yolanda Colesky of Butterfield Holdings (Pty) Ltd. Case study procured by Michael Cant.

MARKETING FEATURES:
CORPORATE CULTURE
CUSTOMER SERVICE
ENTREPRENEURSHIP
GROWTH
INNOVATION
PROMOTION
RELATIONSHIP MARKETING

22

Corporate Services

From small beginnings to continued success[1]

As with many successful business ventures, Corporate Services began as a good idea resulting from an actual business experience. Sandra Millar had spent a frustrating day looking for a company or shop that supplied a specific item. She had visited about ten outlets during that day, and none of them had the item in stock, nor could they tell her where she could perhaps obtain it. Although the day had proved fruitless, it did plant the idea in her head that perhaps she was not the only one who had had this experience and that there must surely be hundreds of customers like her. She thought that there could perhaps be an opportunity for someone to fill the need of supplying and procuring items, and she decided to investigate the possibility of establishing such a business.

This investigation proved difficult to do because Sandra was working at another job at the time. With perseverance and determination she informally researched her friends and business acquaintances as to the viability of the idea. The responses were positive, and coupled with her 'gut feeling' that the concept could be successful, Sandra decided to jump in and establish the company in May 1992. Her initial business vision was to find suppliers for users and users for suppliers.[2] Corporate Services actually started operating as commodity brokers! She had 500 business cards printed (there was no logo – only her name and a phone number) and by the next day she was in business and had begun tele-canvassing for customers.

The beginning

Although Sandra felt positive about trying to establish her business, she had to be careful because her resources were very limited. For example, her husband had to help her finance her first transaction by lending her R7 000 to buy an audio-visual machine, which she then sold to a technikon.[3] She worked from home initially and, as with many small businesses, she was the sole representative of her company. Sandra acknowledges that she was lucky to have two character traits that she considered essential to starting the business. The first was her determination and perseverance to be successful in establishing her business, and the second was her conviction that there was indeed a need for a trustworthy 'supplier'. Her previous business experience had given her the ability to plan well, and she was careful to begin on a small scale to establish some kind of successful track record. Another asset that Sandra had was an enquiring mind, which helped her to not only ask the right questions but overcome all the usual hurdles that a small business faces in trying to establish itself. She also emphasises the importance of good people skills, because if you cannot deal with people in a friendly and courteous manner, then you can neither meet your objectives nor satisfy their needs.

The following year was spent in establishing a track record for Corporate Services. Sandra began contacting potential suppliers and customers, slowly beginning to build up the database of contacts that is so vital in the type of business of which Corporate Services was part. The segments for products varied from the commonplace to the unusual. Sandra had segments from potential customers for 'common products' such as television sets, video cameras, blankets, and toilet paper. Her philosophy with regard to a customer request was to meet that request as soon as possible, to supply the correct product, and to make sure that everything was 100 per cent. As Sandra notes: 'When you start out small, you can't afford to mess up with even one customer, because the name of the game is to survive and establish your business and reputation. Customers give you one chance, often based only on your word that you can perform, and you have to make sure you do it right first time. These early customers have to be treasured, because they are the basis for any later success that you may have'.[4]

The more contacts Sandra built up, the better her business performed. She managed to source and meet requests for products as varied as:
- 2 000 bright orange raincoats for children
- 135 canvas laundry bags
- a quantity of empty gun cartridges for starting pistols
- 281 000 loops to be sewn onto 42 000 pairs of trousers.

There was even an unusual request for post-mortem chisels. In successfully carrying out all these requests, Sandra realised the importance of finding out specifically what was wanted. Customers know exactly what they want, and when they asked for bright orange raincoats, that was what they wanted, not yellow or black. This means that you need to know the customers' needs exactly in order to be able to meet them. In meeting these orders Sandra discovered that sometimes there are no suppliers who have the product in stock, so she had to manufacture or have manufactured some of the products sought by customers, such as raincoats and aluminium watering cans. During this first year she realised that she needed help to handle the increasing number of contacts and administration work that her growing business generated. This was especially crucial in terms of communicating with clients. She hired an administrative assistant to handle the administrative work, leaving her free to concentrate on the important task of generating new business and contacts.

Growth for Corporate Services

The customer database for Corporate Services had grown considerably, and Sandra felt that she needed to keep her customers aware of Corporate Services and its successes, but that she couldn't see them on an individual basis as often as she'd like. After careful consideration, she decided to launch a newsletter to her customers. This would have the twofold objective of keeping customers aware of Corporate Services and what it could do for them, as well as informing them of the growing and ongoing success that the company was achieving.

Excerpts from September 1994 newsletter[5]

We take the time to save you money by

- finding supplies
- obtaining quotes
- expediting deliveries
- handling installations

We will take care of all your ordering and buying.

Need goods or articles that are hard to find? We will find them for you. Need something to be custom built? We will have it made for you. Need supplies urgently? Give us a call.

No other company is more equipped than we are to save you as much money as possible, as quickly as possible.

Our clients include:

- The Medcorp Group (Johannesburg and Tanzania)
- SA Police
- Murray and Roberts
- Transvaal Education Department
- Department of Education and Training
- Waterkloof Primary School
- Alexander Technical College
- SA National Defence Force
- College of Education
- Techno Arms.

From the above, it can be seen that Corporate Services had carved out a customer base from the public sector, which is traditionally a very competitive arena and the focus of many major manufacturers competing for government tenders. Sandra says that she obtained business in this area by supplying commodities that were too small for large suppliers and too big for small suppliers. Corporate Services concentrates mainly on tenders below R75 000, and they have been quite successful because many big companies are not interested in small contracts. Corporate Services often visits state departments and other public bodies to hunt for tenders that are not widely publicised on account of the small amounts involved.[6]

Keeping the momentum going

Early in 1995 Sandra could look back on the typical cycle of ups and downs for a small business. On the positive side, Corporate Services had expanded its customer base by increasing its success with both local and foreign tenders, and had made inroads into and been awarded successful tenders by 'big' clients such as the SA Defence Force, Department of Correctional Services, Johannesburg City Council, and Telkom SA. Her growing success with Corporate Services had also begun to be noticed, because she had been nominated for the 'Businesswoman of the Year' award.

In reviewing the objectives for Corporate Services, Sandra had set specific goals for 1995. She wanted to continue providing excellent service to her existing client base – since they were the ones who had helped Corporate Services become successful. Sandra is a firm believer in the maxim that the only real assets of a business are its customers. A second goal was to widen the South African client base, and to be able to source more goods. This would entail better negotiation skills in order to be competitive with regard to price. Corporate Services could expand its export business, both through other countries and through international organizations. Sandra felt that the firm could make significant inroads into Africa.

These goals were the focus of activities during 1995. Sandra attended the United National Procurement Conference and received her suppliers' vendor number for the UN. Subsequently, tenders for stationery, office furniture, and convoy leaders' kits were favourably received. Efforts to establish contacts in Angola were rewarded with orders to supply a number of products to mining and geological exploration units. Corporate Services also became a member of SAFTO (South African Foreign Trade Association) and met numerous foreign trade delegations. The existing client base was expanded through the addition of a number of 'new' clients – that is, orders and contracts received from clients who were new to Corporate Services. A number of new products were also sourced, and Sandra used her existing client base as a market for these new products. In this way a number of contracts were negotiated and delivered. She also formed a strategic alliance with Mark Kuschke Commodities, who brought in engineering and technical expertise and helped broaden the total product base.

As a result of the increased business, new offices had to be built to handle the heavier workload.

Key success factors for Corporate Services

Corporate Services went from start-up to a turnover of three-and-a-half million rand in only four years. What were the key success factors identified by Sandra in her success? She identifies the following:

The people in the business

Corporate Services currently has six members, all of whom benefit from an employee equity programme and profit-sharing. Sandra believes in a team approach to projects, in order to make use of the synergies that exist between the members. The firm also believes in complete transparency, in that everyone is aware of the current level of profits and potential future profits. The close interaction between the employees ensures that there is good communication across different areas of responsibility and projects. Sandra also encourages training and the attendance of seminars or conferences, and expects those who attend these to come up with suggestions on how to implement the ideas they have heard or on ways to improve the business. There are numerous informal meetings and contacts, so that everyone is informed about what is happening in the business at all times.

Establishing a relationship with the customer

The starting point of the business was to identify potential clients and their needs. Sandra believes that the strategy of networking with both potential clients and suppliers has been vital in helping her meet her customers' needs. Although a number of contacts were established on a one-to-one basis, the nature of the business required much use of the telephone and fax to communicate. Sandra feels that one of her personal strengths is the ability to relate to people, and she had, in fact instituted her newsletter to clients in order to personalise the relationship between Corporate Services and its clients. The newsletter is still used to make clients and suppliers aware of things happening at Corporate Service, such as:

- their achievements
- new products and developments
- special events
- product launches.

Corporate Services sends out roughly 3 000 newsletters to everyone on its database every six weeks. Sandra finds that business has increased after each mailing, and clients often phone to thank them, comment on the contents and, most importantly, to order. The relationship built up is so strong that some customers no longer expect them to submit quotations prior to delivery – a compliment to the integrity and professionalism of the firm. This relationship extends to suppliers, and some of them even deliver orders that are too large for Corporate Services to handle, directly to customers.

Being goal-directed

The staff at Corporate Services are always aware of what the goals for the quarter are, and the performance relative to the goal. A typical set of goals would entail:

- Expanding the contact network.
- Increasing turnover by 50% p.a.
- Improving the price supplied to customers relative to competition.
- Broadening the customer base locally and internationally.

With the emphasis on goals, the effort and time spent by each staff member is directed at meeting these goals. With a small staff and limited resources, a small business cannot afford the luxury of wasting time and effort on activities that do not generate results. The regular informal meetings help the staff to discuss what successful strategies have worked and the networking often leads to identification of areas for follow-up and cross-reference.

Sandra Millar's achievements

- Finalist for 'Business Mover of the Year', 1995–1996
- 'Emergent Marketer of the Year', 1996
- National finalist for 'Marketer of the Year', 1996
- Coverage on national television: 'Your Own Business'
- Accredited trainer to Ntsika Enterprises
- Executive member of IMM (Institute of Marketing Management).

A new direction for Corporate Services

At the end of 2002, Corporate Services was planning to expand its commodity broking services; however, Sandra Millar began to realise that commodity broking was no longer sufficiently challenging and looked for a new avenue in which to invest her talents and energies. Aware of the poverty in the country, she decided to focus on raising funds for people and groups in need of assistance. Corporate Services now services five clients, including Tiqwa School (a school for intellectually disabled children), Cluny Farm (residential care for intellectually disabled adults), Living Link (a training centre to help intellectually disabled adults to be skilled and placed in appropriate employment positions), and The Pretoria Care for the Council of the Aged and Alzheimer's South Africa, which is a national organization.

All fundraising is carried out through approaching people and organizations for sponsorship of the clients, and not through events. Corporate Services mainly approaches big corporates, trusts, Government, the Lotto, and ordinary citizens.

Although Sandra Millar won many awards during the time in which Corporate Services was involved in commodity broking, she feels that the new direction that the company has taken is more personally fulfilling and it also makes a valuable contribution to South African society.

References

1   Case study written by Ricardo Machado.
2   *Corporate Services Newsletter*, June 1994.
3   Small contracts are big sense in commodities. *Business Report*, 4 August 1994.
4   *Corporate Services Newsletter*, September 1994.
5   Extract from *The Sowetan*, 21 November 1996.
6   Small contracts are big sense in commodities. *Business Report*, 4 August 1994.

23

MARKETING FEATURES:
CHANGE
COMMUNICATION
CORPORATE CULTURE
CUSTOMER SERVICE
DIVERSIFICATION

Rooth & Wessels – Since 1889

Background[1]

Rooth & Wessels was established on 12 July 1889, and is one of South Africa's oldest law firms. The firm has grown to become one of the larger and more prestigious law firms in the country. A trademark of the firm is the outstanding stability amongst its partners – over more than 100 years, the firm has had only seven senior partners (or CEOs).

The firm owes its establishment to Edward Rooth. He hailed from the Cape colony and journeyed to the Transvaal as a young boy with his father, when the latter, a land surveyor, was instructed by the Zuid Afrikaansche Republiek (ZAR) to survey and plan the town of Middelburg. After he qualified as an attorney in the Cape, he served his articles at the Riversdale firm of attorneys, Reitz, Versfeld & Rooth, where he later became a partner. When the first opportunity arose he returned to the Transvaal and founded a branch office for his firm in Pretoria. On 1 November 1887, the practice of E Rooth Attorneys was opened in Pretoria.

Two years later, in 1889, ML Wessels, also from the Cape, joined Edward Rooth and on 12 July 1889 their partnership was published in the *Provincial Gazette* as Rooth & Wessels. They practised in the Bank of the Netherlands on Church Square and for many decades the head office of Rooth & Wessels was situated on

Church Square. In 2003, all the different branches of the firm relocated to their own building in the suburb of Brooklyn.

At present, in 2004, the firm has 40 admitted attorneys, consisting of 15 directors, five associate directors, two associates, six professional assistants and three senior consultants. The firm also has eight candidate attorneys and an administrative staff of 119.

Major clients over the years include the Reserve Bank, Absa Bank, First National Bank, Aida, Pam Golding, DaimlerChrysler, Law Society of the Northern Provinces, Law Society of South Africa, Eskom, Unisa, Old Mutual, SA Post Office, South African Mint Company, University of Pretoria, Standard Bank, Nedcor, Health Professions Council of South Africa, Mutual & Federal, ABI (Coke), FOSKOR and the CSIR.

Adapting to a changing environment

Today, the legal environment in South Africa is changing rapidly and transformation and restructuring are on everyone's minds. In the new democratic South Africa, the emphasis is on providing easy and equal access to the law for everyone. The dynamism that drives Rooth & Wessels is reflected in their mission statement:

> Rooth & Wessels strives to become an even better practice for its new and existing clients in the new South Africa; to think creatively and innovatively; and to offer a successful and gratifying career to all its staff.

In order to expand the property law department, and to devise a marketing strategy, Rooth & Wessels conducted a SWOT analysis in the 1990s.

SWOT analysis

The SWOT analysis was a useful instrument for helping Rooth & Wessels to identify its internal strengths and weaknesses and external opportunities and threats facing it. SWOT is an acronym: S = Strengths, W = Weaknesses, O = Opportunities, T = Threats. A SWOT analysis is based on the assumption that an effective strategy maximises a business's strengths and opportunities and minimises its weaknesses and threats. Strengths should be matched to opportunities and threats should be seen as challenges. The main aim is therefore to identify those critical factors that can have a major effect on the business. It should then build on vital strengths, correct obvious weaknesses, exploit significant opportunities and avoid potentially disastrous threats.[2]

A SWOT analysis thus aims to shed light on those environmental variables that in some way either have a positive or negative impact on the success of a business. The Rooth & Wessels SWOT analysis focused in particular on conveyancing, which was in a depression at the time, due to extremely high interest rates, the free fall in the value of the Rand, emigration and severe job losses as a result of restructuring and affirmative action.

Strengths

In their SWOT analysis, Rooth & Wessels identified various strengths of the firm, and these included the following in particular.

Good reputation and honesty

Rooth & Wessels has always been known as a firm of integrity and honesty, a firm with expert legal knowledge capable of providing cutting-edge thinking.

Appointment on the panel of most banking institutions

Rooth & Wessels obtains instructions from a variety of banks to register mortgage bonds on their behalf. This is an advantage, as many estate agents prefer that the same attorney deals with the transfer and bond in order to ensure the expediting of the registration process. This obviously equates to more income being generated.

Location in the community that Rooth & Wessels serves

The new location in Brooklyn is a strength of the firm. Location is critical to any conveyancing practice dealing with local transfers as both the estate agent and clients need easy access to the attorney with safe and convenient parking. It is also critical to be in close proximity to estate agents and bankers.

Skills and experience of professional staff

The professional staff at Rooth & Wessels have a distinct advantage in that they have access to the knowledge and experience of senior colleagues, in the same and associated disciplines. It makes a good impression to the client if you have access to an expert by merely picking up the telephone.

Good support systems

There is good cooperation between the directors. The IT system at the time was adequate and functional, although not state-of-the-art. This has since been addressed and rectified. The firm has an internal network, utilising, among others, e-mail. Communication is efficient and the delivering of documents internally and to clients is thus expedited. Scanners and voice recognition software are also used by the professional staff and Rooth & Wessels is electronically linked to the major banking institutions in order to receive their instructions via the Internet. The latest conveyancing support programmes, including SMS managing via the cellphone have been introduced.

Weaknesses

The weaknesses identified in the SWOT analysis included the following:

Turn around time (in conveyancing)

The turn around time was not as fast as the market leader, from a conveyancing perspective. The Rooth & Wessels process times were slower than those of the market leader. Clients and estate agents are more inclined to refer work to those attorneys getting the transfers registered in the quickest period of time.

Decision-making process

The size of the firm caused problems in decision-making processes. This had always been cumbersome, particularly when a decision was required to embark on a marketing drive from a conveyancing perspective. In many instances opportunities were lost because Rooth & Wessels could not react fast enough to secure the opportunity.

High operational costs

Rooth & Wessels is at a disadvantage with regard to high operational costs. Conveyancing in particular requires high overheads – it is people-driven and requires highly skilled secretaries with the accompanying high salary cost and cost of multiple work stations. This has a substantial impact on bottom-line profit vis-à-vis other branches of the law.

Personnel do not function at full capacity

There was not sufficient incoming work to keep the staff fully occupied (during the 1990s).

Market exposure

This relates to marketing. At the time the minimum was expended on marketing. Rooth & Wessels had to make do with hand-outs they prepared themselves and delivering biscuits while their competitors were offering game safaris. The firm was also not visible enough in the market, that is, Rooth & Wessels was not the name that was thought of first as, for example, conveyancers, in the eyes of the market.

Lack of developers as clients

Residential and office developers as clients can result in a sustainable stream of incoming conveyancing instructions. Rooth & Wessels is still lacking in this department.

Internal communication with staff

Communication with staff was a major weakness. The staff were not adequately informed of new developments. Internal marketing therefore had to become part of the new strategy. In this regard several committees were established to improve the communication between the professional and non-professional staff. Representatives were elected by the staff to facilitate communication and also to address grievances and problem areas.

Training of staff
This was a problem, and recently a committee was established to attend to the training of professional and non-professional staff.

Empowerment
The lack of an empowerment charter in the legal profession was identified as an obvious weakness.

Opportunities
During the SWOT analysis, opportunities to be utilised in the market were identified and included the following:

New sectional title developments
At the time Pretoria, and in particular Centurion, experienced a number of new sectional title developments. None of the Centurion attorneys were, however, privy to those instructions (and none of them has ever been). The developers at the time seemed to favour attorneys based in Johannesburg or certain niche firms in Pretoria.

Lower interest rates
The dramatic drop in the interest rates, which contributed to the buoyant property market, provided an opportunity to expand the conveyancing and property law department.

Focus on the public at large as a source of transfer instructions
In a conveyancing market, numerous transactions are concluded without the intervention of an estate agent. The penetration of the private sale market has the potential to bring in new sources of income. Rooth & Wessels met this challenge and the firm now obtains a substantial portion of income from that source.

Cross-pollination
This refers to the opportunity of cross selling services of other departments of Rooth & Wessels to the client when he attends to sign his documents. In this manner a number of wills, ante nuptial contracts and other work has been generated.

The capacity to deliver a one-stop service
As Rooth & Wessels are on the panel of most of the banks, they can provide the total spectrum of property-related legal services under one roof. Clients in most

instances only need to attend a single consultation to conclude all their business dealings, which is highly valued by the client.

Threats
Capturing of the market by less than ethical attorneys
A number of estate agents give preference in support to those attorneys who provide them with additional incentives. It is an economic reality which Rooth & Wessels will not partake in and they have to accept that they are at a disadvantage in this regard.

Exponential increase in the number of admitted attorneys
The property market does not really expand all that much every year, but the number of attorneys competing for a slice of the cake, does. The number of one-man operations entering the market on a continual basis is a cause for concern. As it is a highly competitive market, the only way to survive in the short term is to pay incentives for work.

Escalating operation costs without a real increase in the fee guidelines
Conveyancing is still largely subject to a prescribed fee structure, albeit that it is nowadays referred to as a recommended tariff. The tariff, unfortunately, is not adjusted as regularly as one would like, with the effect that the ever rising costs bite into profit margins. However, an increase in the tariff in the first quarter of 2000 was given.

Public perception of attorneys
Attorneys have a negative market image. They are in many instances regarded by the public as being dishonest and very expensive. This is a misconception since, although a client may be confronted by an account in excess of R20 000 for a conveyancing transaction, the client does not realise that it is not the attorney fees which constitute the bulk of the expense. Rather, the fact of the matter is that the conveyancer is merely a collection agent for either the Revenue Services (transfer duties) or rates and taxes levied by the local authority. Thus direct and indirect taxes or disbursements account for most of the monies charged.

Prescribed tariff is not in step with rising costs
It is an economic reality that operating costs continually rise although the tariff is only adjusted every once in a while. The tariff could remain unchanged for a number of years while rising costs erode bottom-line profit.

Customer relationship management at Rooth & Wessels

In 2004, a research investigation into customer relationship management (CRM), as practised by law firms in Gauteng, revealed many shortcomings with regard to relationships with clients (customers).[3] In terms of CRM, firms should focus on attracting, maintaining and enhancing customer relationships, and when necessary, terminate relationships with unprofitable customers. After studying this report, Rooth & Wessels concluded that the following findings in particular impacted on their firm.

Role of leadership in CRM

The implementation of CRM strategy may have an impact on the culture of the firm.[4] Leadership, and especially the development of a customer leader, can impact on and change the corporate culture towards that of a customer orientation. Support at executive level is thus essential if CRM is to succeed. The directors need to assume a much more active role in changing the whole culture of the firm to become customer-centred, in order for CRM to become one of the core values of Rooth & Wessels.

Managing customer relationships

Management needs to recognise the fact that the relationship with customers needs to be managed. A relationship manager/supervisor should work with customers to ensure that they receive the value they seek.

Lifetime value of customers

It is essential to look at customer profitability, in order to establish the lifetime value of customers. Lifetime value describes the present value of the stream of future profits expected over the customer's lifetime purchases. The purpose of this is to establish from which companies and customers the firm derives its profit. All costs should be allocated to customers, including marketing, customer service and support and other costs not always attributed to specific customers. This is the cost involved in serving the customer. Rooth & Wessels needs to develop a well-informed financial view of its customer base. This might reveal that a relatively small number of customers account for the majority of their profits.

Adapt processes

Rooth & Wessels keeps strictly to functional areas with no interaction with or dependency on other functions of the firm. If CRM is to be successful, functional silos need to be eliminated so that all processes can be linked, thus enhancing cross-functional teams. All processes should be engineered around the customer; customers should be built into the main processes and should collaborate with management in all the processes that are geared to creating value. This will facilitate tailoring product/service to customer needs.

Customer database

A customer database is at the heart of CRM. Every time a customer comes into contact with any person at Rooth & Wessels, information should be captured.

These data are collected by the contact centre and organized into a data warehouse. Company personnel can then capture, query and analyse the data. Inferences can subsequently be drawn about an individual customer's needs and responses. In this way, a unified view of the customer is achieved, which enables any employee to access all information pertinent to a client, from their contact history to their service record and credit rating.

Customer retention

Rooth & Wessels has spent a great deal of effort seeking new customers, yet has seldom taken equal trouble to retain existing customers. There is a very real and demonstrable relationship between customer retention and profitability.[5] It is thus vital to regularly measure customer satisfaction in a systematic way, so that corrective measures can be taken. What is equally important is to investigate customer migration, upward and downward, before it leads to defection.

Customer service

Excellent service is an integral part of CRM. No company can even contemplate implementing CRM if it does not offer excellent customer service. All Rooth & Wessels staff should thus be trained in rendering excellent service, even those who do not have direct contact with the customer. This could be a mammoth task and might require the services of an external consultant, because it is not easy to establish a service culture in any organization.

In 2004, Rooth & Wessels commissioned an independent consultant to conduct a survey among its established clients in order to ascertain their perceptions of the service rendered by the firm. The findings made by the consultant have provided valuable insight into the perceptions and experiences which the clients had of the firm over the whole spectrum of services rendered by the firm. Remedial action included restructuring of the conveyancing department, while departmental heads were tasked to improve the performance of their departments and individual debit points particularly insofar as client service and satisfaction were concerned. Teams were sent out to meet with those clients who had had negative experiences with the firm's service levels in order to promote personal contact and explain the changes which had been implemented. Customer satisfaction is being monitored on an ongoing basis.

Selecting a CRM technology

Acquiring a suitable CRM software system is usually a large investment. Integrating multiple customer interaction channels with customer service operations, existing business applications, and external business suppliers can be complex, time-consuming and expensive. To have the required knowledge about a customer, Rooth & Wessels thus needs an infrastructure of technology that captures, stores and processes data needed to derive customer knowledge, and an architecture of the technology that places customer data at its strategic heart.

However, it is important to bear in mind that acquiring CRM software is probably one of the last steps in implementing CRM in the firm. Rooth & Wessels has come to recognise the fact that technology would not solve any problems or improve customer service; these should first be solved, then a system can be purchased.

Employees

The idea of CRM needs to be 'sold' to the entire organization, in particular the employees. All employees need to be trained in aspects such as customer service, and how to use the CRM technology. Customer service level standards need to be set and all staff should be informed of these service level standards, and how customer satisfaction should be monitored. Employees also need to be empowered to manage their own activities and to solve certain customer problems. Rooth & Wessels needs to pay particular attention to internal marketing which includes internal communication to motivate staff to 'come on board' the CRM programme.

Empowerment – Anticipating change

The organized legal profession is currently preparing an empowerment charter. In the absence of this charter Rooth & Wessels prepared its own empowerment charter and agreed on the setting of target dates for the implementation of its principles. All the decision-makers at the firm have approved the charter and have resolved to ensure that the charter is implemented by the target dates.

'Every effort will be made to ensure that we become the leading empowerment firm of its size in the Tshwane area,' says current CEO Roland Brink. 'Once this has been achieved, many opportunities to expand our client base will arise. The implementation and expansion of the firm's empowerment charter will also meet the criteria of the empowerment charters which have been or will be adopted by our clients. This will obviously make it easier for our clients to continue supporting our firm.'

References

1   Case study written by Kobus Blignaut, director of Rooth & Wessels, and updated by Roland Brink, current CEO. Case study procured by Annekie Brink.
2   Strydom, JW (ed). 1999. *Introduction to marketing*. Kenwyn: Juta.
3   Brink, A & Gerber-Nel, C. 2004. Research report: Customer relationship management as practised by law firms in Gauteng.
4   Brink, A & Berndt, A. 2004. *Customer relationship management and customer service*. Lansdowne: Juta, p 192.
5   Brink & Berndt, op. cit., p 34.

Ocean Basket

Your seafood house[1]

The first Ocean Basket opened in April 1995, in the Menlyn Park Shopping Centre in Pretoria. Today there are over 60 outlets country-wide and international development of the brand has just begun, with two Master Licence agreements signed. From an initial capital investment of R120 000, the company today has a capital base of over R30 million and over 500 000 customers visit Ocean Basket restaurants monthly.

Changing the industry

Traditionally, the sale of cooked fish products had fallen into the following two categories:
- The traditional fish & chips shop catering to the fast-food lower-income market.
- The fine dining gourmet experience catering to the sit-down top end of the market.

In early 1992, Nick Georgiolakis started serving cooked meals from his retail outlet, called Fishmonger, in Grayston in Johannesburg. He offered a very limited menu, confined to fish, at very reasonable prices. To keep his costs low, he served the food in pans and offered no complimentary or additional items such as bread. The idea was to offer what had previously been considered a very expensive meal (e.g. line fish, prawns, lobsters) at very affordable prices in a relaxed, casual atmosphere. This proved to be an overnight success and people queued for hours to get a seat.

George Nichas (who had originally helped Nick Georgiolakis establish his Fishmonger), a friend 'Fats' Lazarides, and his brother, George Lazarides, decided to emulate the concept and open Ocean Basket in Pretoria. A site was found in Menlyn shopping centre and the combination of good value, limited menu items, and exclusively fish products, proved to be as successful in Pretoria as the Fishmonger was in Johannesburg.

Demand to open in other areas and enquiries for franchises, led to the three original founders of Ocean Basket enlisting the help of a fourth member to expand the group.

Strategy for growth

When determining the strategy for growth, several key decisions were made that later led to Ocean Basket establishing its leadership in the market.

Expansion through joint ventures

It was decided to effect growth through joint ventures rather than through franchising, mainly because Ocean Basket did not have the expertise or infrastructure to support franchisees. It was therefore decided to copy Nando's success and expand through joint ventures in terms of which Ocean Basket provided the lease, knowledge and product, while the joint-venture partner provided limited capital and labour.

Locate outlets in high-traffic areas

As there were no funds for marketing, and because Ocean Basket believed that the market would soon be full of copy-cat concepts, it was decided that all restaurants had to be located in high-traffic areas for visibility and to assist in establishing brand awareness, as well as to ensure that even when the novelty of the concept wore off, customers would still 'fall' into Ocean Basket stores.

Limited menu

It was decided to keep the menu limited in terms of variety and to have a simple cooking process and taste. The limited menu allowed for more efficient stock control and production that lead to lower stock losses and better control over product quality. The simple cooking process meant that no special skills needed to be taught to the staff and the simple taste allowed customers to eat regularly at an Ocean Basket without getting that 'tired of all the rich food' feeling.

Central buying

Management decided that all fish would be bought centrally and distributed by head office, because fish is a hunted product, so price and availability fluctuate regularly. It was also important to retain control over quality. This gave management the ability to utilise their buying power and to minimise price fluctuations. These four key decisions led to rapid expansion of the group. It grew from one company store and one franchise outlet in April 1996, when the strategy was adopted, to market leadership with 20 company and 10 franchise stores two years later.

Setting the standards

Expanding through joint ventures enabled the management of Ocean Basket to learn and develop operating standards and procedures as the business grew. They soon learnt about the operating standards called QSCV – quality, service, cleanliness, and value.

Quality

Ocean Basket believes that quality, that is, the state of the product, its freshness and taste must never be compromised. They would rather lose the sale than serve an inferior product. They firmly believe that this philosophy will expand their customer base over time.

Service

In an industry where your product is mainly indistinguishable from that of your competitors, it is service that sets you apart. As more and more copy-cat concepts appear on the scene and other restaurants expand their fish selection, it is only the Ocean Basket commitment to higher levels of service that will allow them to maintain market leadership. That commitment requires large investments in training, particularly in South Africa where waitering and managing a restaurant are not seen as professions but rather as 'fill-in employment' until the next job, or 'pocket money' while studying. The Ocean Basket management endeavour to encourage a culture of professionalism in their industry and teach their waiters that their allotment of tables is in fact a micro-enterprise that they own and control for the day.

Cleanliness

Cleanliness is a never-ending issue in the food industry and particularly with fish where it is incorrectly perceived as a 'dangerous food', that is, food that must be refrigerated at all times. Proper food handling procedures are taught to all the staff at all levels.

Value

Value is the elusive perception that differentiates one store from the other. It is a combination of price, service and ambience, and starts even before the customer enters the store. It is the most difficult concept to understand but it is ultimately the result of complying with all the rules, regulations, and procedures developed over time.

Operations

Sites identified as 'prime' or 'flagship' are developed as Franchise stores. Location criteria are regional shopping centres or entertainment venues with due regard to visibility and proximity to offices and residential areas. In smaller towns the rule of the above criteria can be negated as stand-alone sites have, in the experience of Ocean Basket, proven to be very successful when intelligently situated.

- Store size ranges from 200 to 250 square metres with outside seating.
- Set-up costs are approximately R1,5 million.
- Average turnover exceeds R300 000 per month.
- A staff of 18 is needed to operate each store.
- Rental is 6-9% of turnover.
- Gross profit is 60%.
- Target net profit before income tax is 20%.
- Gross profit cannot be guaranteed.

Serving the customer

To enhance the casual, relaxed atmosphere that Ocean Basket aims to project, management will not accept bookings during the busy periods. They try to design their stores to open onto a busy mall or path so that 'see and be seen' becomes part of the eating experience. They also encourage their staff to be loud and dramatic when interacting with one another. They strive to please as many guests as possible but they do teach their staff that you cannot be everything to all customers and that they will not expend effort and time trying to meet unreasonable demands.

The Ocean Basket concept originated with retail sales of fresh fish equal to restaurant sales. However, the retail section has deteriorated to the extent where it no longer exists in most shops. But it has left a legacy of the daily display of fresh fish and this Ocean Basket believes, enhances the customers' perception of the freshness of their products. Retail is an area they are endeavouring to understand and revive in their shops. The potential benefits are huge, given the marginal costs incurred to sell fresh fish from the existing shops. This will, however, also bring new competitors into play.

Marketing

The management of Ocean Basket learnt over time that the best marketing is by word-of-mouth and the queues that formed outside their restaurants. They deliberately kept their shop seating areas small so that there would be queues outside the restaurant most evenings. These queues attracted interest and drew many customers into their shops.

'When we reached the stage that we could afford to do formal marketing, we took a view that we would concentrate on creating brand awareness and never discount our product which is in effect discounting the brand. We also took a strong view on never making a promise that we could not guarantee would be kept', they say. Instead, they try to communicate an attitude and lifestyle that appeals to their customers and they promise them an overall experience rather than making specific promises such as 'lower price, more comfortable chairs, broader smiles'. They maintain that 'Our view on the recent rush towards loyalty programmes is that no loyalty programme can match the satisfaction that a customer feels when he/she is recognised by the staff and management and his/her personal preferences are remembered'. Management has the discretion to reward customers for their loyalty with drinks and the occasional meal on the house.

Moving to controlled franchising

Now that the management of Ocean Basket has acquired the knowledge and developed the infrastructure, expansion will be through the sale of franchises and master licences, that is, the right to open shops for own operation. Company-owned shops still form part of their strategy as these provide the critical function of keeping Ocean Basket, as the franchisor, in touch with the franchisee's perspective of the business. They also allow management to develop yardsticks by which the performance of franchisees can be measured.

The company currently (in 2004) owns two stores while the balance of the stores are all franchised. Manny Nichas, operations manager of Ocean Basket says that 'Over the years we have learnt that there is no better operator of a business than the person who invested his or her money and has a personal interest in his or her business. The decision to sell off the company-owned stores, 32 of them three years ago in 2001, was a critical decision for the success and growth of the brand. We have an infrastructure that is geared to monitor and control the standards within the stores in quite a unique way. We firmly believe that we are business partners with all our franchisees and it is critical that we operate in that fashion. We are not policemen or inspectors that check a store once every few weeks; we get physically involved regularly with each store and assist in the growth of each individual franchisee.'

Threats and opportunities in the marketing environment

Externally the supply of fish is Ocean Basket's biggest threat. Over-fishing and the plundering of this natural resource can and will make certain products unavailable. Fish farming is still in its infancy and needs many years before it will form a significant and stable source of supply.

Until very recently, the international market for fish restaurants was exactly like the South African market when Ocean Basket started, namely that only the upper end and lower end of the market were being serviced. Ocean Basket believes that although there is some movement to try to service the middle market, a great opportunity exists for Ocean Basket to fill that gap and introduce its concept internationally. Also, the consumption of fish is growing worldwide and as more people learn the benefits of healthy eating, and red-meat scares, such as foot-and-mouth and Mad Cow disease, turn people away from meat, Ocean Basket's potential market continues to expand. The restriction to only fish products on the menu makes Ocean Basket an easy and natural brand to comply with the Halal requirements of the Muslim community, a community whose needs have been undercatered for and whose economic power is rapidly expanding.

The future

Ocean Basket has been sailing the high seas of seafood fare for the past eight years. The company has provided millions of customers with its famous fish, fantastic service and friendly atmosphere. For the years to come Ocean Basket plans on sailing even further, both locally and internationally, with plans to open more international stores being finalised now.

The new look of Ocean Basket comprises new pastel colours, being blues, greens and creams with its distinctive wooden railing demarcating the dining area. The company has also brought in a fresh new training programme for both the waiters and kitchen staff to ensure that not only is the seafood the highest quality, but that the standard of service is maintained and improved. Regular customers will find that the 'fish in the pan' concept has been retained, portions sizes are the same, and the fish is as fresh as ever.

Ocean Basket has identified its two main assets as its people and its brand, recognising that it is its people who determine the brand's value. This means that the way to continued expansion is through developing its people by helping them realise their full potential and giving them the opportunity to grow within the group.

References

1   This case is based on information supplied by Ocean Basket, and updated by Manny Nichas, Operations Manager. Case study procured by Annekie Brink.

25

MARKETING FEATURES:

COMMUNICATION
DISTRIBUTION
ENVIRONMENT
INTEGRATED MARKETING
MARKETING STRATEGY
MISSION
PROMOTION
QUALITY

Envirogreen

Background

In 1991 the South African government introduced legislation to compel organizations to rehabilitate sites which are ecologically disturbed by mining, industrial, and other activities. An abstract of the Minerals Act, 1991 (Act 50 of 1991), section 12, reads as follows: 'On the lapse, cessation or abandonment of operations, the mining/prospecting permit holder remains liable for environmental issues on site, until issued with a certificate releasing him or her of such responsibility.'

This Act prompted Lambert van der Nest and Gerard Heydenrych, two men with vision and an entrepreneurial spirit, to form a new company, Heydenrych & Van der Nest (Pty) Ltd, in 1993. Heydenrych & Van der Nest's main goal was to assist mines, industry and relevant government departments with rehabilitation solutions. By 1997, Heydenrych & Van der Nest (Pty) Ltd had become the rehabilitation market leader in southern Africa. Management decided to enter the international market if opportunities arise. The more globally accepted name of Envirogreen was adopted to brand the name over international and cultural boundaries.[1]

Envirogreen's major customers include both small and large mining and industrial companies with interests around the globe, as well as governments. Its core business is to provide innovative holistic solutions in terms of mine closure, rehabilitation, and remediation of ecologically disturbed sites. The company's unique structure also strengthens its ability to deliver world-class integrated solutions in all major mining centres of the world. This is encapsulated in Envirogreen's vision and mission, as described below.

Envirogreen's vision and mission

The vision
Envirogreen's vision is an employee-owned dream based on shared experience that inspires and motivates every member of the Envirogreen team to consistently aspire to new levels of achievement. The vision of a company includes daring and far-sightedness about the direction of a company, as well as what the company should do to get there. Envirogreen's vision is: Greening the world's waste and tailings.[2]

The mission
A company's mission, on the other hand, embodies the reason for the existence of a company in terms of the nature and extent of present and future company activities. Aspects that should be described in a mission statement include the product range or service of the company, the market, the management philosophy, the company image, and the technology used by the company.[3]

> Envirogreen's mission is to add value through professional, innovative, cost-effective, and scientifically based environmental solutions. Furthermore, Envirogreen uses their multidisciplinary team to apply scientific and engineering skills to solve environmental rehabilitation problems in the most cost-effective and technically sound manner.[4]

Envirogreen's shared value system is an integral part of the culture of Envirogreen. This is a crucial factor in ensuring an aligned commitment within the company. Envirogreen believes that by increasing its market share and influence, it offers itself the opportunity of controlling the destiny of the environment industry and thereby its own destiny. The company plans to achieve this through its service reliability, added value, innovative approach through products, as well as its marketing strategy.

Marketing strategy

A marketing strategy consists of a company's target market as well as the company's marketing mix.[5] A target market is the specific group of customers at which a company aims its products and services. The target market is determined by the process of segmentation and the marketing mix specifies how the target market will be served. Using this definition as background, the target market of Envirogreen is discussed below.

Target market

Envirogreen defines its target market as follows: 'Our target market ranges from the smallest to the largest mining and industrial companies, as well as governments in the world.' Many governments have the responsibility to rehabilitate and close mining sites. Good examples in South Africa are the abandoned and derelict ownerless asbestos mines in the Northern Cape, which are being rehabilitated by the South African government.

Markets that are targeted are those that are attractive and best match Envirogreen's objectives and resources. The company selects its target market on very specialised criteria. These criteria include the rehabilitation of sites that, for example, need specialised and holistic solutions. The nature of this work is very complex and cannot be addressed by an individual. These solutions, therefore, require input from a wide range of expertise, namely civil engineering, ecology, soil science, hydrology, etc. A recent example would be the gold mine industry, where a specialised and holistic solution is needed for the rehabilitation of the gold slimes dams, such as the Hartebeestfontein No 7 slimes dam of Durban Roodepoort Deep.[6]

Envirogreen's client approach

The quality of the unique and world-class environmental rehabilitation services Envirogreen renders to its customers is defined by their expectations. At Envirogreen outstanding customer service means [...] carefully listening to and responding to [customers'] needs, aspirations, and concerns every step of the way. By placing the customers at the very centre of its organization's philosophy Envirogreen ensures that every member of its team continuously strives toward optimal customer satisfaction. At Envirogreen they continuously evaluate every process, every task, and every decision by asking: 'How will this add to our customer's value?' The company dictum is that there is no minimum at the outset and no maximum at the conclusion.[7]

Marketing mix

A company's marketing mix defines the company's product or service offerings, the price and distribution of these product or service offerings and, finally, how the company will communicate the product or service offerings to its target market. Envirogreen's marketing mix includes the following:

Product or service strategy

The product strategy of Envirogreen is to assure its customers of the highest quality, by providing them with innovative and sustainable environmental rehabilitation solutions. Specific products that are offered to Envirogreen's different market segments include vegetating and/or rehabilitation of gold slime dams, such as Crown Mines in Johannesburg. The rehabilitation of the gold slimes dam was started in 1997 and is an ongoing process. Another product which the company offers includes the rehabilitation of polluted soil areas, such as the work done at Yskor in Vanderbijlpark, which commenced in 1998.[8]

Envirogreen is a product as well as a service company. The company has managed to develop consulting services which include, among others, mine closure plans, such as ERGO Daggafontein on the East Rand, and rehabilitation planning. This unique product offering of Envirogreen is indicated in the turnkey solutions described below.[9]

Turnkey solutions

Envirogreen has adopted a multidisciplinary team approach. This implies that the company has combined two major aspects of mine rehabilitation. These two major aspects are, firstly, the consulting aspect of mine rehabilitation and secondly, the operational practical vegetating and/or rehabilitation activities of mine rehabilitation.

The company has a highly qualified, skilled, and experienced multidisciplinary team of professionals and technicians who offer the comprehensive range of environmental services. Some disciplines include ecology, civil engineering, soil science, hydrology, and plant toxicology.

Price strategy

The perceived value of a product or service can be linked to the specific price of the product or service. Price is used not only as an indicator of the cost that a buyer must incur, but also serves as a signal of the quality of a product.[10] Envirogreen emphasises value and professionalism rather than price. This implies that the company does not compete on a price level, but rather emphasises the quality and uniqueness of its products and services. Therefore, the multidisciplinary team approach of Envirogreen implies that the company can present innovative and cost-effective solutions to its customers on a high quality level.

Distribution strategy

Envirogreen's distribution channels consist of a combination of the company's own structures in the target market, as well as the alliance partners which the company has access to through its co-operation with other companies, such as Fraser Alexander and Wates, and Meiring and Barnard.[11] Envirogreen shares the same client base with both these companies. Individuals of these companies are in contact with clients on a daily basis and inform Envirogreen of any opportunities to follow up in terms of rehabilitation.

Rehabilitation specialists of Envirogreen are located as close as possible to the company's target markets through satellite offices that are sited in close proximity to the company's target markets, which ensures quality customer interaction.

Marketing communication (promotion) strategy

Marketing communication refers to the methods used by a company to communicate its products to the target market. The main thrust that Envirogreen wishes to achieve in its promotional strategy is to emphasise value-amplified professional service. The marketing communication techniques Envirogreen applies include personal selling, promotional days for existing and potential customers, media exposure, and selective advertising.

Firstly, Envirogreen applies personal selling as a marketing communication technique by approaching existing and potential customers with its products and services. The company then informs its customers of legislation, and educates them in problems concerning the environment. Secondly, Envirogreen has promotional days where customers from different sectors, such as mining and industrial, are given information in a discreet way regarding their obligation to rehabilitate the environment. The company then also offers a cost-effective solution to the customer. Thirdly, Envirogreen applies media exposure and selective advertising through magazines such as *Mining World, Mining Weekly,* and *Mining Mirror.*[12]

Envirogreen's market strategy is illustrated in Table 25.1. It is therefore clear that the spirit of Envirogreen is one of striving towards personal excellence through a shared value system that constantly guides the company to quality performance. The quality of the unique and world-class environmental rehabilitation services that Envirogreen renders to its customers has made the company a market leader in southern Africa. To remain a market leader, a company needs to keep ahead of its competition. Envirogreen's two main competitors are Viridus Technologies and EMPR Services, but they are significantly smaller in terms of market share. By being pro-active and by developing new products the company can succeed in staying ahead of its competitors. This key process for future success is explained below.

New product development

New product development is essential for survival, as it gives a company a competitive advantage over its competitors. To identify new product opportunities, companies should use their knowledge of their target market and competitor actions to look for possible profitable gaps in the market. Companies can follow a new product development process to enable them to develop new products. A typical process in new product development entails the following: idea

---

Price

Emphasis on:

- Value and professionalism
- Quality and uniqueness

Product

- Innovative and sustainable environmental rehabilitation

Distribution

Combination of:

- Own distribution structure
- Alliance partners

Marketing communication

Value-amplified professional service through:

- Personal selling and promotional days
- Media exposure and selective advertising

Target market

- International local mining and industrial companies
- Governments across the world.

Table 25.1: Envirogreen's marketing strategy

generation, screening of ideas, product concept testing, financial and marketing projections and analysis, product development and testing, test marketing of the product, and the commercialisation of the product.

According to Envirogreen, the company applies the steps of the new product development process in an informal and spontaneous manner to develop new products.[13] When, for example, the company worked on a project for the Water Research Commission, they came up with an idea to plant vegetables on the dam. As the new product idea progressed through the different stages of the new product development process, it was clear that vegetables could be planted on the dams. This is, however, not a simplistic process. These products have to be tested for toxicity before they can be commercially distributed. At present, Envirogreen is investigating the possibility of farming on slimes dams.

Quality performance

The quality performance of Envirogreen can be seen in many rehabilitated mine sites in South Africa. Quality performance is measured by means of chemical analysis through sample testing, as well as scientific-based plant survey techniques. The company has, for example, transformed the Hartebeestfontein No 7 slimes dam.[14] The barren moonscape is now covered in a diverse community of plants.

Projects completed by Envirogreen emphasise the company's philosophy that there should be no minimum at the outset of a project and no maximum at the conclusion thereof. The Envirogreen passion is built on its dream of assisting its customers to create an environment that future generations will be proud of and cherish.

Future plans

Envirogreen is strongly focused on its vision, namely: **Greening the world's waste and tailings.** This main goal is especially supported by the fact that Envirogreen has, for example, expanded its market by buying a water management company. The company has applied its existing business plan to the water management company, which shares a similar mission and vision to the rehabilitation and mine closure division. The mission of the water management company 'To provide innovative, cost-effective, practical and scientific solutions in all aspects of water and waste water management' and the concomitant vision 'To be a water management solutions provider of undisputed choice' demonstrates Envirogreen's awareness of the further responsibilities – and opportunities – involved in environmental rehabilitation.

Envirogreen plans to continue its social responsibility towards its consumers through good management under the co-operation of the government, in a cost-effective manner to the advantage of the company, the community, as well as future generations of people living in a harmonious ecology.

References

1   Steenekamp, S. J. 2001. Personal interview. Potchefstroom. (Notes in possession of author.) Case study procured by Charlene Gerber-Nel.
2   Corporate Company Profile. 2000. Potchefstroom.
3   Kroon, J. 1997. General and strategic management. In L. R. J. van Rensburg. Ed, *Business management: An introduction*. Pretoria: Van Schaik.
4   Corporate Company Profile, op. cit.
5   McCarthy, E. J. & Perreault, W. D. 1993. *Basic marketing: A global approach*, 11th ed. Boston, Mass.: Irwin.
6   Steenekamp, S. J., op. cit.
7   Corporate Company Profile, op. cit.
8   Steenekamp, S. J. 2001. Personal interview. Potchefstroom. (Notes in possession of author.)
9   Corporate Company Profile, op. cit.
10 Strydom, J. W.; Jooste, C. J.; & Cant, M. C. 2000. *Marketing management*. 4th ed. Kenwyn: Juta.
11 Corporate Company Profile, op. cit.
12 Steenekamp, S. J., op. cit.
13 Steenekamp, S. J., Ibid.
14 Steenekamp, S. J., op. cit.

MARKETING FEATURES:
ADVERTISING
FRANCHISING
GROWTH
INTERNATIONAL MARKETING
NICHE MARKETING
PRODUCT STRATEGY
QUALITY

26

King Pie

Capturing a slice of the pie[1]

King Pie opened its first franchised outlet in December 1993. Today, it boasts over 300 outlets countrywide, selling in excess of 8 million pies per month with a capital base of around R11 million. The freshly baked pie market as a whole is estimated at a whopping R350 million rand industry and is still considered to be in its growth stage. At under R3,00 per pie, that's quite an achievement! Sceptics, both in franchising and business, thought the concept would never take off, and that it would fizzle out.

KING☗PIE

Freshly baked all day

'Who', they intoned, 'could make money out of a R2,75 pie?' King Pie's reply to that was: 'With 43 million South Africans who love pies and, above all, can afford to buy them, there is no doubt that it will be a success!'[2]

The starting point

Although the franchised pie industry is a phenomenon of the nineties, pie-making has a long and uniquely South African history. King Pie's origin and inspiration can be traced back a few generations to the great-grandfather of Hennie Andrews, the descendent who founded King Pie. A photograph shows old man Andrews with his horse-drawn bakery buggy. Well known in the centre of Pretoria not only for his freshly baked breads, he was also famous for his home-style pies. That proud pie tradition was handed down with every generation who then became master bakers in their own right.

Hennie Andrews was no exception. As a master baker, he opened his King Pie bakery in Pretoria in 1990. Knowing that South Africans were devout pie-lovers, but over the years had had to make do with rather suspect pies, Hennie decided to give the public honest-to-goodness quality with no surprises! This meant using only the very best ingredients in pies that were made and baked fresh each day. He also designed his bakery in such a way that the pie-making process took place in an open area inside the shop, in full view of the customers. People queued to buy his pies, knowing and seeing exactly what they were getting. The result was phenomenal and King Pie was established! In 1993 the King Pie franchise was born, with Kobus Nieuwoudt joining the company to take responsibility for the financial and administrative set-up of the holding company. Within a year there were over 50 King Pie franchises and by the end of 1997 there were more than 300 around the country.

Indication of a niche

What was the key that unlocked the dramatic success of King Pie? There were essentially three factors that stood out as key elements.

- The first is undoubtedly the turnaround of the pie from the soggy, low-quality mass of fatty pastry and grizzly meat which had been left for days in a café's pie-warmer, to the freshly-baked-all-day concept of King Pie. Previously, one tended to ask 'Where did they come from?' 'What was in them?' 'How fresh were they?' Under the controlled production standards of a franchise, however, South Africans rediscovered their love of pies and the market welcomed a new take-out alternative.

- The second factor related to South Africa's fast-changing socio-economic situation and the subsequent expanding market for the 'universally affordable commodity'. King Pie was a franchised food concept that through good quality and a good price appealed not only to the privileged few million but was something that the other 43 million could afford as well!

- The impulse purchase versus a planned meal was a factor in cementing the pie market's success. Chicken, pizza and burgers are substantially more expensive and appeal to a select market. Pies have a much broader appeal. In addition to being bought by the dozen by the homemaker who plans to serve them as a complete meal, pies, because of their affordability, are also bought on impulse. They can be eaten as a snack to fill the gap between breakfast and lunch, or before going home to dinner. The other undisputed advantage was the quick turnaround time of pies, which are available fresh at all times of the day and the customer does not have to wait while the order is prepared.

The changing face of franchising

The fast-food franchising industry in South Africa has, during the past ten years, remained rather static. Although the franchise statistics are impressive, with an estimated total turnover of R9,278 billion generated by all types of franchise, the consumer which the industry served remained in the upper and middle class. For most franchisers, the size of a country's upper and middle class was of more interest than the absolute number of people, and most franchises had only ever catered to that sector of the population. South Africa's past isolation and its subsequent lack of competitiveness resulted in a limited selection of fast-food concepts – with very few of them offering a take-out item under R5,00...or even R10,00. Consumers had a limited choice and fast food had become prohibitively expensive. No one had seriously looked at whether it was possible to service the entire spectrum of the population, and not just pockets of consumers determined by race and income. The political, social and economic changes of the past few years have brought about the most astounding entrepreneurial opportunities, and suddenly the market has opened up and thrown off the blinkers of the past. King Pie was undoubtedly at the forefront of that new enterprising spirit and the snowballing effect of the pie industry can only be described as a uniquely South African phenomenon. It has spearheaded a spin-off of related concepts that today form part of a growing small business boom which is fast forming the backbone of our country.

Selecting the target market

King Pie is the first truly South African fast-food franchise to break all barriers of race, culture and status. Knowing your market in franchising in South Africa has always been crucial to success. It has always been a case of identifying your market sector, positioning yourself in the correct area and marketing your product to that specific market through the appropriate medium. King Pie entered the fast-food market knowing that pies appealed to all sectors. There was never any conscious effort to position itself in any one particular slot. The initial outlets were determined by the type of franchisee who bought the franchise, and the outlets were opened in busy urban areas.

King Pie has recognised, however, that although the South African market is united in its love of pies, there are geographical, ethnic and economic considerations that have prompted it to fine-tune its range of products and cater to targeted groups in some areas. For example, the consumer market in KwaZulu-Natal demands a 'hotter' pie and sales of 'curried' pies are high. Some Western Cape franchises have converted to the 'halaal' requirements to service their market sector. The Western Cape market prefers mutton to beef, and adjustments to that effect have been made. The pricing of pies has also come under the spotlight, with certain 'poorer' areas requesting a cheaper pie, while the more discerning pie customer wants a bigger and more substantial pie and is quite willing to pay more for it. Once again, taking into consideration the fact that King Pie services the entire spectrum of the market, it was decided to offer a variety and choice in all the shops, thereby satisfying every consumer's taste and pocket. The King Pie traditional range of pies at just under R3,00 appeals to the broader market, while the royal range offers the more substantial and exotic pies like the burger pie, the tuna pie, the giant chicken and mushroom and, the lamb and mint pie, at a higher price. In addition, every King Pie outlet has a 'pie of the day' which is available at a special, affordable price.

Setting the standards: Product quality

In its short existence, King Pie has been one of the leaders in setting the standards for the rest of the franchised pie industry. 'Freshly baked all day' is the philosophy at the core of King Pie's success and encompasses the three most important ingredients for success:

- **Freshness** The appeal of a pie is in the aromatic smell as it comes out of the oven, piping hot, golden brown and crisp, with a delicious, mouth-watering filling in the centre.
- **Quality** Only the best ingredients are used in the pie-making process. Top grade flour is used, as well as superior fat that will give the best puff pastry results, only 100% pure South African beef, fresh vegetables, no soya and no preservatives.
- **Value** The pie remains the most affordable meal on the market. At an average price of under R3,00, it offers unbelievable value for money and is regarded as a wholesome and nourishing meal.

Branding and packaging

In order to maintain the highest possible standards, it was necessary to form partnerships with suppliers and bring a strong level of consistency to the ingredients and equipment used in the pie-making process. Some of South Africa's biggest raw material suppliers supply King Pie throughout the country with branded products, and MacAdams, the manufacturers and suppliers of bakery equipment, look after the equipment side of the business. The centralised buying power of the holding company ensures that the best prices are negotiated, and with a total of 600 tons of Cape flour and 220 tons of first-grade meat being used per month, the group can ensure the most competitive prices, while the consumer is guaranteed consistency. The branding on packaging has been reinforced with a new-look King Pie logo that is stronger and more visible, while retaining the sharp, clean look against a pristine white background that has become synonymous with King Pie. As the franchise has grown, it has become necessary to update the shop 'image', bringing it more into line with market trends. New interior improvements include a new light-box menu board, bar counter and stools for customers to use, together with a stronger focus on point-of-sale material.

Distribution

With the rapid expansion of the King Pie franchise, distribution became crucial to the success of the outlets. King Pie shops in all four corners of the country needed regular deliveries of raw materials, spices and packaging. It was therefore decided to form an exclusive partnership with a distribution company that would focus its core business on King Pie. The unprecedented expansion of the King Pie group also necessitated the rapid expansion of the distribution company and today it has warehouses in Pretoria, Durban and Cape Town, and a fleet of six trucks dedicated to servicing the needs of King Pie.

Requirements for a franchise

The King Pie franchisees come from all walks of life and it is not a pre-requisite to have any baking experience since all training, including all aspects of management, marketing and production, is provided by the holding company. The cross-section of people who own a King Pie franchise is varied, from school teachers to doctors, and former civil servants to auditors. It will cost a prospective investor approximately R380 000 to set up a full King Pie franchise. A smaller satellite bake-off costs in the region of R150 000. The average turnover of the full King Pie franchise is in the region of R120 000 per month, with a return on capital of around 40%. King Pie's royalty structure differs from the standard norm in that royalties are pegged at a fixed rate, depending on the size and type of outlet. In the structure of full franchises (which incorporate full production facilities) and bake-offs (which take deliveries of prepared raw pies for baking), there are various categories of royalty payments. The advantage in this system lies in the fact that, without the constraints of controlling and verifying exact turnover figures, the relationship between franchiser and franchisee is at its optimum best. The advertising contribution, which in a standard franchise set-up is included as a percentage of the royalty, is administered completely separately by a national executive committee comprising representatives of the franchiser and regional franchisee representatives who determine the advertising strategy for the group.

Requirements to set up a King Pie franchise include:
- The ideal site should be between 60 m² and 80 m² in size.
- It must be aesthetically appealing, with a large, attractive shopfront.
- It must have good visibility to be easily seen and noticed. A corner stand is preferable.
- A high volume of people traffic is important, with a feet count of between 6 000 and 8 000 per day past a potential shop.
- The expendable income of the residents in the area is taken into consideration.
- Observing trading neighbours to assess the market trends. A good, strong anchor tenant is an advantage.

An ideal King Pie shopfront

Operational standards

A strong operations and technical team guides the new franchisee through all the stages of a set-up – from the site selection to marketing, from training to technical support, and a team is on hand on opening day when the queues may go around the block and sales can top 10 000 pies in a day! The different pie recipes are thoroughly researched and tested, and franchisees follow these tried and tested recipes in their own outlets. Training in the various vernaculars is done at shop level by a team of technical consultants, and periodic on-site refresher courses are held country-wide. Ongoing training and regular seminars are provided for franchisees, and service standards are maintained through regular visits by the operations managers who provide training on sales techniques, counter sales methods, and customer service. A 'mystery shopper' is employed to visit shops as a customer, buying pies and reporting on aspects such as quality, hygiene and service. Reports are sent to individual franchisees with a full analysis of their performance and steps taken to rectify any problems. Hygiene remains one of King Pie's top priorities, especially because it promotes its open-plan bakery. The entire franchise group is on contract with an internationally accredited hygiene laboratory which monitors, trains and accredits outlets to maintain the highest levels of hygiene. Regular swab tests are taken of working surfaces, coldrooms and products, and King Pie maintains a health and hygiene level of 75% and above, which is well above the industry norm.

Product development

Research and new product development play a major role in the long-term success of the King Pie franchise. The pie industry offers a wide range of pie variants, with the traditional pies forming the foundation of the range. Such popular variants as steak and kidney, pepper steak, steak and onion, cornish and chicken, as well as sausage rolls, will always remain the favourites. However, the consumer needs to be tempted by new taste sensations and the product development division has as many as ten new variants in different stages of development at any one time. Factors such as international culinary trends, local ethnic tastes and consumer demand, play a role in determining new additions to the range. There is also a growing line of 'add-on' lines, ranging from gravies to 'dessert' pies, as well as doughnuts, biscuits, and scones.

When is a burger not a burger?

Having taken a slice (roughly 17%) of the food franchise concept market in 1996, King Pie went one step further and decided to challenge the traditional burger market by introducing its very own 'burger pie' in a bid to capture an even larger slice of the fast-food market. The test team at King Pie developed a burger pie patty, complete with onion rings and relish, encased in crispy puff pastry and baked to perfection. This alternative to the traditional hamburger has proved highly successful and is taking the fast-food market by storm.

Advertising

King Pie has spearheaded a strong national advertising and promotional support programme to further its marketing efforts and to position King Pie as the strongest pie franchise in the country. As a totally new concept in fast food, it was imperative that King Pie should capture the Number One position in the pie market and be the first to advertise on television. The advertising agency AM-C was briefed to produce a television commercial that would make an indelible impression on the consumers' minds that pie franchisers, and King Pie in particular, had been the first to introduce this new food trend. In researching their approach, the agency visited the outlets and asked: 'Who buys pies?' They were told: 'Everyone!' – from the early morning commuter going to work and the office worker buying pies for lunch, to the construction worker buying an in-between snack and the career woman picking up a dozen to serve for dinner. As a result the King Pie 'Mr Bean' television commercial took a neutral stance, with the focus on a humorous look at 'freshness'. Subsequent research conducted on whether people noted and liked the King Pie ads, showed an almost equal liking pattern throughout all cultural groups, with an above-average percentage than the norm for fast-food advertisements. The ads won an international advertising award and now that King Pie is well established as the Number One in pies, it has taken a more flexible approach to its advertising and is broadening its base to include advertising in targeted areas for specific markets.

Competition within the food services industry is fierce, and with the pie market capturing an immediate 17% share of the fast-food market in a 1996 survey, the industry is poised for some interesting marketing battles. One can already see the drop in prices of take-out items such as hamburgers to counteract the effect of the pie industry's competitive pricing. This is a welcome move since fast food, because of South Africa's past isolation, has always been prohibitively expensive. So aware are the market leaders of the impact of the pie industry, that King Pie's original advertising agency DD-B were forced to relinquish the King Pie account because McDonalds was being handled by the international arm of that agency and objected to King Pie's presence as a small, but threatening account.

The international connection

King Pie and the pie franchise, as a uniquely South African concept, is also working successfully in neighbouring countries such as Namibia, Botswana, Swaziland, Lesotho, Zimbabwe, and Mozambique. With such an overwhelmingly successful formula, King Pie lost no time in researching the international market with a view to expanding into foreign countries. Pies are essentially a colonial tradition from England and research into other former colonial countries like Australia, New Zealand, Canada, and the USA, showed that the introduction of pie franchising would be welcomed and would prove viable. A King Pie International division was set up and in May 1996 the first King Pie had opened in Auckland, New Zealand. Several more outlets were opened and Australia soon followed suit. Franchises in Canada, Britain, and the USA are in the process of being set up.

Conclusion

South Africa might have been left out in the cold during our years of isolation; we may be experiencing monetary and labour problems; we might be considered a Third World country in many respects, and we've always thought the rest of the world had the blueprint for franchising, but King Pie is proud to have proved everyone wrong with their uniquely South African concept that is taking the world by storm.

References

1   This case study was written by Giuli Osso, Communications, for King Pie. Case study procured by Michael Cant.

MARKETING FEATURES:
BRANDING
CHANGE
IMAGE
POSITIONING
SEGMENTATION
SLOGANS

27

Brand South Africa

Past positioning: Sun, surf, and leisure

The traditional South African positioning of its country revolved around the usual slogans punting the sun, Zulu dancing, and the Big five game experience. These attractions had been the focal point around which the whole of the country's positioning and marketing in respect to tourism had been based. Promotional videos, posters, brochures, and packages had used these as the main selling points in marketing the country.[1] In spite of this, Africa had been one of the losers in world tourism since 1975. In 1975 East Asia and the Pacific had accounted for 5,3% of the world's tourism receipts, while Africa had earned 3,1%. This had changed significantly by 1996, where East Asia/Pacific accounted for 19,1% of the receipts, mostly at the expense of Europe, the Middle East, and Africa. Africa had shrunk to 1,9%, as a result of factors such as war, instability, and loss of infra-structure.[2]

Mid-1990s: Relook at positioning

In the mid-1990s Satour, the body responsible for marketing South Africa's image both locally and abroad, decided to refocus its efforts to capitalise on the surge of interest in South Africa's recent history. The important areas of focus would be history, culture, and ecotourism. This was in line with the outlook of the World Tourism Organisation at the time which identified socio-environmental aware-ness as one of the major motivational forces in tourism during that period.[3] Efforts were made to include the history and heritage of the disadvantaged to cre-ate a form of African-based tourism that was uniquely South African but that also benefited and appealed to the beneficiary communities. In combining ecotourism with sport and cultural heritage tourism a unique spread of offerings from leisure to conferencing could be offered to domestic and international travellers. The payoff line was 'A world in one country'.

In order to support this Satour also negotiated with government for a substan-tial increase in its budget. Allied with this was an attempt to create new and emerging businesses to help deal with the delivery of the product. This encour-aged emerging entrepreneurs to enter the business or ally themselves with estab-lished players. Criteria for the awarding of tenders would be relooked at to favour emerging and previously disadvantaged groups.[4] A planned upgrade of the exist-ing information technology system was also planned. Results were achieved; for example, a Satour survey at the time found that Soweto was rated a more desir-able tourist destination than Sun City. Cultural destinations such as the former Mandela home in Soweto and the Robben Island prison became prime tourist des-tinations. Private enterprise also got involved, with SABMiller starting a shebeen tour and the Lesedi Cultural Village outside of Pretoria.[5]

South African tourism boom

Tourism in South Africa is growing, and prospects are good that it will be sus-tained. Statistics show that South Africa was the fastest growing tourist destina-tion in the world.[6] The projected tourism growth has been exceeded, which con-founded the global industry trend of flat growth. This is in spite of the problems faced by many tourism authorities throughout the world due to the continued economic downturn and the political storms evident around the globe.

This is as a result of the strategies to make South Africa a preferred tourist destination. All of South Africa's key markets have posted double-digit growth, despite the overall general reluctance by tourists to travel long-haul. Regions such as the Western Cape have set ambitious targets to reap the benefits of this predicted surge of overseas visitors.[7] One of the key drivers of this success has been the Brand SA initiative.

The Brand South Africa initiative

This is an initiative launched in 2001 by the recently formed International Marketing Council[8] (IMC). Brand SA, a private/public initiative, has the task of enhancing perceptions about South Africa by managing the image of the country so as to impact favourably on domestic and foreign investment and tourism.

It strives to do this by co-ordinating and helping to enable efforts to create a unified and consistent image of South Africa as a successfully evolving country. It focuses on both local and international markets.

Intensive research was conducted among 25 000 people in eleven different languages from ten different countries. This was done to generate clear personal information on people's perceptions of South Africa from grassroots level to the level of international business leaders. The research also included a representative cross-section of the South African community.

A task team from many of the important stakeholders – business, tourism, investment, government, and society in general worked on the design of the brand positioning, by analysing the current and future desired positioning. The Unilever brand development process was the basis for this process, and this was the first time that this process had been shared outside of Unilever.[9] The Unilever model develops two images of a brand – the current image and the desired image – in detail. This is done through generating clear descriptions of the brand that include the reason for its existence, its personality, and its key differentiators. Once this step has been taken the model then develops the road map of how to move the brand from its current position towards the planned future position, keeping in mind the time and resource constraints.

The end result of this process is the positioning that South Africa is the world's most competitive emerging market and a winning nation sharing a common vision. This image will be the basis of the marketing drive by government and coordinated by the International Marketing Council to drive all the marketing of Brand SA under one brand identity.[10]

Key issues impacting on the development of the new Brand SA positioning

A number of key issues have impacted on the brand development process.[11] These include:

- The fact that people the world over are looking for new role models. This is due to the global and political developments such as the September 11 2001 attacks, the Iraqi conflict, the volatility of the world financial markets, and the search for a new world order after the demise of Communism.
- South Africa is increasingly seen as a desirable destination for tourism and financial investments in the developing world. The success of the economy in generating consistent growth – albeit not at the levels sought – has made it an attractive destination. Coupled with a generally more positive community, this is having positive spin-offs for both tourism and business. One problem has been the inconsistent communications by a variety of bodies to the world community, as well as the need to evolve the country from the Rainbow Nation after the 1994 elections to a new stage of transformation that reflects its achievements and future directions.
- The inspiring transformation of the country means that South Africa has the

image of a new emerging country with unique history, resources, and society that is a role model for others. This is as a result of the developments in the country and South Africa is increasingly seen as a role model for others in many fields.

These issues have helped to form the overarching brand positioning, and will be used to develop more detailed and refined positioning for both tourism and trade and investment.

The brand essence revolves around the points noted above, and the payoff line chosen to help communicate this is 'South Africa – Alive with possibility', which developed out of research among opinion formers, tourists, figures regarded as national icons, and business. This was to ensure that the process had a hard business edge and was not limited to tourism.[12] The other 'legs' of the initiative include the Proudly South African campaign and a planned investment drive.

Communication of the Brand South Africa message

A number of communication efforts have been established or are planned to help attain the Brand South Africa objectives.[13] These include:

- The establishment of a Communication Resource Centre to monitor all communications around the world for all mentions of the country. It is proactive in that it responds to requests for information but also helps inform those that are misinformed; it manages responses to articles about the country; it advises government on media trends and appropriate responses, and helps to actively disseminate positive news about South Africa to help create a balanced perception of the country.
- It has created a unique web portal at www.safrica.info to help promote both business and tourism for the country.
- It will perform strategic public relations projects in key cities of the world through Country Managers so as to communicate the brand message. This will be done in liaison with the Department of Foreign Affairs and other leading South African personalities.
- South African communities both at home and abroad will be targeted with communication in both above-the-line form as well as experiential processes to help make the communities representatives of the new initiative.
- This will include key communities such as business, sports, arts and culture, government, and civil society.

The SA Tourism marketing strategy

The development of the SA Tourism marketing strategy falls under the Brand SA umbrella. In the first phase of the strategy the objectives[14] included the following:

- Clarify the goals for tourism against which the strategy for international tourism had to deliver.
- Bring together and evaluate all existing data.

- Draw in stakeholders from government, industry, and SA Tourism.
- Help establish attractive target markets for the strategic effort.

More importantly, five specific objectives were established which formed the basis of deciding where to market.[15] These were:
- Increase tourism volumes at high and sustainable rates.
- Increase total spend by tourists in South Africa.
- Optimise the length of stay in SA to maximise revenue yield.
- Improve the volume and spend distribution throughout the year and around the country.
- Improve activity and spend patterns to enable transformation and promote black economic empowerment.

A set of attractiveness criteria was established and used to filter the possible market choices as well as to rank the relative attractiveness of markets. The basis of these criteria was to test the ability of a market choice to deliver against these objectives.

By using the filtering method a list of 70 countries was established, which were further filtered on the basis of volume and revenue growth to come up with a list of 40 countries which formed the basis of the portfolio of countries for SA Tourism to focus on.[16]

Redefining the brand

Once the segments were identified, SA Tourism redefined the tourism brand to be customer-focused so as to be aligned between the attributes of South Africa as a destination and the needs and desires of the key audiences for the specific chosen segments. The research conducted in phase 1 showed that South Africa, in most cases, did not own any significant key attributes in the minds of the consumers.[17] The overall aim was to ensure that the value proposition was tailored to each segment so as to be considered as a destination of choice for that segment and to facilitate the selling process that converts potential customers to actual buyers of South African tourism products. All of this was to be done under the umbrella of the Brand SA initiative, which holds the segment specific activities and messages together. Key to the marketing was the effort to ensure the alignment of the product, service, and experience behind the messages so as to deliver the brand promise beyond the customer's expectations.

The first step in this process of redefining the brand was a categorisation of the segment portfolio into four specific brand audiences, with similar needs and desires.[18] The four segments are:
- 'Luxury in Africa' segment. This is the segment that was the focus of most of the marketing in the past. Growth in this segment will be achieved through product development and innovation, so as to retain the business and encourage repeat visits.

- 'Value for money in Africa' segment. This segment has been relatively ignored in the past and represents a broad category that includes family travel and mass tourism. This will require significant product development and packaging of products that are cost-competitive.
- 'Africa is hip' segment. These are very demanding young professionals looking for luxury, adventure experiences, culture, and entertainment but at cost-competitive prices. The positive aspect of this demanding segment is that they are very positive about South Africa, but no work has been done in this segment in the past. They also provide channel opportunities, as they are users of the Web and the Internet.
- 'South Africa for business and entertainment' segment. The key attraction for this segment is South Africa as a developed, world-class location. It will require work in terms of an extended product that includes entertainment and transport before and after events, and not just shopping malls and conference centres.

Each of these segments will have brand and segment activation strategies to establish the marketing details in a segment-specific manner. This would include competitive positioning, messages, channels, and product and price points, aligned with the overarching Brand SA process.

As an example, a campaign was launched in the United States marketing two value-for-money holiday deals aimed at key segments in the USA market. These two packages are called the 'Next Stop South Africa' and the 'Upscale Wanderlust' package.[19] The Next Stop South Africa package is aimed at active, older travellers with lots of travel experience and the desire and money to support their travel. The package is at the $2 999 price point that includes return international air flight, 12 nights accommodation and a safari. The Upscale Wanderlust package is aimed at customers who are more interested in travel than any other USA segment. They want comfortable destinations that are soft and offer relaxation. The price point for this package starts at $1 999 and includes return international air flight, 8 nights accommodation, and a safari. The communication campaign for these packages includes high-profile magazine and newspaper advertising, direct mail, and online and retail promotions. They have both been designed to encourage travel in the traditional low season of March–June. These products are the direct result of the research undertaken by Tourism SA to establish which segments of the tourism market would generate the most revenue for the industry.[20]

Criticism of, and concerns with, the initiative

As with all attempts to reposition, there has been some criticism of the efforts in some quarters. One criticism[21] is that the term 'Alive with possibility' is a bit meaningless in operational terms. It does not clearly identify or communicate the value proposition of South Africa nor differentiate it sufficiently from its competitors, as it is seen as too general and not actionable by all of the stakeholders. The value proposition, it is felt, should incorporate something that ties together the complete value chain of people, resources, animals, and weather that is relevant in terms of differences with South Africa's competitors, and the feeling is that the slogan does not do that. In response to this criticism it is noted that many confuse the payoff line with the total brand essence. The communications plan will take the payoff line and the brand essence and make it relevant to specific audiences so that it resonates with as many people as possible.

Another problem is the alignment of all levels of the tourism industry under the umbrella of the Brand SA initiative.[22] This implies the cooperation and support of both regional and local tourism initiatives, and this has always been problematic at best. As an example, a plan to establish a single marketing body for Cape Town and the Western Cape has had mixed response because it has been seen as too 'top-down' and designed and driven by officialdom. It was also feared that smaller attractions, such as Knysna, might be ignored in a unified marketing strategy. The essence of the problem is that the initiative was seen as driven by politicians and that private sector input was insufficient. These types of alignment problems will have to be addressed in the communications efforts by the IMC within South Africa itself.

Another concern is that the politicians running the country have to put the integrity of the national brand ahead of political one-upmanship and manage the perceptions of the country. Issues such as the situation in Zimbabwe and the all too common round of wars and coups in Africa will have an influence on the brand, irrespective of how unfair it may seem.[23]

Other issues that will need attention are the crime levels in the country, public transport and service levels.[24] The crime situation has been much talked about, and more significant improvement will have to be seen to ensure that the benefits of South Africa being seen as a 'safe haven' due to its politically neutral world position do not get eroded. The public transport system is in dire straits, and in the big cities it is either unsafe or non-existent. Travel in South Africa can be a logistical nightmare and private transport is almost essential to be able to move around with ease. Lastly, the service levels in the tourism industry have to improve. Although there are programmes and plans in progress to address this there needs to be a concerted effort by all players in the industry to create a world class service sector.

The Brand SA journey

One would be tempted to already judge whether the Brand SA and Proudly South African campaign have been successful. Yvonne Johnston, the CEO of the International Marketing Council, is of the opinion that it's too early still to judge the campaign.[25] She feels that the effort will take years to reach fruition, and that many countries launched branding campaigns twenty or thirty years ago that were not that successful. She does feel that there has been a shift in national pride, and that the campaign is one of the factors impacting on that shift. She cites the recent exercise by BrandMetrics, which developed a model to put a commercial value on the SA brand.[26] By their calculation, the Brand SA is worth US$5 billion, and Johnston feels that this is a benchmark which can be used to measure the success of its branding efforts.

References

1   Digging for tourism. January/February 1998. *Marketing Mix.* p. 36.
    Case study by Ricardo Machado.
2   Ibid, p. 39.
3   Ibid, p. 36.
4   Ibid, p. 37.
5   Village of culture a boost to tourism. 13 January 2003. *Pretoria News.* p. 6.
6   Joy and pride at SA tourism boom. 10 March 2003. *Citizen.* p. 4.
    This growth is, however, starting to slow in 2005 as a result of the stronger rand which is discouraging part of the tourist market.
7   Tourism authorities set ambitious goals to benefit all sectors. 17 February 2003. *Cape Times.* p. 6.
8   Nation Branding. 2002. theMARKETINGSITE.com. p.1. Accessed: 15 April 2002.
9   Ibid.
10 Padayachy, L. Glossy new image designed for SA. 25 November 2001. *Sunday Times.*
11 Ibid, p. 2.
12 Bulger, P. Marketing SA as brand to beat the best. October 4 2004. *Business Day.*
13 Ibid.
14 Introduction and Executive Summary of Phase 1. August 2001. SA Tourism. www.southafrica.net. p. 10. Accessed: 15 April 2003.
15 Ibid, p. 13.
16 Ibid, p. 36.
17 Ibid, p. 26.
18 Ibid, pp. 27–28.
19 New holiday deals to lure US tourists to South Africa. 26 January 2003. *Sunday Independent.* p. 4.
20 SA Tourism launches $2 m US campaign. 26 January 2003. *Sunday Times.* p. 3.
21 Alive with possibility or bored to death? 2002. Bolt, J & Johnson, Y. Reality Bytes. M2. p. 72.
22 Plan for single tourism marketing body faces flak. 20 January 2003. *Cape Times.* p. 4.
23 Moerdyk, C. Brand SA is our only real selling point. 29 September 2002. *Sunday Times.*
24 Lazar, C. SA showcase. 3 May 2003. *Pretoria News*, Travel Section. p. 2.
25 Shevel, A. Branding of a nation. 11 July 2004. *Sunday Times* Business Times. p. 5.
26 Maggs, J. What are we worth? *Financial Mail.* 10 October 2003. p. 90.

Tourism marketing:
A public-private partnership
in Zululand

Introduction[1]

The province of KwaZulu-Natal has long been underdeveloped in national terms and yet, at the same time, has been a magnet for tourists, both local and foreign. The situation began to change for the better when in December 2000 a new municipal dispensation was launched in South Africa, reducing the number of municipalities nation-wide from over 800 to a more manageable 284. This dispensation was people driven rather than ideologically driven and it concentrated on development and job creation. These development driven municipalities were to be achieved by means of the Integrated Development Plan (IDP). The IDP would be both instrument and process and through a system of structured reviews would be constantly adjusted to variables in the management environment. The needs analysis for implementing the IDPs focused on tourism possibilities and realities for this region. Tourism creates jobs and in carrying out their mandates to encourage job creation, municipalities need to look critically at tourism.

This critical look entails an analysis of existing (mainly private sector) tourism developments as well as drafting marketing strategies for developing new tourist attractions.

The tourism marketing environment of uMlalazi

Background to uMlalazi

In KZN, local authorities are grouped together under a District Municipality. Known as KZ284, uMlalazi is together with five other constituent local authorities – Mbonambi (KZ281), Nkandla (KZ286), Mthonjaneni (KZ283), uMhlathuze (KZ282), and Ntambanana (KZ283) – part of the District Municipality of uThungulu, known as District Council (DC28). This area is situated in north-eastern KZN and wholly in what is traditionally referred to as Zululand.

The newly created (December 2000) municipality of uMlalazi, is named for a local river. The entire area of uMlalazi has low levels of urbanisation and more than 80% of the population is rural. uMlalazi is typical of the whole area, with the added advantage of having access to an 80 km pristine shoreline on the warm Indian Ocean. More than half of its formally employed population is involved in agriculture while statistics show that the area benefits heavily from tourism. These are two main areas of economic activity, which have also been identified as areas ideally suited for further growth. uMlalazi is one of the largest municipalities in South Africa at 2 300 square kilometers. The population stands at an estimated 250 000, and women make up close to 60% of the population. uMlalazi has the highest rainfall in South Africa.

Challenges to marketing initiatives

The uMlalazi Council recognises that while specific agricultural and tourism developments are optimally launched and managed within the free-market system by entrepreneurs, it also has a duty to develop infrastructures which would support the major job-creating sectors. Some of these infrastructures are already in place, particularly in urbanised areas, for example, there is a high-standard airport at Richards Bay with car hire facilities. However, there are certain challenges: transport infrastructure, for instance, has an urban bias and the rural areas, including much of the beach areas, face problems of accessibility.

Apart from issues related to infrastructure, in the tourism-marketing environment, marketers are faced with various challenges. One such challenge is the government ban on 4 x 4 vehicles on the beaches in this region, which has dealt a heavy blow to businesses in the area. General trends indicating a sharp fall-off of inland visitors to resorts like Mtunzini are evident since the announcement of the ban in 2002. The onus of imposing the beach ban in formerly popular stretches of beach fell on uMlalazi since it is within the ambit of Ezemvelo KZN Wildlife. Sales of crafters' curios specifically have been affected by the vehicles-on-the-beach ban, which is serious as these crafters are among the poorest of the poor.

B&Bs are also affected, as are sports shops, garages, charter vessels, and day visitors to the beaches.

Tourism attractions

Part of the functions of the District Municipality includes deliberating on tourism policy for its constituent local authorities. It also modestly finances the establishment of local tourism associations, usually consisting of groups of private tour operators, B&B establishments, hoteliers, chalet and lodge owners, and backpackers' establishments (which are proving very popular with that market segment).

Tourism activities

Any serious study of the tourism potential of the Zululand area is informed by the fact that the whole area boasts historical sites, battlefields, cultural villages as well as expansive and impressive, if remote beaches. Some of the uMlalazi tourism attractions include:

- Game viewing and day safaris, adjacent to Zululand's world famous game reserves.
- Deep sea and shore angling.
- Whale watching by boat along the uMlalazi coastline (statistically the best in Africa, at 700% higher than Hermanus, the `traditional' whale watchers' spot).
- Cultural experiences such as Shakaland and Simunye which despite atrocious road conditions for the former still attract the most tour bus traffic (80% foreign) in the uThungulu region at 70 000 between them.
- Lodges and B&Bs.
- Hiking trails and horse riding.
- Aerial Boardwalk in Eshowe
- Canoeing on lagoons and rivers.
- Biking trails.
- Camping of all sorts.
- Irrigation (agricultural) tourism in conjunction with agri-tours from Holland to this region.
- Religious interest tourism (missionary interest, e.g. Norwegians/Lutherans).

With the exception of the Aerial Boardwalk and the last item, which is loosely coordinated by the Museum staff of the Municipality, the above activities are mainly privately owned.

The natural heritage

Furthermore, the bird life in the uMlalazi area is one of five world-class eco-tourist attractions in the area. The others are rhino conservation, the coelacanths off Sodwana, trees, butterflies, and moths. Other natural assets have also been identified and will require carefully applied conservation measures. These include the following:

- Siyala Coastal Park, which offers a coastline for major developments. Mixed land uses such as hotels, camping sites, chalets, walks, boating, and fishing facilities can be developed.
- Ongoye Forest is one of South Africa's most unique forests. The development plan, together with access roads is near completion.
- The Zululand Birding Route, is training birding guides from among the local people.
- The Nkandla and Quedeni Forest areas are among the most impressive in the country, but the access roads are beset by mists at certain times of the year.
- The Phobane dam offers a wide range of water sports, angling, camping, and picnic sports. A floating lodge is a favourite feature.

These and other areas are natural assets and increased visits will depend to a large extent on upgrading the roads. Facilitating job creation in these areas requires educating the local people to the economic value of their heritage. Apart from these two issues, ensuring increased visits also requires good marketing and promotion of the attractions. In the main, marketing of the region's tourist attractions has been carried out most profitably by independent operators using specialised publications. Examples of these include the article of July 2002 *Getaway* regarding the Aerial Boardwalk and shows such as the yearly Getaway Show in Johannesburg. Word of mouth also plays a part in generating publicity for the region. While the Council may play a role in the development of tourism infrastructures, marketing tourist attractions is not its core business.

Tourism marketing communication

In tourism marketing, marketers also need to inform the public about various sites and attractions that could be visited. The uMlalazi Council has, amongst other things, produced a promotional video, in which tourist attractions feature together with sketching a general view of amenities in the towns of Eshowe, Mtunzini, and Gingindlovu.

Promotional video

The target audience for this video, which has been produced to accommodate modular inserts and amendments, is the local population as well as groups of interested visitors. The Council has established tourist information offices in Eshowe where visitors are assisted. Evaluations have recently commenced on the numbers of visitors to this office, from whence they come, nature of enquiries and whether these visitors are foreign or local. The video has also been edited and produced in Mandarin Chinese for use in China and Taiwan.

The uMlalazi Council has also produced a Chinese language video for the

KwaZulu Municipal Marketing Initiative (KMMI) whose function it is to attract Chinese investment to member areas (Newcastle, Ladysmith and uMlalazi, Eshowe). This video has attracted investments pledges, with deposits paid to the value of R25 million. This is no insignificant result and an excellent return on the original production investment of about R70 000. Included in this Chinese investment package is a hotel complex, which according to the investors from Taiwan will offer package tours to visitors from the East, to the uMlalazi area and beyond. This is a good example of foreign interests being aware of, and wanting to take advantage of the tourism attractions of the uMlalazi region.

Aims of marketing communication

The uMlalazi Council encourages private enterprise to promote tourist attractions by utilising other forms of tourism marketing communication. Their communication strategy includes the following aims:

- Participation by way of exhibition stalls, brochures, videos in shows like Getaway and Indaba, which are among the biggest in the world.
- To encourage small and medium (private) tourism enterprises.
- To promote tourism to and investment in uMlalazi area by means of marketing aids like videos, brochures, media releases, news-making events, and other reactive responses.
- To help coordinate tourism marketing efforts in the area without being prescriptive.
- To sponsor events, routes, and shows.
- To develop crafters (e.g. Vukani which has sales worldwide).
- To bring about a greater awareness of the value of tourism to the area.
- To inspire news-making (tourism-related) events for media.

Marketing strategies in the pipeline

Furthermore, the Council has formulated the following objectives as being part of their tourism marketing strategy for future efforts:

- To request surveys by the District Municipality on tourism trends in the area.
- To update accommodation statistics in the municipal area (currently at 1 900 beds).
- To deliberate on B&B applications to ensure acceptable standards.
- To conduct regular health/safety related inspections of tourist facilities and to report on same.
- To encourage local tourism operators' participation in supplying inputs to strategies for District Municipal consideration.
- To take an active interest in developments spearheaded by Tourism KZN, the Elephant Coast (Branding) Committee activities, Ezemvelo KZN Wildlife events/activities and those of the Greater St Lucia Wetlands Park Authority (The Wetlands Park).
- To report on matters of tourism interest in the Municipal newsletters.

Conclusion

The marketing of individual tourist attractions within the uMlalazi Municipal area is currently the responsibility of individual private enterprise stakeholders. The Municipality has identified tourism (with agriculture) as the growth area to create jobs and encourage development with the most potential. The development of the tourist potential of the area is an amalgam of the identification of a wide variety of tourism possibilities by the municipality, plus the selection and involvement of the right developers to bring projects to fruition.

References

1   Case study written by D. Rezelman, consultant for the uMlalazi Municipality. Information in this case study based on communication by uMlalazi Municipal Manager, Eshowe, February 2004. Case study procured by Charlene Gerber-Nel.

PART FOUR

OVERCOMING MARKETING OBSTACLES

Introduction

This fourth and final part differs from the preceding parts in two ways. Firstly, only one of the companies involved – Hahn & Hahn – is South African and secondly, the cases do something other than describe and analyse the (generally) straightforward path to marketing success exemplified in the other case studies.

Lane Crawford describes an instance of a marketing failure within the otherwise highly successful Lane Crawford Group. Marketing failures can represent an opportunity to gain insight and perspective into the way marketing works, particularly when the failure is used as springboard for re-evaluation and a change in direction.

The expansion strategies aimed at by Eu Yan Sang can be described as 'work-in-progress' as the case study discusses the background to, and the implications of, the decisions the company is currently facing. A dilemma is involved since although Eu Yan Sang is a strong regional brand in Singapore looking to expand internationally, at present the company is uncertain as to the best strategy to adopt in approaching major international markets.

The case study on the organ donation drive of the National Kidney Foundation of Singapore also concerns whether a marketing strategy (a charity show involving daredevil stunts performed by celebrities) which has proved successful in one sphere of their activities (kidney dialysis) could prove equally successful when applied to fundraising for organ donation.

The case study on the importance of intellectual property alerts marketers to the importance of being fully knowledgeable about the laws concerning the protection of intellectual property. This is both in order to protect the intellectual property of one's own company and to avoid breaking the law, for example in the case of trade mark infringement.

Eu Yan Sang – Building a global brand

Eu Yan Sang company background

Eu Yan Sang (EYS) is a company that dispenses effective and quality traditional Chinese medicines (TMC) and herbs. Founded in 1979 by Eu Kwong Pai, the name of the company is made up of the words 'Yan' and 'Sang'. The former means benevolent, kind or humane in the Cantonese dialect while the latter represents birth, life or livelihood. 'Yan Sang' literally means 'caring for mankind'. Eu Kwong Pai's eldest son, Eu Tong Sen grew up dedicating himself to the family business and realising his father's goal. With determination and astute foresight, Eu Tong Sen established himself very quickly in Malaya and Singapore. Eventually, Eu Tong Sen expanded EYS's business to Hong Kong and China.

In the 1990s EYS's business operations were fragmented. There were six retail outlets in Malaysia and Singapore, and two stores in Hong Kong. Business turnover for the total region was S$10 million in Malaysia and Singapore, and HK$50 million in Hong Kong. The business operations were supported by a total of 170 staff. Business operations became fortified when EYS went from being a family-owned business to a company and this move also gave it a competitive advantage over the other TCM businesses in the market.

Since the late 1980s, the number of Chinese medicine shops has been in almost permanent decline, mainly due to the fact that less than 8% of the total TCM stores are owned by companies and family businesses close down as the owner retires. EYS, however, has gone from strength to strength and is Singapore's number one Chinese medicine business. The EYS brand of products is one of the best known of local consumer product brands in Singapore.

Eu Yan Sang today

EYS has currently established itself as a regional company, with a prominent market presence in the TCM markets (refer to appendix 29.A). EYS's business operations are consolidated at the Singapore headquarters. In 2000, EYS became a public-listed company, Eu Yan Sang International.

EYS retails, wholesales, and manufactures TCM products under the EYS brand name. The company also distributes and sells western and other medicines, invests in properties and provides management services, biomedical and applied life science technologies products and services. Currently, EYS has two factories in Hong Kong and one factory in Malaysia. Its regional chain of 72 self-operated retail stores and over 5 000 point-of-sale outlets in drugstores, supermarkets, medical halls and convenience stores worldwide make it a major player in the TCM industry. As of June 2002, business turnover is S$97,2 million with growth of over 18% from the previous year. Total staff strength is over 600 members strong.

No. of outlets	Dec 2002	Dec 2001
Hong Kong	23	18
Singapore	18	16
Malaysia	31	27
Total	**72**	**61**

Source: Eu Yan Sang Website (http://www.euyansang.com.sg/hk/content/en_US/aboutus/business.php)

Table 29.1: Number of EYS stores

Eu Yan Sang branding

EYS has shown that older, more traditional brands need not tread the path of obsolescence. With reinvention, EYS has succeeded in refreshing its brand, stayed relevant and continue to appeal to the consumers of today.

The 120-year 'Eu Yan Sang' brand name, synonymous with quality, has entrenched its presence in the key markets of Hong Kong, Singapore and Malaysia. With such brand recognition, EYS is differentiated from most other players in the fragmented TCM market.

Eu Yan Sang structure

EYS is divided into four arms, namely, Products, Services, Science, and Location. Each function works towards attaining the EYS vision:

> To be a leading global healthcare company leading the way to Integrative Healthcare with the core focus in Traditional Chinese Medicine.

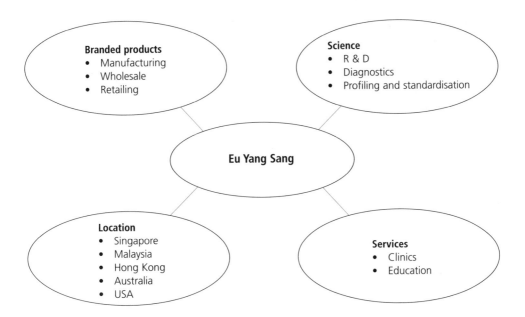

Figure 29.1: Structure of EYS – the four arms

Eu Yan Sang products

EYS manufactures and markets fine quality Chinese herbs and medicines under the 'Eu Yan Sang' brand name. The Group operates a regional chain of branded traditional Chinese medicine shops offering more than 150 products under its EYS brand name and over 1 000 different types of Chinese herbs and other medicinal products.

EYS's flagship products are Bo Ying Compound (wellness for infants) and Bak Foong Pills (wellness for women, a preparation of Chinese ginseng, deer antlers, black-bone chicken, and selected Chinese herbs). The other top selling product is the Bottled Bird's Nest (prepared from swallow's nest and rock sugar). EYS also offers a range of branded products like health foods e.g. Essence of Chicken and health supplements e.g. Lingzhi Cracked Spores Powder Capsules.

Product premium

EYS is known for its high product premium given its strong brand name supported by superior quality. Consumers pay a premium for the high grade raw materials, reliable control and scientific approach over the detoxification process. Most other Chinese medical halls do not have their own production facilities. Therefore, EYS is able to command a premium for its products.

Integrative Medicine Centers (IMC) & TCM clinics

EYS has also invested in a chain of fusion East/West Medical Centers in Australia known as YourHealth. The first center was opened in Sydney over a year ago, and recently, a second in Sydney, one in Melbourne and one in Brisbane. These four medical centers offer both modern western medicine and TCM. Each IMC would have a group of specialists, and in addition to doctors trained in western medicine, there are TCM Herbalists, Acupuncturists, Osteopaths, Clinical Nutritionists, Massage Therapists, Naturopaths, Biological Dentists, and Homeopaths to attend to the needs of patients.

In Singapore, YourHealth Singapore has modified the TCM concept to establish a chain of three clinics and centers, namely YourHealth Clinic, YourHealth Natural Therapy Centre, and YourHealth TCM Centre. EYS has also opened several TCM clinics attached to several retail outlets. There are four such clinics each, in Singapore and Malaysia.

Wholesale

Some of the more popular Eu Yan Sang products, like Bak Foong Pill, Bo Ying Compound, herbal candies and packaged food products, are sold through a network of over 5 000 drugstores, supermarkets, medical halls and convenience stores worldwide. These include outlets of wholesale chains such as Mannings, Watson's, Park 'n Shop, Wellcome and Jusco in Hong Kong; Carrefour, Jaya Jusco, Giant, Makro, Parkson's and The Store in Malaysia; and Guardian, Cold Storage, NTUC FairPrice, Watson's, Nature's Farm, and selected polyclinics under the National Healthcare Group Pharmacies in Singapore.

Manufacturing

EYS's manufacturing activities are carried out primarily at its two Good Manufacturing Practice (GMP)-certified factories located in Chai Wan, Hong Kong and Cheras, Kuala Lumpur, Malaysia. They produce more than 50 different types of powder, pill and capsule products. The manufacture of other packaged food products like bottled birds' nest, chicken essence, herbal jellies, herbal candies, and ginseng wines are sub-contracted to third parties.

The branding dilemma in international markets

Although EYS's local branding strategy has successfully differentiated EYS from other Traditional Chinese Medicine players, the EYS annual survey report shows that EYS's international brand name recognition is very low. In order to develop EYS's competitive advantage in the international market such as Australia and the United States, the company needs to find ways to innovate, leverage on knowledge and to establish a clearer branding direction in those countries.

On of the main threats to EYS international expansion is that such markets are predominately influenced by western medicines rather than Chinese medicines. EYS cannot simply apply the local strategy to other markets as each market differs and communications need to be localised to suit the particular culture.

EYS currently has two alternatives at its disposal. Firstly, EPS can market its products by their product names only, for example, the Bak Foong Pills. There are many products and every product has a different market positioning. The second alternative would be to pursue a global branding under the EYS brand name. This would mean that all the products come under the global EYS branding umbrella, and share a common branding. The two alternatives present divergent paths with major implications for the entire groups' marketing strategy.

At present EYS has undertaken to analyse its markets in order to make a more informed decision as to which strategy the company should undertake in order to attain its branding objectives.

Conclusion

EYS aims to transform from a Chinese medical hall to a global consumer healthcare group. This is evident by the shift in existing product mix and efforts in new product developments. With the introduction of integrative medical centers and further expansion of TCM clinics, EYS has brought TCM as a complementary medicine closer to consumers. It remains to be seen how the regional brand will leverage its strengths in approaching major international markets in the future.

SINGAPORE
Eu Yan Sang (Singapore) Private Limited
Eu Realty (Singapore) Private Limited
Eu Yan Sang Marketing Private Limited
Applied Biomedical International Pte Ltd
EYS Kang Hong Herbal Pte Ltd
Yin Yang Spa products Pte Ltd

HONG KONG
Eu Yan Sang (Hong Kong) Ltd
EYS Medical Services Limited

Eu Yang Sang International Ltd.

MALAYSIA
Eu Yan Sang (1959) Sdn. Berhad
Weng Li Sdn. Bhd.
Eu Yan Sang Heritage Sdn. Bhd.
Degree Achievement Sdn. Bhd.

AUSTRALIA
Eu Yan Sang (Australia) Pty Ltd

Appendix 29.A: EYS regional structure

References

1   This case study was provided by May Lwin and Jacqueline Chow. May Lwin is an Assistant
     Professor of Marketing, National University of Singapore Business School. Jacqueline Chow is a
     post-graduate student, National University of Singapore Business School. This case was prepared
     as a basis for class discussion. The cooperation of Eu Yan Sang is gratefully acknowledged.
     Selected financial and market data have been disguised for confidentiality reasons.
     Case study procured by Michael Cant.

Lane Crawford: To be or not to be... in Singapore

History[1]

Lane Crawford's history extends back 155 years to 1850 when T.A. Lane and his friend Ninian Crawford went into partnership and started a business in the new and flourishing territory of Hong Kong. Now owned by the Wheelock Group, a trading and property conglomerate, Lane Crawford has since grown into one of Hong Kong's leading local department store chains with five operating stores as well as more than 20 specialty and shoe shops in Hong Kong, China and Singapore. In Hong Kong, Lane Crawford has four locations, each occupying an average of 50 000 square feet, including Central, Pacific Place in Admiralty, Ocean Terminal in Tsim Sha Tsui, and Times Square in Causeway Bay, all in key shopping areas. Lane Crawford also operates designers' boutiques, including Alberta Ferretti, Bruno Magli, On Pedder, Sergio Rossi as well as Lane Crawford Luggage and Lane Crawford Jewellery.

Positioned as a specialty store operator that caters primarily to the upper end of the market, Lane Crawford is synonymous with the world's best known luxury brands in fashion, jewellery, home furnishings and accessories. It prides itself on merchandise excellence and has a philosophy of service superiority and an enjoyable shopping environment. Through the years, the name Lane Crawford has become a brand (LC) unto itself, an iconic watch tower for fashion-conscious consumers as well as retailers throughout Hong Kong and in mainland China. It has always been a trendsetter for the Hong Kong market and is regarded as the Harrods of the territory for its branded goods and high-class image. Offering the most premium and international brands, Lane Crawford is also considered a market leader in Southeast Asia and a prime retailer of the most fashionable accessories brands, carrying big names such as Sergio Rossi, Manolo Blahnik and Jimmy Choo.

Despite its sound management and leadership status in Hong Kong, Lane Crawford's expansion into the region, especially Singapore, has not been smooth sailing. Although top officials from the company have regularly indicated their interest to set up more stores in China, till now it only operates one Lane Crawford store and five Hugo Boss boutiques in China. It had also planned for an expansion into Taiwan at the beginning of the decade, which faltered and then faded away. More importantly, the store's disastrous attempt to break into the Singapore retail market lasted for only two years despite bouts of downsizing, renovating and changes in management.

Its foray into Singapore was cited as one of the main reasons for Lane Crawford's huge decline in revenue during its operation and eventually resulted in the company being de-listed and taken private[2] by its owner, the Wheelock Group. Lane Crawford's 200 000 sq ft Singapore store opened on June 17 1994, marking its first major extension of retailing activities into the region outside Hong Kong and China. Being Lane Crawford's maiden foreign venture, it was initially planned as a test-bed for setting up more stores in the region. Analysts and Lane Crawford's management have both offered various reasons behind the store's failure in Singapore, such as the bad economic climate, management problems, etc. What exactly went wrong? Could its Singapore closure have been prevented if things had been done differently? This case study discusses the market failure of the Singapore Lane Crawford store and then goes on to examine the company's change in strategy and the subsequent renewed and increased success of its On Pedder stores.

Opening of Lane Crawford – Rocky start

Wheelock Group planned to enter the Singapore market with a view to using Singapore as a springboard for retail expansion throughout the region, including Malaysia, Thailand and China. The Group considered Singapore to be a good market given the increasing sophistication of the Singaporean shopper. Initially the Group planned to open a 60 000 sq ft store but eventually settled on a 200 000 sq ft retail space in Orchard Road, chosen since it was owned by the Group's Marco Polo Developments. Moreover, its location was inside the city centre but just outside the central business district and was seen by the management as having great potential, particularly for the middle-income earner market.

Right from its opening in May 1994, the new department store did not take the Lion City shopping market by storm. People criticised the location and merchandising and the store also struggled to come to terms with the difficult local market from day one (see Table 30.1 below for full chronology). Market conditions and government retail policy had changed and the store was hit by a major downturn in retail demand. The Singapore store was the biggest contributor to Lane Crawford's fall in net profit in 1994, and operations were not expected to improve for at least another twelve months.

Sequence of Events

Jun-94	Opening of a 200 000 sq-ft Lane Crawford store
Apr-95	Revamp of the store to 42 400 sq-ft; from 5 storeys to 2 storeys
Sep-96	Lane Crawford announced that it would give up the remaining space due to consistent losses
Oct-96	Closure of Lane Crawford's Singapore store
Dec-96	Lane Crawford bounced back into Singapore with On Pedder, a speciality shoes and accessories store

Table 30.1: Chronology of Lane Crawford's operations in Singapore

Revamp – Attempt at recovery

In April 1995, barely a year after opening Lane Crawford was faced with the task of planning a recovery strategy for the failed store. The Group announced that it would give up the top three levels of the five-storey store, shrinking the size of the store from 204 000 sq ft to 42 400 sq ft – less than a quarter of its original size. Major changes were also made in the senior management and merchandising teams for Singapore in order to put the store back in the black. The previous expatriate general manager was replaced by one who had grown up in Singapore and a local team of buyers was formed to guide the Hong Kong unit on the appropriate purchases for Singapore. Following its decision to cut its retail space by a drastic 80%, Lane Crawford also carried out a retrenchment exercise where it reduced up to half of its staff.

In order to achieve better returns from the smaller selling space, and realising that the mid-price market was overcrowded, Lane Crawford planned to reposition itself from being a department store with a vast core to pull in the masses to being a specialty fashion store, refocusing on selling upmarket and quality fashion. This move consequently required a major rethink of its product lines in order to decide what would most appeal to its new target market as well as which departments had to be scrapped. As part of the makeover, the store underwent a S$1,8 million storewide retrofit.

With the reduction of dedicated retail space, the loss-incurring store did away with its children's and fragrance departments in addition to downsizing its remaining departments. It also made a variety of other plans, the outcome of which is discussed in the next section. The plans largely involved the prioritising of the target market. For instance, Lane Crawford Express, which sells young fashion, could be spun off and relocated. The refitted store could continue to sell fashion wear, home furnishings and gifts. It could be anchored by its popular shoes and leather accessories department, which accounted for a third of sales and could be targeted at stylish women. The current 7 000 sq ft shoe and accessories department could be enlarged by 2 000–3 000 sq ft to make it the mainstay of the new Lane Crawford store.

In addition, to add variety to all the departments, Lane Crawford could complement its own merchandise mix by inviting concessionaires of upmarket branded goods. The store was especially keen on concessionaires that feature shoes as an important part of their overall merchandise. With the addition of such concessionaires, the 7 000 sq ft shoe and accessories department could increase in size by about 35%. There would also be the addition of cosmetics counters for the first time. Lane Crawford was expected to sub-let half to 70% of its space to these cosmetics and branded goods concessionaires.

The store was also out to capture more tourists and local shoppers by making the store a more 'happening place'. On the agenda were more 'stylish food and beverage outlets' such as outdoor cafés. Lane Crawford would have within six months a café fronting the main entrance facing Orchard Road, and another at the Globe Piazza, facing Orchard Boulevard. Negotiations were ongoing with Olio-Dome to manage the proposed outlets. Lane Crawford was also in talks with theme restaurant operators Planet Hollywood and Fashion Café to clinch either of the chains as a sub-tenant. Securing either of the two operators could boost the image that Lane Crawford had been building up as a specialty fashion store, after slashing its store size from five levels to two.

Closure

However, most of the plans did not materialise and the Singapore store continued to post losses and to drag down its Hong Kong-listed parent's earnings. Talks with Fashion Café fell through, while Planet Hollywood settled for a location next to the store at Liat Towers. Lane Crawford also abandoned the plan to search for concessionaires, deciding to let the store consolidate first before taking the next step. Lane Crawford Singapore lost HK$132,5 million (S$23,8 million) for the year ended March 31 1995. During that period, the parent group's net profit plunged 64% to HK$131,7 million, from HK$362,1 million previously, with much of the drain on profits blamed on the company's ill-fated Singapore venture. For the six months ended September 30 1995, the store was again blamed for a 50% decline in Lane Crawford International's group net profit, from HK$52,6 million to HK$26,4 million. Earnings at Lane Crawford also collapsed for the year to March 31 1996, with operating profit plunging 45% to HK$16,8 million and the Singapore store taking most of the blame once again.

As a last resort, Lane Crawford sought to cut the size of its store again to only the ground floor in a bid to reduce its overheads and operate as an exclusive specialty store. However, Lane Crawford's Singapore landlord and sister company, Wheelock-owned Marco Polo Developments, rejected the request because it could make more in rents from smaller shops. Marco Polo felt it would be unable to maximise its returns on the two storeys and would continue to run the risk that Lane Crawford might eventually terminate its seven-year lease prematurely. Marco Polo and Lane Crawford then agreed to end the lease four years ahead of schedule. In September 1996, it announced that it would give up the remaining space of its loss-making Singapore operation, after a drastic move to make it profitable by halving the size of the store failed.

The closure would cost Marco Polo S$21,35 million in contracted potential rentals and S$2,92 million in service charges receivable. Marco Polo also needed to spend another S$6,3 million to convert the first two floors of Lane Crawford into small shops which it would rent out individually. In return, Marco Polo would receive a compensation of only S$3,15 million in a one-off payment from Lane Crawford. This was paltry compensation for Marco Polo, which spent S$460 million to build Lane Crawford Place, of which $308 million went to buying the land on a 99-year lease from the government. The assurance of a constant rental stream from Lane Crawford could have had a part in this. In fact, the building was named Lane Crawford Place even as Marco Polo was putting in its first bid. For a start, it had earlier agreed to reduce Lane Crawford's space from five to two floors just a year ago, and take over the two basements, with a total rental loss of S$54 million. So the relationship between the two was more than mere tenant and landlord. They were more like partners, in spirit at least. Now the partnership broke up and Marco Polo left with what seems the short end of the stick. What Lane Crawford did was to put up a cash security deposit of S$1,18 million and a bank guarantee of S$2 million against default and early termination of lease. With the lease given a premature four-year demise, even this S$2 million could not be 'called upon' (Marco Polo's words) as the termination was by mutual agreement. In the market, it was unheard of for a retailer to break a firm, long-term contract on such terms even once, let alone twice.

Lane Crawford's $2\frac{1}{2}$-year-old Singapore store closed on 1 October 1996, thus ending one of the most disastrous forays in Lane Crawford's 150-year history. Other retailers who had also bowed out from the Singapore retail market included CK Tang's Nex.is and Tangs Studio outlets, Tanglin Place, Galeries Lafayette, Tanglin General Store as well as Kmart. The move to Singapore had cost HK$132,5 million, and the store had been expected to be nearing the break-even point at March 1996. Lane Crawford said it was pulling out in such a short time because it had suffered further losses, and its business hadn't improved despite its downsizing and further efforts and investments in promotion, advertising as well as changing its merchandise mixes. The closure, cost the company HK$57,4 million (S$10,47 million) and contributed to a loss of HK$90,8 million in the six

months ended September 30 1996. Coinciding with a downturn in the retail
sector across Asia, the closure officially put an end to Lane Crawford's regional
ambitions.

Reasons why Lane Crawford failed in Singapore

Analysts have persistently criticised Lane Crawford's decision to open a store in
Singapore. There are several reasons why Lane Crawford in Singapore foundered.
One was government policy. Early in 1994, the Singapore government introduced
measures to lure shoppers away from the central district, creating more shopping
districts in the city state. This ultimately resulted in a huge increase in rental space
as well as a dilution of human traffic. As a result, department stores in the city
centre were badly hurt as people began to shop more at suburban shopping malls
closer to their homes. Lane Crawford chose exactly this time to open their store
at the junction of Orchard Road.

Another crucial factor was the bad economic climate at that time. Lane
Crawford's woes here have been partly attributed to the highly competitive local
retail market which had claimed several victims including listed retailers C K
Tang, Metro and Isetan which lost money for three years running. Soaring rentals
and staffing costs, coupled with consumers' decreasing disposable incomes due to
high property prices and a stock market fall, crushed the territory's retailers. The
industry was 'scraping the bottom of the barrel' while coming under pressure
from a tight labour market, rising wages and an economic slowdown.

Furthermore, although Singapore had long been famous as a shopper's para-
dise, its department stores faced increasing competition from new giant shopping
malls opening all over South-East Asia such as Jakarta, Kuala Lumpur, Bangkok
and Manila. With all the big brand names in their backyard, Orchard Road thus
lost many big spending visitors from neighbouring countries, especially Indonesia
and Malaysia. Another serious problem lay in the continued strengthening of the
Singapore dollar, which kept even the most enthusiastic Japanese shopper at bay.
A strengthening yen combined with the recession in Japan had curbed some of
the Japanese instinct to shop in the region. Those who still came were keeping
their wallets zipped and spending 40% less than they were before. At the same
time, the increasing popularity of Singaporeans travelling overseas also meant
that local retailers could no longer count on local shoppers in times of low tourist
spending. Singaporeans are becoming great travellers, many taking two foreign
holidays a year, and with the strong Singapore dollar in their pocket they are
prepared to spend when they go. The competition to Lane Crawford, Robinsons
and other up-market stores was not solely from their rivals across the road but
included the houses of Los Angeles, Sydney, Paris, London and Milan.

Although most see Lane Crawford's problems as a result of Singapore's difficult
retail scene, the store's concept and management difficulties have also contributed to its problems: the merchandising was wrong and the store was too big

(200 000 sq ft compared with the average 50 000 sq feet Hong Kong store) and also too expensive for the market conditions in Singapore.

Some also attributed Lane Crawford's poor performance to its merchandising plan that went terribly wrong. From the start, it had been a mistake to have placed a British manager with no Asian experience to head the store. Furthermore, its merchandising team was inexperienced in choosing the right product mix for such a large outlet. It certainly did not help that none of the Hong Kong buyers for the new store had even done a Singapore market survey before Lane Crawford opened its doors. The Singapore outlet thus ended up replicating Hong Kong stocks which did not appeal to a more casual society living in a tropical climate. It even stocked as much, if not more, goods than all the Hong Kong stores put together. More importantly, Lane Crawford had a reputation for non-aggressive management.

Lane Crawford's fate also showed how crucial a role marketing strategies play in the survival of retailers in the face of tough conditions in the industry. First, there was a lack of marketing done to promote the launch of the Singapore store. Neither did the store spend much on advertising (minimal compared to other retailers) to market the many brands completely unfamiliar to the local shopper. It was as if the store was relying on the strength of Lane Crawford's reputation in Hong Kong and the sheer size of the Singapore store to sell the merchandise. Furthermore, their products were often deemed too expensive and overpriced for the local market. What was worse, they failed to create sufficient public awareness when they changed their product mix. This all contributed to a recipe for disaster which led Lane Crawford to suffer a massive loss of S$10,47 million.

Further closures

Following the closure of the Singapore store, Lane Crawford also announced the closure and transfer of its Causeway Bay operation in Windsor House, a core shopping area, to Times Square. The slump in retail sales has also forced Lane Crawford to abandon plans to open a HK$30 million flagship store in Kowloon as well as to lease 50 000 sq ft, or five of the seven retailing floors, at Titus Square, Tsim Sha Tsui. Earnings from its outlets in China have also been flat since the stores were still at a 'developmental stage' and Lane Crawford opted to take a 'selective and cautious' approach in China.

Effect on company image

In its home territory in Hong Kong, Lane Crawford, once regarded as the Hong Kong equivalent of Harrods had also blown away its strong name and consequently acquired a poor image. The brand name – based on almost 150 years of business – had possessed immense goodwill as a quality retailer. The store used to be the place to leave your wedding list. But over the years, competitors, especially swish Japanese retailers such as Matsusakaya and Sogo, had come to dominate the upper end of the market. Lane Crawford's product lines were now not moving. The company also lost the distribution rights to the Escada and Hugo Boss lines, and analysts predict that more defections are sure to follow. Analysts observed that the stores were old and tired and lacked sex appeal. The company once again recorded an operating loss of HK$54,5 million for the six months to September 30 1999, following a loss of about HK$46,2 million for the whole of the financial year to March 31 in 1998.

The failure of expansion overseas to significantly contribute to profits – such as Singapore – and the horrid retail recession in Hong Kong affected investor confidence in the stock's profit outlook. The three-year slump also led to continued speculation that the concern would be sold – either privately within the massive Wheelock Group or to another party.

Privatisation

The Wheelock Group later announced that it would buy the one-quarter of the company's stock it didn't already own and take the ailing department-store chain private for HK$384 million. However, Wheelock was forced to raise its offer to HK$406,7 million when a group of shareholders holding 10% of Lane Crawford's shares complained that Wheelock was taking advantage of a temporary downturn in Asian consumer spending to snap up a grand old brand name at a substantial discount for less than its net asset value. Its initial offer price also failed to take into consideration the current market value of its investment portfolio and its flagship property in Central. The shareholders said the company had poured 'as much doom and gloom as possible' into last year's profit and loss account to boost the chances of a successful takeover. With those objecting to its privatisation pacified by an increase in the offer price, Lane Crawford was successfully taken private on 30 July 1999.

Management changes – Moving forwards

With its privatisation completed, Lane Crawford now had to find ways to revamp its business and restore its former glory. Analysts adhered to the fact that the underlying business of Lane Crawford was sound and that with restructuring it could counter its competition. Hence, the store underwent a major management rethink and decisions were made to improve its marketing and merchandising strategies. While Lane Crawford had always catered to the top end, it obviously hadn't been doing well at all. Attempts had to be made to re-brand part of the Lane Crawford image to attract a younger luxury shopper in order to become viable.

Lane Crawford was also consistently renovating and expanding its stores. For example, the company invested heavily in its flagship store on Queen's Road in Central. A facelift was given to the Shoes and Accessories, Jewellery, Cosmetic and Men's Departments in order to create a state-of-the-art environment for a more rewarding shopping experience. The revamped store will also boast a personal shopping corner that will provide a link to what is happening elsewhere in the store. The personal shopping service, the first of its kind in Hong Kong, is complimentary. Also, in its quest for opportunities, Lane Crawford opened its latest outlet on Canton Road in Tsim Sha Tsui, dedicating 15 000 sq ft of its 55 000 sq ft area to a men's department – a niche market not catered for in Hong Kong. This department provides everything a man needs, from games to cuff links to socks and suits. Besides giving their stores a facelift, Lane Crawford's management has also expanded into China, with a joint-venture department store in Shanghai – Maison Mode Department Store – as well as boutiques in Shanghai, Beijing and Guangzhou. It also has a Lane Crawford in Shanghai, and a Lane Crawford joint venture in Harbin, and a a similar operation planned in Hangzhou.

Merchandise-wise, Lane Crawford felt that it was important to develop a real personality in terms of its product mix. The store would thus keep its focus on fashion-forward footwear and accessories. The Accessories Department, one of its best selling departments, is being expanded to accommodate more designer shoes, bags and jewellery. In order to attract its new target market consisting of the young luxury shopper, there also will be a new designer area on the first floor for special, young, designer, couture-quality fashion. Lane Crawford's latest fashion and accessories brand acquisitions are summarised in Table 30.2 below. In addition, the beauty floor has recently acquired popular brands such as Bobbi Brown, MAC and Shiseido, in addition to cabins for skin care treatments. New products were also introduced. For example, a first of its kind Period Jewelry Corner was opened at the flagship store with special antique jewellery pieces selected from capitals of the world. Further, the store added its own creations named the Lane Crawford Jewelry Collection to its jewellery department. Lane Crawford also became the only Asian outlet to secure a series of exclusives. These include being able to debut the collection of womenswear newcomer Lambertson Truex, Michael Kors' bags and shoes line and Stockholm menswear name J. Lindeberg, at the same time as Europe. The jewel in the crown of the Group's achievements lay in the store's launch of Prada cosmetics on March 17 2001. Exclusivity has always been part of Lane Crawford's history, and Wong says that about 85% of its merchandise is exclusive to Lane Crawford.

There was also an increased emphasis on home goods. Its selection of modern, contemporary and classic home accessories has always been a trendsetter for the local market. Following the success of the East Meets West Collection launched in 1999, Lane Crawford will continue its search for quality home products from all over the world to offer a whole new dimension of home deco and lifestyle.

Lane Crawford said that the management changes were already starting to produce encouraging results with an improved merchandising mix and a revitalised brand portfolio. The store has seen an increase in customers as well as increased spending per customer. For the year 2002, Lane Crawford remained profitable (HK$10,5 million) despite the overall retail sector heading a downturn. According to its general manager the profit margin was achieved through merchandising, diligent expansion and value building, enhanced by improvements in performance and market conditions. However, the store is certainly not resting on its laurels. Besides introducing new international designer brands during the different seasons, there will also be a constant process of sourcing new items for all its departments.

Australia	**United Kingdom**
Akira Isogawa	Hussein Chalayan
	Jimmy Choo
France	Matthew Williamson
Olivier Theyskens	
Courreges	**United States**
Christian Louboutin	Daryl K
	John Varvatos
Germany	Lambertson Truex
Strenesse Gabriele Strehle	
	Sweden
Italy	J. Lindeberg
Alberta Ferretti, Tuleh	
Armani Le Collezioni	

Table 30.2: Lane Crawford's latest fashion and accessories brand acquisitions

Bouncing back in Singapore with On Pedder

After the failure in Singapore Lane Crawford underwent major changes in merchandise management and strategy and was able to bounce back into Singapore with On Pedder, a 2 600 sq ft shoes and accessories shop in Ngee Ann City just three months after the Singapore closure. On Pedder, which first opened in Hong Kong's Pedder Street in 1996, was one of the first concept shops in the world to put the trendiest selection of both the big names and the no-names together in a series of free-standing stores. The On Pedder chain now operates four stores in Hong Kong, one in Singapore, one in Taipei and another three are slated to open in the coming season. Singapore is Lane Crawford's third On Pedder outlet. More than 70% of the merchandise in the Singapore outlet comprises of footwear by big names such as Jimmy Choo, Moschino, Isaac Mizrahi, Todd Oldham and other designers, with accessories such as handbags, scarves, belts and hats making up the rest. Sales were more than encouraging, with shoppers snapping up more than 40 pairs of shoes worth over $300 each in just three hours on the opening day. On Pedder, which has become one of Singapore's best-selling shoe stores, now moves 12 000 pairs of soles a year and in 2000 it added up to more than 20% of the Group's total HK$102,5 million (S$22,5 million) profit.

It seemed that Lane Crawford had hit the jackpot with its product decisions – the shoes and accessories business had been a success from day one, even during 1994–1996 when Lane Crawford was headed toward closure. During Lane Crawford's first year of operations in the new Singapore store, footwear unexpectedly turned out to be the most profitable department. Even as the Singapore store was bleeding its Hong Kong-listed parent company, Lane Crawford International, of HK$90,8 million (S$16,4 million) in losses in 2002, its shoe sales were tops in the region. Its shoe department not only accounted for 40% of its total domestic trade, but was also growing at 12% every three months. When Lane Crawford was closing down a lot of customers expressed disappointment that they were going to be losing what had become a destination for footwear and accessories shopping.

Lane Crawford was thus alerted to an opening new market for specialty shoes in Asia, if not the world. The company had realised that women were turning their attention from clothes to accessories, particularly shoes. With clothes becoming simpler, sales in accessories such as shoes, bags and belts – to dress up the clothes – have never been better. The store expected that the current interest in footwear would develop into a fetish for expensive bags and related accessories, hence explaining its foray into a specialty shoes and accessories shop. Up until then, only luxury shoemakers such as Charles Jourdan and Sergio Rossi dared to open their own shoe shops based on the power of their names. Small boutiques and big stores would only run inconsequential mixed-brand corners of lesser-known footwear names, as an alternative to better-priced heels.

The success of the first two shops in Shanghai and Hong Kong also spurred the Group to open the Singapore outlet. Shoes bought were not only in the latest styles – graduated wedge heels and conical stilettos – they were also no longer in the budget price range of $200 and below, but all above $500. Such 'surprising' sales figures made it feasible to stage a comeback for Lane Crawford in Singapore that year in order to capitalise on the unique success. While Tangs and Tangs Studio successfully introduced the concept of multi-brand shoe shops to Singapore in the early '90s, when most branded shoes were sold in their own shops, it was Lane Crawford who made the one-stop, multi-brand shoe boutique a hit with its thematic approach of grouping several shoe labels of a similar theme together. In this way, Lane Crawford catered to a broad range of shoe tastes, from the dainty and formal to the chunky and casual in various corners of the store.

The sale of shoes helped to identify two niches in the Asian market: brand-name shoes, like Moschino, for label-conscious shoppers who may not be able to afford the clothing but can buy footwear at a tenth of its prices; and designer look-a-likes at a fraction of designer prices. For the former target market, Lane Crawford had the exclusive rights to retail and distribute the bulk of the best footwear brands, from the Italian Sergio Rossi and Bruno Magli, to Sigerson Morrison and Todd Oldham from the United States, in Hong Kong and China. Most of the brands are also exclusive to the store in Singapore. Furthermore, its wide retail network gave Lane Crawford a unique advantage in possessing the means to commission Italian and Spanish manufacturers of designer shoes such as Armani and Moschino to develop specialised products such as mixed animal-print boots, as well as create private labels like Lane Crawford and Giglio, for Lane Crawford stores. Thanks to this approach, 'designer-look' shoes, with an almost-identical European make, can start at prices from as low as S$79.

Setting its sights on conquering Asia, Lane Crawford has spun its footwear division into a separate company called Pedder Group, which will be in charge of ladies footwear and accessories for all Lane Crawford stores as well as the On Pedder boutique chain and branded freestanding stores including high-end labels such as Sergio Rossi and Bruno Magli. Future plans involve expanding in the current markets and investigating opportunities in new markets like Korea.

The losses incurred by the Lane Crawford store in Singapore between 1994 and 1996 not only led to the birth of the successful On Pedder shoe business, it also led to the most up-to-date overhaul of what was once considered the dinosaur of Hong Kong retail scene. Its On Pedder business hence enabled Lane Crawford to regain its firm footing eventually. Now, it is looking to expand with more On Pedder outlets as well as Lane Crawford stores in China, Singapore, Taiwan and Sydney.

The future of Lane Crawford

With the success of its On Pedder outlet, Lane Crawford considered setting up another shop in Orchard Road, this time selling clothes, shoes and accessories, as well as another On Pedder outlet. Some questioned whether it was too soon for Lane Crawford to expand given its limited success in Singapore. Has Lane Crawford fully learned its lesson? Will it face the same predicament as Galeries Lafayette who was forced to exit the difficult local retail scene in January 1996 for a second time after another failed attempt to establish itself in Singapore?

Given its intention of opening new stores, the question of location comes up. After all, this particular factor contributed to its failure in 1996. Should it continue to operate in Orchard Road, or consider setting up shops in the suburbs such as Tampines, Bishan or Jurong? Additionally, what sort of positioning should the new stores adopt? Should Lane Crawford continue chasing the high-end market, or should it change its target market to the middle-income earners? What sort of merchandise should they sell this time to guarantee success? Lots of questions abound, and hopefully Lane Crawford can learn from the mistakes made from its first foray into the local scene to find a perfect strategy for its second attempt to conquer the Singapore retail market. The strategy should also propel Lane Crawford into expansion mode among existing locations and ignite the plans for the opening of Lane Crawford stores in new markets. The future of Lane Crawford depends on implementing the correct solutions to issues the company faces.[3]

Lane Crawford in China (Shanghai)

Lane Crawford in Hong Kong

Lane Crawford – Store interior

On Pedder store in Singapore at Ngee Ann City

Appendix 30.A*:External façade and store interior of Lane Crawford's department and On Pedder Stores

*All pictures are property of the Lane Crawford website

References

1   Case study by Dr Prem Shamdasani, Associate Professor of Marketing, NUS Business School. This case study was prepared with information from public sources as the basis for class discussion rather than to illustrate either effective or ineffective handling of an administrative situation. The author gratefully acknowledges the research assistance of Juliana Tan and Emily Kwok and the research funding from the NUS Business School.
Copyright © 2003 Dr Prem Shamdasani. No part of this publication may be reproduced or transmitted in any form or by any means without the permission of the author.
Case study procured by Michael Cant.

2   Wheelock & Co has proposed divesting its entire retail portfolio – Lane Crawford and City Super department stores and Joyce Boutique Holdings – in deals worth HK$589.8 million. The bulk of the assets will be sold to family trusts linked to Wheelock chairman Peter Woo Kwong-ching – *South China Morning Post* (23 February 2003).

3   Information in this case study was gathered with grateful acknowledgement from the following publications: *Far Eastern Economic Review, South China Morning Post, Footwear News, The Straits Times, Hong Kong Standard, Business Times Singapore, Singapore Straits Times, Business Times, Dow Jones International News, The Asian Wall Street Journal, Dow Jones Asian Equities Report.*

The importance of intellectual property

Consider the details of the court case between South African Breweries (SAB) and Laugh it Off Promotions CC (LIOP). At what point does resourceful marketing cross the boundaries to become a case of trade mark infringement? Judgment of the case described below took place in April 2003.[1]

> In *South African Breweries International (Finance) BV t/a Sabmark International v Laugh It Off Promotions CC*, SAB had trade mark registrations for the words Carling Black Label, and for a depiction of its product's label. LIOP manufactured shirts featuring the Black Label beer logo containing the words 'Black Labour – Africa's lusty lively exploitation since 1952'. The words 'Carling Beer' were replaced with the words 'White guilt' in the same colour and font.
>
> SAB argued that it owned the Black Label trade mark and had used it in South Africa since 1966. It was submitted that Black Label is a well-known mark in South Africa and that LIOP's use took unfair advantage of, and was detrimental to, the distinctive character and repute of the trade mark. The use was said to be distasteful and undesirable. LIOP countered by saying that its use amounted to freedom of speech, but the court was not impressed and LIOP was ordered to cease its infringing use and pay SAB's legal costs. LIOP is taking the matter to the Appeal Court and the case has yet to be finalised.

The marketing strategy used by Laugh it Off Promotions consisted of riding on the fame of, and subverting, the slogans of other famous brand names, for Laugh it Off's own positive brand building. Regardless of whether or not this particular strategy is good marketing, the case provides a powerful lesson for marketers: successful marketers need to take cognisance of the laws on the protection of intellectual property and avoid trade mark infringement. This chapter discusses some of the intellectual property concepts and laws which marketers need to be aware of.

Intellectual property

Intellectual property can be described as any asset(s), which has been developed through the application of the intellect of a person or group. The worth of intellectual property is often undervalued, considering that it can be a company's most valuable asset in a marketing campaign. A prime example of an intellectual property right with huge economic worth is the Coca-Cola trade mark. It is imperative that companies identify their intellectual property and properly protect their intellectual property rights.

As intellectual property may become an asset of great value to a company, it is advisable to approach intellectual property experts to discuss the protection of rights in intellectual property, rather than later losing those rights to other competitors. There are various forms of intellectual property and the most relevant of these are briefly discussed below:

Patents

Patents may be granted for new inventions which involve an inventive step and which are capable of being used or applied in trade, industry or agriculture. The South African patent system is governed by the Patents Act of 1978, which affords protection to patents for inventions. Novelty is an absolute requirement for patentability in South Africa. This means that inventions that are already known (either because the person responsible for the invention has made his invention available or because someone else has already made the invention and distributed it) cannot form the subject of patent rights. Protection is refused to obvious inventions. An obvious invention lacks inventiveness: typically this happens where a person takes the invention of another person and makes a minor change to that invention and that change would be obvious to anyone skilled in the craft of the invention in question.

The Patents Office will examine patent applications to ensure compliance to form only: no examination on the merits takes place. This means that the registrar will not search his records to determine whether the filed patent covers an invention which is the subject of a prior patent. It is therefore possible to spend vast resources on the filing of a patent that cannot be protected (because, for example, it is not novel or it is obvious). Accordingly, it is imperative to obtain assistance from a registered patent agent when filing patent applications. A further reason to consult a patent agent is because the patent specification (the wording that describes the invention and the various parts and working thereof) must be precise. Patent agents have had years of training in the drafting of patent specifications.

The importance of precise wording was illustrated in the case of *Nampak Products and Another v Man-Dirk* (a matter heard in the Supreme Court of Appeal in 1999). In this matter, Nampak's Pressure Resistant Bag was described as consisting of:

(a) a pressure resistant bag including

(b) a first bag ...;

(c) an envelope... in which the first bag is located;

(d) a second bag... in which the envelope is located; and

(e) a filter arrangement which is attached to and opens into the first bag and passes through apertures in the envelope and second bag.

Man-Dirk manufactured a similar article, differing only in that it had a 'sleeve' rather than a 'second bag'. The court decided that the normal meaning of 'bag' is 'a receptacle of flexible material open only at the top (where it can be closed)' and Man-Dirk's product was accordingly found not to contain one of the essential elements of the patented product. Accordingly Man-Dirk's product did not infringe.

The patent term is twenty years from the date of filing of the complete specification. A patent must be renewed every year from the fourth following the filing date. One of the great values of patent registrations is their capacity to reserve for the patent rights holder the right to make, use, exercise and dispose of the invention during the validity period of the patent.

This was of importance to Monsanto Company in 1986. Monsanto acquired a patent in respect of its 'Phytotoxicants' product (a fertiliser). This right expired on 1 March 1986. On 4 April 1986, Stauffer Chemical SA (Pty) Ltd filed application for registration of its 'WENNER' product (a 'phytotoxicant' for maize).

Although the application for the WENNER patent was made after expiry of Monsanto's phytotoxicant patent, the court found that the tests and field trials conducted in order to develop the WENNER product took place prior to 1 March 1986 and these amounted to infringing use. Stauffer was ordered to cease all disposals of phytotoxicants and also to deliver all stocks of its WENNER product to Monsanto. Naturally, this would have been a major commercial setback for Stauffer and would have artificially assisted Monsanto to retain the exclusiveness of its product in the marketplace.

Trade marks

The Trade Marks Act of 1993 (as amended) governs the South African trade mark registration system. Distinctive signs of all kinds and descriptions which are capable of graphical representation are registrable as trade marks. An effective trade mark registration grants the proprietor of the trade mark protection against unauthorised use of both identical and confusingly similar marks in relation to the goods or services in respect of which a mark is registered or similar goods and/or services.

It is also possible to obtain rights in a trade mark in terms of the common law if the trade mark is used to such an extent that a reputation and goodwill is acquired therein. It is, however, fairly costly to prove the existence of common law trade marks in court and it is therefore preferable to obtain registration of trade marks.

Another trade mark related case that made headlines in 1997 was the McDonald's case. This case hinged on the concept of well-known trade marks. In terms of the new Trade Marks Act (which came into effect during the course of arguments between the parties), a well-known trade mark is afforded protection, even if it is unregistered in South Africa. Between 1968 and 1985 McDonalds obtained registration of a number of its trade marks in South Africa although it wasn't trading in this country. Joburgers Drive-Inn Restaurant (Pty) Ltd (Joburgers) and Dax Prop CC applied for removal of the McDonalds trade marks from the register on the basis that they had not been used in South Africa and that McDonalds had no intention of using them in the foreseeable future.

In the court of first instance, judgment was granted against McDonalds, to which McDonalds appealed. The Appeal Court found that McDonalds is a well-known trade mark and that, accordingly, even if the McDonalds trade mark registrations could, in law, be expunged, it made no practical sense to order their removal from the register, because the provisions of the Act protecting well-known marks would prevent anyone but McDonalds from using and registering the McDonalds trade mark.

Copyright

Copyright is conferred by the Copyright Act, 1978: no registration is required. Owners of copyright are encouraged to keep drafts which may assist in proving the existence of their rights in copyright works, should this later be required by a court.

The Act protects literary, artistic and musical works, sound recordings, cinematographic films, computer programs, radio and television broadcasts, satellite transmissions and published editions. The categories of persons who are afforded copyright protection are defined in the Act and include certain foreign persons and incorporated bodies.

An interesting case that illustrates the importance of copyright is the *Waylite Diary CC v First National Bank Ltd* case (1995):

FNB commissioned Waylite to provide it with diaries in 1987, 1999, 1990 and 1991. In 1992 another firm won FNB's contract to supply it with diaries. The diaries supplied by the other firm were basically identical to those supplied by Waylite. Waylite claimed that FNB was infringing its copyright in the layout of the diary pages. The court found that Waylite expended insufficient skill and effort in development of the diary pages (they were not original) and that they accordingly did not qualify as works capable of protection in terms of the Copyright Act.

In contrast, in the matter of *Da Gama Textile Co Ltd v Vision Creations CC* (1995), the court found that copyright existed in an ornate pattern applied by Da Gama to textile used for curtaining, upholstery, clothing, etc. Vision started manufacturing a virtually identical cloth. The court applied a two-pronged test: firstly, there was objective similarity between the pattern used by both parties on their fabrics, and, secondly, it was proven that Vision had specimens of Da Gama's cloth in its possession (a subjective test).

It is interesting to note that the artist who designed the pattern on Da Gama's fabric used another example of fabric as an example upon which to base her pattern. The court found that, although there were similarities in the artwork, the Da Gama fabric pattern was sufficiently dissimilar to conclude that skill and effort had been expended in its creation and it was accordingly judged a copyright work.

Designs

The Designs Act of 1993 provides protection to aesthetic and functional designs through registration. Functional designs have features which are necessitated by the function of the article to which the design is applied, and include integrated circuit topography and mask works related thereto. Aesthetic designs relate to designs applied to articles of manufacture because of the pattern, shape, configuration or ornamentation of the design which is judged solely by the eye. Aesthetic designs must be new and original while functional designs must be new and not commonplace.

Plant breeder's rights

South Africa is the only country on the continent of Africa which is a member of the UPOV Convention. This has the effect that South Africa is bound to protect the plant breeders' rights of foreign nationals, whilst the rest of the countries on the African continent are not. The rights cover propagating material for the relevant variety as well as harvested material, including plants. These exclusive rights consist of the production or reproduction of the aforementioned plant material, the conditioning thereof for the purpose of propagation, the sale or any form of marketing thereof, as well as the exporting, importing and stocking thereof.

Counterfeit goods

The Counterfeit Goods Act provides enhanced means for dealing with counterfeit goods, i.e. those incorporating or featuring trade marks or copyright belonging to another party.

Intellectual property valuation

Apart from Capital Gains Tax (CGT) requirements, significant tax advantages may be realised when acquiring a business which owns intellectual property. In particular, the South African, UK and Australian tax regimes provide that any company purchasing intellectual property (excluding trade marks) is entitled to deduct the purchase price from its pre-tax earnings over the lifetime of the intellectual property. The company would still be able to depreciate the intellectual property whether or not it takes advantage of the above tax relief.

Whilst companies often spend considerable amounts on securing intellectual property rights, experience has shown that a proper valuation of such intellectual property, in particular a valuation of the technology aspects, is rarely carried out. By properly reflecting the intellectual property as an asset in the balance sheet as required by the Generally Accepted Accounting Practices (GAAP), a company could significantly improve its shareholder value and benefit from an often neglected, yet important source of value creation.

Conclusion

As can be seen from the above discussion, the protection of intellectual property is vitally important for the continued success of an organization, as well as the fact that intellectual property is an important marketing tool for any company. Companies wishing to obtain advice on the managing of their intellectual property can apply to intellectual property experts, such as the firm Hahn & Hahn. Hahn & Hahn Inc plays a vitally important role in the registration and protection of intellectual property in South Africa, and has gone from strength to strength based on their ability to determine the ongoing legal needs of companies and individuals in South Africa. The consequences of marketers not properly managing their company's intellectual property have been illustrated in the court cases referred to in this case study.

Reference

1   This article was provided by Hahn & Hahn, Inc, a firm established in 1951 that specialises in the provision of expertise in the field of Intellectual Property Law. For more information see www.hahn.co.za. Case study procured by Cindy Erdis.

32

MARKETING FEATURES:

IMAGE
MEDIA STRATEGY
PROMOTION
PUBLIC RELATIONS
STRATEGIC MARKETING

Ethical concerns in social marketing: Organ donation drive in Singapore

Introduction[1]

The National Kidney Foundation of Singapore (NKFS) has two functions: it raises funds for patients suffering from kidney failure and it promotes organ donation. NKF has recognised a serious lack of organ donors not only in Singapore but world-wide. In the United States, the waiting list of the United Network for Organ Sharing has grown about 250% from 1987 to 1995. The first major step NKF has taken was to set up a Multi-Organ Donation Development (MODD) in 1999 as an effort to encourage nationwide organ donation. The NKF has a very pro-active marketing division and its promotional and marketing efforts have been increasingly success-ful with the launch of its first NKF Star Charity Show, particularly with dialysis aid efforts. However, controversies arose regarding the risk that the local TV station artistes were put through in order to raise funds. The public was also highly concern about the commercialisation of NKF's fundraising strategies. This has created some disagreement within the NKF has to whether the aggressive marketing strategy used for the dialysis promotion could be equally well applied in other areas, such as the promotion of organ donation. Misapplication of the marketing plan could result in it being more difficult for the NKF to implement any future marketing plans.

History of NKF

The National Kidney Foundation of Singapore was founded in 1969 by Dr. Khoo Oon Teik, a nephrologist, after his brother died of kidney failure. The establishment of Singapore's first dialysis unit at the Singapore General Hospital (SGH) was the result of Dr. Khoo's determination to save others from the debilitating and life-threatening affliction of kidney failure. That dialysis unit has since grown to become the NKF. Over the past 14 years, the NKF has built dialysis centres all over Singapore, providing patients with quality dialysis at heavily subsidised rates near their homes or workplaces.

During this period, NKF also became the main proponent of organ donation. The Human Organ Transplant Act (HOTA) passed in May 1987, applies to Singaporean and permanent residents between the ages of 21 and 60. HOTA 1987 allows the kidneys of accident victims to be used for transplants, unless they have opted out (HOTA 1987). However, Muslims are excluded.

Organ donation scene in Singapore

There is a severe shortage of organ donors in Singapore. The major problem is the long wait for suitable donors. The statistics shown in tables 1, 2 and 3 briefly sum up the acute organ shortages in Singapore.

Year	Kidneys	Heart	Liver	Lungs	Cornea
1998	574	14	15	–	–
1999	607	9	12	11	–
2000	638	4	21	2	–
2001	650	5	25	2	–
2002	666	7	20	0	19

Table 32.1: No. of patients on waiting list for transplant as of 31 Dec 2002

Year	Kidneys		Heart	Liver	Lungs	Cornea	TOTAL
	Cadaveric	Living					
1998	54	34	5	18	0	191	302
1999	44	30	1	11	1	165	252
2000	30	22	1	8	0	79	140
2001	46	46	2	10	1	194	299
2002	30	44	2	12	1	158	247

Table 32.2: No. of patients who have received a transplant as of 31 Dec 2002

Year	Kidneys	Heart	Liver	Lungs
2001	5	1	8	0
2002	5	3	14	2

Source: 2002 Multi-Organ Donation Development, National Kidney Foundation Singapore
(http://www.thegift.org.sg/why_organ_donation/critical_statistics.html)

Table 32.3: No. of patients who died while waiting for a transplant as of 31 Dec 2002

Organ donation marketing

Faced with the challenges of shortage of donors and the cultural issues, NKF has carried out its marketing plans using two different units, namely the Muslim Kidney Action Committee (MKAC) and the Multi-Organ Donation Development unit.

Muslim Kidney Action Committee (MKAC)

The Muslim Kidney Action Committee (MKAC) was set up in 1990. The objectives are to increase awareness among Singapore Muslims on issues relating to kidney disease, pledging and transplantation. MKAC works with the NKF to help kidney patients and to promote kidney pledging within the Singapore Muslim community.

In 1994, the NKF launched a year-long kidney donation and transplantation programme to educate the Singapore Muslim community (NKF 1999). MKAC also had a 'Kempen Suara Hati' or 'Voices of the Heart Campaign', a 4 month programme aimed at promoting the newly proposed kidney law for Muslims. The proposal seeks to amend the Human Organ Transplant Act (HOTA) to include Muslims as automatic kidney pledgers. The proposal was well received with 56 212 individuals signing the 'Book of Hope' to show they supported the proposal. Additionally, more than 150 Singapore Muslim organizations, including mosques and grassroots organizations came forward to support (MKAC 2000). However, doctors must still seek the consent of two waris, or close paternal male relatives, before the kidneys can be removed. MKAC's marketing efforts has been successful with the number of Muslim pledgers increasing from a paltry 404 before MKAC formation to an encouraging 12 000 after the formation.

Multi-Organ Donation Development

The Multi-Organ Donation Development (MODD) unit was established by NKF in 1999 to organize a nationwide effort to encourage organ donation. One key activity is the launch of the Multi-Organ Pledge Appeal (MOPA) Campaign (a five-year long public education and awareness campaign) in 1999.

One of the strategies of the campaign was its Ambassadors of Life programme which recruits volunteers to become spokespersons on the Organ Donation cause.

The job of the Ambassador is to spread the word among his/her family, friends and colleagues and encourage them to become pledgers. The MODD also conducted talks in schools as part of its public education programme. Other marketing activities include the MODD Viva Life celebration held in conjunction with the local newspaper. This whole day event was meant to celebrate the true essence of life. More than 150 Ambassadors of Life turned up to provide hope and chances for new lives to nearly 3 000 organ failure victims and their families.

Given the current situation, the NKF team recognised that the organ donation drive was in dire need of funding. Mr Joseph Tan, Marketing Manager of the NKF, verbalised two important decisions:

1   Strategically, whether organ donation should be approached in the same manner as the dialysis programme.
2   Tactically, whether to continue to depend on the Star Charity Show for the bulk of NKF and MODD's fund generation.

NKF Star Charity Show

The NKF Star Charity Show was seen as a marketing breakthrough for charitable organizations. The NKF Star Charity Show is a live telethon where local and foreign stars gather to perform for a night with the purpose of raising awareness on kidney failure and the plight of kidney patients and to garner donations to fund their subsidised dialysis programme. The first Star Charity prompted 1,3 million phone calls to come in. In 2001, the annual NKF show was divided into two parts, consisting of celebrities enticing people to give throughout performances and the enactment of daredevil stunts. For example, one celebrity had to kiss a fully-fanged cobra. Another typical stunt involved an actress waiting helplessly for her male counterpart to come to her aid while fully submerged underwater with her limbs tied. These stunts certainly converted into money as the most recent show in 2001 raised a record-breaking $11,6 million.

With such daredevil efforts, the NKF show has attracted much public concern. Members of the public have written into the forum expressing their concern over the safety of the stars. The Senior Manager of Communications of the local TV station Mr. Thomas Heng addressed the concerns: 'The production team for the charity show conceives new and innovative performances to encourage viewers to make donations. The artistes involved are consulted beforehand on their comfort and level of confidence in attempting the proposed stunts. None of the acts are physically endangering or life-threatening. They are just a combination of illusions and well-coordinated acts.' Such answers further fueled critics. Some even went as far to say that the show borders on emotional blackmail.

While controversy raged regarding NKF's in-your-face methods, millions of dollars were still donated. Besides the glitzy show, emails and phone text messages were also sent out. These marketing tactics received mixed reviews from the public. Although some found these tactics enterprising, others believed they were being aggressive and invasive. In addition, attractive prizes such as a private condominium, a car, and cash were offered to the donors. The public voiced concern that donors were not genuinely altruistic but merely taking a shot at the prizes.

At the NKF board meeting, differing opinions were voiced. The Marketing Manager said that since the Star Charity show had proved to be a success the NKF should seriously consider applying the same concept to the organ donation drive to generate the funds needed. The Public Relations Manager Mr J. Siva, on the other hand, had his reservations, commenting that as the NKF was a non-profit charitable organization, the public expected it to hold moral high ground by supporting patients and nurturing altruism and the hard sell nature of the Star Charity Show conflicted with this public expectation.

Dr Matthew Tan, chairman of the organ transplantation board expressed his concerns pertaining to organ donation marketing, adding that the NKF should also consider the ethical and cultural issues involved, especially in the promotion of organ donation to the Muslim community. He agreed with the Public Relations Manager that Star Charity approach could not be applied to organ donation as it required a different set of considerations.

Conclusion

Even in developed countries, current policies on procuring organs still rely on the ethical principles of voluntarism and altruism. Organ donation marketing in Singapore is in its infancy. As the country continues to face an acute shortage of organs, the two units set up by NKF need to carefully examine all relevant issues before embarking on a full-scale marketing programme.

References

1   Case study by May Lwin and Jacqueline Chow. May Lwin is an Assistant Professor of Marketing, National University of Singapore Business School. Jacqueline Chow is a post-graduate, National University of Singapore Business School. This case was prepared as a basis for class discussion. The cooperation of Eu Yan Sang is gratefully acknowledged. Selected financial and market data have been disguised for confidentiality reasons. Case study procured by Michael Cant.

2   List of websites from which information was derived:
    http://eyeball.asia1.com.sg/Eyeball
    http://www.nkfs.org
    http://straitstimes.asia1.com.sg
    http://mediacorptv.com
    http://www.thegift.org.sg
    http://upenn.edu/ldi/issuebrief2_5.html
    http://www.cota.org
    http://www.unos.org
    http://www.transweb.org